TWENTIETH-CENTURY CHAUCER CRITICISM

Shifting ideas about Geoffrey Chaucer's audience have produced radically different readings of Chaucer's work over the course of the past century. Kathy Cawsey, in her book on the changing relationship among Chaucer, critics, and theories of audience, draws on Michel Foucault's concept of the "author-function" to propose the idea of an "audience function" which shows the ways critics' concepts of audience affect and condition their criticism. Focusing on six trend-setting Chaucerian scholars, Cawsey identifies the assumptions about Chaucer's audience underpinning each critic's work, arguing these ideas best explain the diversity of interpretation in Chaucer criticism. Further, Cawsey suggests few studies of Chaucer's own understanding of audience have been done, in part because Chaucer criticism has been conditioned by scholars' latent suppositions about Chaucer's own audience. In making sense of the confusing and conflicting mass of modern Chaucer criticism, Cawsey also provides insights into the development of twentieth-century literary criticism and theory.

For Jim Weldon, Helen Cooper and Will Robins
with gratitude

Twentieth-Century Chaucer Criticism
Reading Audiences

KATHY CAWSEY
Dalhousie University, Canada

Routledge
Taylor & Francis Group
LONDON AND NEW YORK

First published in paperback 2024

First published 2011 by Ashgate Publishing

Published 2016
by Routledge
4 Park Square, Milton Park, Abingdon, Oxon OX14 4RN

and by Routledge
605 Third Avenue, New York, NY 10158

Routledge is an imprint of the Taylor & Francis Group, an informa business

Copyright © 2011, 2016, 2024 Kathy Cawsey

The right of Kathy Cawsey to be identified as author of this work has been asserted in
accordance with sections 77 and 78 of the Copyright, Designs and Patents Act 1988.

All rights reserved. No part of this book may be reprinted or reproduced or utilised in
any form or by any electronic, mechanical, or other means, now known or hereafter
invented, including photocopying and recording, or in any information storage or
retrieval system, without permission in writing from the publishers.

Trademark notice: Product or corporate names may be trademarks or registered
trademarks, and are used only for identification and explanation without intent to
infringe.

Publisher's Note
The publisher has gone to great lengths to ensure the quality of this reprint but points
out that some imperfections in the original copies may be apparent.

British Library Cataloguing in Publication Data
Cawsey, Kathy.
    Twentieth-century Chaucer criticism : reading audiences. 1. Chaucer, Geoffrey, d. 1400
    – Criticism and interpretation – History – 20th century. 2. Chaucer, Geoffrey, d. 1400
    – Appreciation – History. 3. Reader-response criticism. 4. English literature – Middle
    English, 1100–1500 – History and criticism – Theory, etc. 5. Criticism – Social aspects.
    6. Critics – Attitudes.
    I. Title
    821.1-dc22

Library of Congress Cataloging-in-Publication Data
Cawsey, Kathy.
    Twentieth-century Chaucer criticism : reading audiences / Kathy Cawsey.
        p. cm.
    Includes index.
    ISBN 978-1-4094-0478-1 (hardback : alk. paper)
    1. Chaucer, Geoffrey, d. 1400 – Criticism and interpretation – History – 20th century. 2.
    Chaucer, Geoffrey, d. 1400 – Appreciation – Great Britain. 3. Authors and readers – Great
    Britain – History – 20th century. I. Title.
    PR1924.C33 2011
    821'.1–dc22

2010046915

ISBN: 978-1-4094-0478-1 (hbk)
ISBN: 978-1-03-292808-1 (pbk)
ISBN: 978-1-315-54950-7 (ebk)

DOI: 10.4324/9781315549507

Contents

Acknowledgments		*vii*
Preface		*ix*
Introduction: Chaucer, Audiences and Critics		1
1	George Lyman Kittredge (1860–1941): The Dramatic Reader	19
2	C.S. Lewis (1894–1963): The Psychological Reader	39
3	E. Talbot Donaldson (1910–1987): The Careful Reader	59
4	D.W. Robertson (1914–1992): The Allegorical Reader	85
5	Carolyn Dinshaw (1957–): The Gendered Reader	109
6	Lee Patterson (1940–): The Subjective Reader	131
Conclusion: Readers Then, Now, and In Between		155
Bibliography		*163*
Index		*179*

Acknowledgments

I am indebted to numerous individuals and institutions who helped me see this book through to completion. I owe major thanks to Carolyn Dinshaw and Lee Patterson for their generosity—and bravery!—in communicating with me and providing me with information for the chapters on their scholarship. I also owe thanks to John Fleming and Judith Anderson for sharing personal reminiscences of D.W. Robertson and E. Talbot Donaldson. One of the advantages of being a medievalist is that one's research subjects have been dead for many centuries; one does not expect to have to talk to one's "topics" or to their partners or students, or to run into them at conferences. I thus approached this project with some major trepidation. I hope that I have done justice to the spirit of the work of these scholars, and that they will read this book with the same generosity they showed in communicating with me.

I am grateful for questions and advice from audiences at the Canadian Society of Medievalists and the New Chaucer Society conferences, especially to the student of Lee Patterson's who reminded me of the importance of the "subject" with regards to Patterson's work. Major thanks and gratitude are also due to Will Robins—who somehow managed a one-night turnaround on chapter readings—and to Suzanne Akbari and Ruth Harvey who provided cogent suggestions for an earlier draft of the book. To Helen Cooper and Jim Weldon I also owe thanks for their inspiration and encouragement.

Finally, my gratitude goes to my family—to my parents, for support emotional, material and editorial; to my grandmother and sister, for phone calls and hugs; to Kenneth, indexer extraordinaire, for invaluable work Fridays during my maternity leave; and to Ria, for confirming my priorities in life.

The original research for this book was done while I was supported by a doctoral grant from the Social Sciences and Humanities Council of Canada, as well as several scholarships and grants from the University of Toronto and the Centre for Humanities at Toronto.

Preface

During my graduate studies at the University of Toronto, I managed to score a prime study carrel, on the thirteenth floor of Robarts library, overlooking Toronto, the CN Tower, and Lake Ontario—but more importantly, right at the end of the row starting with call number PR1900: the Chaucer shelves. Most mornings the English grad students would go down the row of carrels collecting people for a coffee break. On one of these occasions, I got talking to a fellow student about the work we were doing for our just-begun dissertations. "Well, I've read my three books," he announced. I looked at him blankly. "There are only three books written so far on my author," he explained. I felt the crushing weight of the unfairness of the universe—or at least of graduate studies—descend upon me. "I have five *bookcases*," I said. "And that's not counting articles."

This book is written primarily for graduate students and upper-level undergraduate students who are in the same position I was: staring overwhelmed at the multiple bookcases on Chaucer in their libraries, perplexed by the mass, variety, and sheer contrariness of Chaucer criticism.[1] This book will provide students with a means of sorting through and making sense of that overwhelming mass of scholarship. It will also give one explanation—there are others, for sure—for why such diversity of scholarship exists, and why different critics come to such different conclusions about how to read Chaucer. Excellent books summarizing major trends in Chaucerian scholarship have been written before, of course, among them Gillian Rudd's *The Complete Critical Guide to Geoffrey Chaucer* and Corinne Saunders's *Chaucer* in the Blackwell Guides to Criticism Series. Anthologies of criticism such as Derek Pearsall's *Chaucer to Spenser: A Critical Reader* and handbooks such as the Oxford, Cambridge and Yale *Companions to Chaucer* also give students a good sense of the dominant schools of thought in Chaucerian criticism. However, most of these books are historical summaries, and do not provide explanations for *why* completely contradictory ways of reading Chaucer arose over the course of the twentieth century.[2] Nor do these books provide

---

[1]   Thirty-five years ago Larry Benson wrote, "Many readers today, confronted by the vast quantity of critical and schlolarly work about Chaucer ... may wish that everyone had been a good deal less learned about the poet, for all our sakes." The number of books and articles on Chaucer has only grown exponentially since then. L.D. Benson, "A Reader's Guide to Writings on Chaucer," *Geoffrey Chaucer*, ed. Derek Brewer (London: G. Bell & Sons, 1974) 321.

[2]   Several articles have also been written surveying Chaucer criticism: see Ethan Knapp, "Chaucer Criticism and its Legacies," *The Yale Companion to Chaucer*, ed. Seth Lerer (New Haven: Yale University Press, 2006) 324–56; Glenn A. Steinberg, "Chaucer and the

x   *Twentieth-Century Chaucer Criticism*

students with a theoretical framework which can be used when they encounter new schools of thought or works of Chaucer criticism, ones not covered by the surveys so far. My hope is that this book will be useful not only in making sense of the abundance of Chaucer scholarship produced over the course of the twentieth century, but in continuing to make sense of the scholarship that will be produced in equal abundance, I am sure, in the century to come.

This book is also written for more mature scholars of Chaucer who have already come to terms with the diversity of Chaucer scholarship, but who are interested specifically in Chaucer's audiences and readers. The subtitle of the work, *Reading Audiences*, speaks to this concern. I hope that I have provided a new way of thinking about Chaucer's audiences, by framing them as a theoretical concept which a critic needs to define before the work of criticism begins, rather than as a self-evident category. This book will provide scholars of Chaucer's audiences an overview of the changing understanding of those audiences over the course of the twentieth century. It will also, I hope, prompt them to think more explicitly about their own assumptions with regards to the concept of audience, and the ways those assumptions condition their scholarship.

Finally, this work will be of interest to more general English scholars concerned with theoretical issues surrounding the concepts of audience, readers, and criticism. For these scholars, the idea of the "audience function," outlined in the Introduction, will be most useful, since that idea is transferrable to authors and criticism beyond Chaucerian Studies. Issues of audience and the problems they cause for criticism may be particularly evident when it comes to Chaucer, but I believe all English scholars use an "audience function" when carrying out their scholarship. Just as Chaucerian scholars need to be more explicit about the assumptions they are making about audiences when they provide readings of

---

Critical Tradition," *Approaches to Teaching Chaucer's* Troilus and Criseyde *and the Shorter Poems*, ed. Tison Pugh and Angela Jane Weisl (New York: Modern Language Association of America, 2007) 87–91; Albert C. Baugh, "Fifty Years of Chaucer Scholarship," *Speculum* 26.4 (Fall 1951) 659–72; Derek Pearsall, "The Criticism of Chaucer in the Twentieth Century," *Chaucer's Mind and Art*, ed. A.C. Cawley (Edinburgh: Oliver and Boyd, 1969) 1–25; Derek Pearsall, "Chaucer's Poetry and Its Modern Commentators: The Necessity of History," *Medieval Literature: Criticism, Ideology, and History*, ed. David Aers (New York: St. Martin's, 1986) 123–47; Charles Muscatine, "Chaucer's Religion and the Chaucer Religion," *Chaucer Traditions: Studies in Honour of Derek Brewer*, ed. Ruth Morse and Barry Windeatt (Cambridge: Cambridge University Press, 1990) 249–62; Florence Ridley, "The State of Chaucer Studies: A Brief Survey," *Studies in the Age of Chaucer* 1 (1979) 3–16; Florence Ridley, "Questions without Answers—Yet or Ever? New Critical Modes and Chaucer," *Chaucer Review* 16.2 (Fall 1981) 101–6; Morton Bloomfield, "Contemporary Literary Theory and Chaucer," Florence Ridley, "A Response to 'Contemporary Literary Theory and Chaucer'," and Winthrop Wetherbee, "Convention and Authority: a Comment on Some Recent Critical Approaches to Chaucer," all in *New Perspectives in Chaucer Criticism*, ed. Donald Rose (Norman, OK: Pilgrim, 1981) 23–36, 37–51 and 71–81; Benson, "A Reader's Guide."

Chaucer's works, so too I believe that other scholars would benefit from thinking explicitly about the assumptions they make with regard to the audiences of other authors.

Introduction: Chaucer, Audiences and Critics

Geoffrey Chaucer was fascinated by audiences. His main works all contain embedded audiences—both his narrators, audiences of ancient "auctores" in their own right, and characters who listen to stories-within-the-story. Chaucer worried about how the members of his own real-life audience would read his poems; how they might interpret them in ways he didn't foresee or intend; how they might take his words and twist them into something unrecognizable. He was intrigued by the ways stories function: how the communication process works, how meanings are transmitted from person to person, how people tell and retell and change the stories they hear. More importantly, he was interested in how stories apparently *don't* work—how people misinterpret things they hear; how stories become carriers of meanings in contexts and situations their original authors never imagined; how tellers betray to their audiences information they never intended. Chaucer returned, over and over again, to the role that audiences and readers play in the creation of meaning: the way a story is not a stable entity, which conveys exactly the meaning the author intends, but instead is a moveable, changing thing, as much created by the reading process as completed by it. This interest is evident as early as *The Book of the Duchess*, in the Dreamer's lack of comprehension—be it real or strategic—of the Black Knight's tale of his love and woe. It continues in *The House of Fame*, Chaucer's most explicit exploration of the story-telling process before the *Canterbury Tales*. *The House of Fame*, as the title indicates, shows that Chaucer's interest in audiences and reception started early: he is bemused by the fact that some stories become famous, while others, equally good or important, are poorly received by their audiences and are doomed to obscurity.

The short lines of "Adam Scriveyn" show that Chaucer's concerns about the transmission and reception of stories were not just academic. He complains about the "negligence and rape" of his scribe, which forces the author to "renewe ... corecte and eke to rubbe and scrape" the manuscripts of Boethius and Troilus that Adam has copied.[1] In the Middle Ages there was a real possibility of scribes mistranscribing an author's poems, and with such errors, Chaucer's audience, even if they were perfect readers (which Chaucer seems to doubt), would never be able to capture the meaning Chaucer intended. Likewise, the G Prologue to the *Legend of Good Women* may reflect Chaucer's actual experiences with his own audience: Cupid complains about Chaucer's translations of the *Romance of the Rose* and of *Troilus and Criseyde*, saying that Chaucer only writes about bad women; Chaucer is then given the task of writing stories about good, true women.

---

[1]   Geoffrey Chaucer, *The Riverside Chaucer*, ed. Larry Benson, 3rd ed. (Oxford: Oxford University Press, 1987) 650. All quotations from Chaucer are taken from this edition.

As Carolyn Dinshaw writes, "If, as seems likely, this palinode was indeed written in response to discussion at court of his works, Chaucer's analysis [in the Prologue to the *Legend of Good Women*] reveals ... the demands for simplicity and closure made by his own audience."[2] Chaucer may have known first-hand what it was like to have an audience reinterpret, rework, or simply dislike his poetry.

Chaucer's poems also detail the very real dilemma every author in the Middle Ages felt acutely: not only is Chaucer an author, but he is an audience, himself a reader of the classical and early medieval "auctors." How is he to be a "good" audience to these writers, to remain faithful to the spirit and intentions of their works, while establishing himself as an original writer, retelling and re-interpreting the stories for a new age, language and society? In his writing Chaucer often denies himself any strong claim to authorship, emphasizing instead his role as audience. He maintains that he is retelling, compiling, translating, or passing on something he has heard, rather than creating or "writing." Yet he knows well that even a simple act of transmission or translation can irrevocably change what the "auctor" wrote.[3] Chaucer's interest in the functioning of audiences is not a light or passing concern, but an issue he faced throughout his life.

At times, Chaucer transfers his worries about audience reception to his characters. In this way he can explore the workings and problems of transmission and reception without necessarily adopting a particular stance, or coming to a definitive answer. Criseyde expresses a fear that people who hear her story will judge her poorly—and this fear is not mere paranoia, if the condemnation of *Troilus and Criseyde* in the Prologue to the *Legend of Good Women* or Henryson's *Testament of Cresseid* is anything to go by. In the *Book of the Duchess* the Black Knight has great difficulty making himself understood to the Dreamer, and expresses frustration at the Dreamer's incomprehension of his story about his love for Blanche. But Chaucer's most thorough exploration of the problematics of audience reception comes in the *Canterbury Tales*. In the *Tales*, Chaucer creates a story-telling situation, and shows it at work: characters misinterpret stories (the Host); they react negatively to stories, taking them personally when they may not have been intended as personal attacks (the Reeve); they craft their own stories in response to other stories (the Miller; the Summoner); they see in stories meanings and implications their original tellers apparently did not see (the Host again); they reject stories completely (the Host, the Knight); they laugh, they approve, they condemn. This interest in audience response and participation is apparent in the very structure of the *Canterbury Tales*. It also becomes acute in several instances. Fragment VII, with its interruptions and re-formulations, brings audience participation in the story-telling event to the fore: first the pilgrim Chaucer is

---

[2] Carolyn Dinshaw, *Chaucer's Sexual Poetics* (Madison: University of Wisconsin Press, 1989) 66–7.

[3] For Chaucer as a reader, see Jill Mann, "The Authority of the Audience in Chaucer," *Poetics: Theory and Practice in Medieval English Literature*, ed. Piero Boitani and Anna Torti (Cambridge: D.S. Brewer, 1991) 1–12.

Introduction: Chaucer, Audiences and Critics 3

interrupted in his story, which is condemned by the Host as "drasty rymyng" (VII.930), and, in a manner reminiscent of the instructions the Dreamer receives in the Prologue to the *Legend of Good Women*, he is told to tell a story in prose "in which ther be som murthe or som doctryne" (VII.935). Then the Monk is cut off by the Knight's objection to the dreary quality of the Monk's list of tragedies, and Host tells the Monk, "Youre tale anoyeth al this compagnye" (VII.2789). The Host emphasizes the importance of the audience, saying, "Whereas a man may have noon audience, / Noght helpeth it to tellen his sentence" (VII.2801–2). In Fragment IX, this playful exploration of audience control takes a darker turn, as the Manciple warns about the problems of audience reception:

> He that hath mysseyd, I dar wel sayn,
> He may by no wey clepe his word agayn.
> Though hym repente, or be hym nevere so looth.
> He is his thral to whom that he hath sayd
> A tale of which he is now yvele apayd. (IX.353–7)

Once a tale is told, the author loses control of it, and becomes the "thral" of his audience; the audience may put the tale to purposes for which it was never intended, and those purposes may harm the author. The author cannot control the consequences of tale-telling, and thus, the Manciple concludes, it is better to stay silent: "be noon auctour newe / Of tidynges" (IX.359–60). Nevertheless, Chaucer himself does try to "call back" some of his writings at the end of the *Canterbury Tales*. This retraction of the greater part of his writings is prompted by a concern with the way in which they will be received. Chaucer closes the *Canterbury Tales* with an address to his audience, "all that herkne this litel tretys or rede" (X.1081). He asks that if they find "any thyng that displese hem," that they attribute it to "the defaute of myn unkonnynge and nat to my wyl" (X.1083). He is concerned too with the moral effect of the tales on his audience: he "revokes" all his writings that "sownen into synne" (X.1086). From his first writings to what seem to be the last, therefore, Chaucer was concerned about the response his audience would have to him and his writing.[4]

The Audience Function

An interest in audience and reception is so pervasive in Chaucer's writings that it seems crucial to an understanding of Chaucer's ideas about stories, story-telling, and writing. Yet there is little scholarly agreement about Chaucer's understanding of audience. Different critics perceive different "implicit audiences" in the works, and few critics agree about the way the explicit audiences depicted within the

---

[4] Seth Lerer, "Introduction," *The Yale Companion to Chaucer* (New Haven: Yale University Press, 2006) 7, 20.

works should be interpreted. Moreover, the assumptions—whether latent or explicit—that critics make about Chaucer's audience seem to dictate, to a large extent, their criticism. In this book I want to explore the ways in which modern scholars of Chaucer have understood and envisioned Chaucer's audience. The concern with audience that I have described above is central to Chaucer criticism and scholarship, yet the central role that a critic's own understanding of Chaucer's audience plays in his or her criticism has often gone unexamined. This book will trace the narrative of the changing understanding of the concept of "audience" over the course of the twentieth century, and evaluate the effect of differing ideas about Chaucer's audience on Chaucerian scholarship. The importance of ideas of audience and reception to Chaucer's writing has almost become a commonplace in Chaucer criticism. I want to argue a parallel importance of ideas about audience for Chaucer scholarship itself.

Michel Foucault, in the article "What is an author?" introduced the concept of the "author function." He argued that, at least structurally, the author was not a "person," but worked as a "function" which enabled interpretation. Whatever or whoever the real author of a literary text might be, a text always contains "a certain number of signs referring to the author," such as the grammatical position of the "subject," and these signs together create a "function" upon which the structures of critical interpretation depend. The "author function" may or may not have any connection to the "real" writer of the work, but its status as a structural element of criticism is crucial. Whether or not criticism is concerned with the actual author's biography, identity, or authenticity, it still depends upon the "author function": the concept of an author enables a critic to explain a text because in the author, the critic locates "a point where contradictions are resolved, where incompatible elements are at last tied together or organized around a fundamental or originating contradiction."[5] In other words, the assumption that a literary text "makes sense" is predicated upon the idea of a controlling individual behind the work. Foucault gives four criteria by which St. Jerome defined "authorship," and argues that, for the most part, we define the "author" in much the same way today: the author is defined in terms of value (the works are "good"), conceptual coherence (the works could plausibly have been produced by one mind), stylistic coherence (the works share a style which stays within the plausible limits of change), and historical limitation (the works were produced within one lifetime).[6] These definitions of authorship function as limitations. They limit literary works, turning them into something manageable and enabling us to sort "meaning" into categories such as genre, time period, tone, style, etc.[7] Leaving aside the ideological and political side of Foucault's argument (he sees this limiting role of the "author function"

---

[5] Michel Foucault, "What is an Author?" *Modern Criticism and Theory: A Reader*, ed. David Lodge (London: Longman, 1988) 204. This essay was originally printed in the *Bulletin de la Société française de Philosophie* 63.3 (1969) 73–104.

[6] Foucault, "What is an Author?" 204.

[7] Foucault, "What is an Author?" 209.

as a restriction upon freedom, a tool of ideological control), we can see the way in which the "author function" works within the realm of literary criticism as such a "limit": as English scholars in academic institutions, we make our work manageable by dividing up the immense realm of all "written work" into authors, themselves categorized in terms of history, value, style, genre, theme, and so on.

Since Foucault's article was written, literary criticism has explored the implications of his argument in a variety of ways with reference to the concept of authorship. Less use, however, has been made of his theoretical idea of "function," in terms of asking what other functions might also be operative in a literary text. In this book, I use the notion of "audience function," in the same way that Foucault uses the idea of the "author function." As critics, we depend upon an "audience function" in limiting and making manageable our critical task. This "audience function" works in a similar manner to the "author function," as a limit to and enabler of interpretation, and is as fractured from the "real" audience as the "real" author is from the "author function" of a text. In the same way that interpretation can be limited with reference to the author (what s/he could have known, could have thought, or was likely to have written), interpretation is also limited with reference to the audience (what they would know, how they would read/hear, how they would experience the text, how they would interpret ambiguity or irony or humour). This audience might be defined as the medieval audience of Chaucer's day, or all people for all time; in either case, the "reader" functions as a control upon the critic's interpretation. The way in which a critic defines or envisions the "reader" determines what interpretations are valid, plausible, and convincing for that critic.

We can see the way this function works in the theories of Hans Robert Jauss, who in many ways presages my concept of "audience function." In his model, the task of a critic is to establish the "horizon of expectations" an audience of a work would have had, and limit his/her readings accordingly, to interpretations which would fit within this horizon.[8] A valid interpretation of a piece of literature is one which would work within the pre-established expectations held by the envisioned audience. The audience here, as far as Jauss is concerned, is a real audience, but if we consider it from a structural point of view it works as a "function," a way of shaping and limiting interpretation. Where I differ from Jauss is that, while his "horizon of expectations" theory accurately describes the way in which the audience function often works, he limits his theory to his own definition of audience: that is, the historical audience who would have been the first readers or listeners of a particular work or text. I contend, by contrast, that *all* literary critics work on the basis of what they think the audience's "horizon of expectations" is; however, the crucial aspect, and the reason different theories produce

---

[8]   Jauss's most influential work was "Literaturgeschichte als Provokation" or "Literary History as a Challenge to Literary Theory" translated in Hans Robert Jauss, *Toward an Aesthetic of Reception*, trans. Timothy Bahti (Minneapolis: University of Minnesota Press, 1982).

6 *Twentieth-Century Chaucer Criticism*

such widely different interpretations of text, is the way in which that "audience" is defined. How the critic defines the audience will determine the "horizon of expectations" that is established.

Many critics, therefore, who do not explicitly subscribe to Jauss's "horizon of expectations" methodology nonetheless implicitly or explicitly use an "audience function" in a similar manner, and this manner parallels the way the "author function" works. The same categories that Foucault outlines are operative. The audience, however the particular critic defines it, limits possible interpretations in terms of "value": interpretations must not involve readings which the audience would not like, would consider worthless, or which would mean they did not value the text being discussed. The audience provides a limit in terms of conceptual coherence: interpretations must fit within the realm of what the audience would consider plausible or logical; apparent contradictions must be "tied together or organized around a fundamental or originating contradiction"[9] within the audience. The audience also limits our understanding in terms of style: interpretations must not read the text according to stylistic considerations the audience would not know or understand. Most importantly, the audience provides a historical limitation: interpretations must fit within the historical limitations which the critic has used in defining the audience. Like the "author function," the "audience function" makes criticism and interpretation manageable and understandable. It defines the limits of what interpretations are acceptable and viable, eliminating other interpretations because they are not plausible according to the parameters with which the critic defines the audience. Indeed, the "audience function" is in some cases anterior to the "author function." Many critics use the "audience function" in constructing the "author function": they conclude that an author could not have written a text to mean a particular thing, because his/her audience would not have understood that meaning. So, for example, D.W. Robertson uses the "audience function" to determine Chaucer's intentions: since, according to him, medieval audiences were trained to read exegetically and allegorically, Robertson believes that Chaucer wrote works which were meant to be interpreted in such a way.

Because this "audience function" or "reader function" is fundamental to the structures of criticism, it is difficult to disentangle a critic's concept of Chaucer's audience from the criticism itself. In studying Chaucer's understanding of audiences, we cannot depend upon a pre-established concept with which everyone agrees; instead, ideas about audience are so wrapped up in critics' readings of Chaucer's works that "audience-analysis" becomes almost indistinguishable from "interpretation." And if interpretations of Chaucer's works are incredibly varied and contested—as any student of Chaucer knows—then so too are the images of Chaucer's audience. Chaucer's own ideas about audience are obscured by the ideas about audience which have conditioned and influenced the interpretations we have inherited.

---

[9] Foucault, "What is an Author?" 204.

Introduction: Chaucer, Audiences and Critics   7

Studies of Chaucer's actual audience have, of course, been done. Yet these studies suffer from a dearth of evidence. Anne Middleton, Richard Firth Green and Paul Strohm have studied Chaucer's literary circle, the "new men" at court such as Gower, Strode, and Bukton (all of whom Chaucer mentions), but we do not know how far Chaucer's immediate audience extended beyond this circle, nor how representative these men are of Chaucer's overall audience.[10] Derek Pearsall focuses on a portrait illumination which depicts Chaucer reading to a courtly audience, yet this illumination was created after Chaucer's death, and we have no contemporary portraits or illuminations of him.[11] Several historical records mention Chaucer, but these records all deal with Chaucer's Chancery or court work, and never mention his literary endeavours. We have no autograph manuscripts of Chaucer's work, nor do we have any manuscripts of his poems which date from before his death. Linne Mooney's recent work on Adam Scriveyn and the Ellesmere and Hengwrt scribe may bear fruit in terms of making those manuscripts more "authoritative";[12] nonetheless, any evidence about audience they might provide will remain, for the most part, speculative. *Legend of Good Women* is dedicated to Queen Anne, but we do not know whether this dedication is a formal trope or an indication that she was an actual reader (or listener) of Chaucer's works, nor do we know whether the other women at court would have been a part of Chaucer's audience.[13] Of Chaucer's "secondary audience," the readers of the fifteenth century, we have slightly more evidence: references to Chaucer's work by writers such as Lydgate, Hoccleve, and the Scottish poets, and evidence of manuscript ownership which suggests that Chaucer's audience extended beyond the court circle and upper class.[14] But

---

[10]   Anne Middleton, "Chaucer's 'New Men' and the Good of Literature in the *Canterbury Tales,*" *Literature and Society,* ed. Edward Said (Baltimore: Johns Hopkins University Press, 1978) 15–56; Paul Strohm, *Social Chaucer* (Cambridge, Mass.: Harvard University Press, 1989); Richard Firth Green, *Poets and Princepleasers* (Toronto: University of Toronto Press, 1980); Paul Strohm, "Chaucer's Audience(s): Fictional, Implied, Intended, Actual," *Chaucer Review* 18.2 (1983) 137–45; "Chaucer's Audiences: Discussion," *Chaucer Review* 18.2 (1983) 175–81; Paul Strohm, *Hochon's Arrow: The Social Imagination of Fourteenth-Century Texts* (Princeton, New Jersey: Princeton University Press, 1992). See also Derek Pearsall, "The Chaucer Circle," *Old and Middle English Poetry* (London: Routledge and Kegan Paul, 1977) 194–7; R.T. Lenaghan, "Chaucer's Circle of Gentlemen and Clerks," *Chaucer Review* 18.2 (1983) 155–60; Dieter Mehl, "The Audience of Chaucer's *Troilus and Criseyde,*" *Chaucer and Middle English Studies in Honour of Rossell Hope Robbins,* ed. Beryl Rowland and Lloyd A. Duchemin (London: Allen and Unwin, 1974) 173–89; Edmund Reiss, "Chaucer and His Audience," *Chaucer Review* 14 (1980) 390–402.

[11]   Derek Pearsall, "The *Troilus* Frontispiece and Chaucer's Audience," *Yearbook of English Studies* 7 (1977) 68–74.

[12]   Linne Mooney, "Chaucer's Scribes," *Speculum* 81.1 (January 2006) 97–138.

[13]   See Richard Firth Green, "Women in Chaucer's Audience," *Chaucer Review* 18.2 (1983) 137–45.

[14]   For the most extensive work on Chaucer's fifteenth-century audience, see Seth Lerer, *Chaucer and His Readers: Imagining the Author in Late-Medieval England* (Princeton:

8   *Twentieth-Century Chaucer Criticism*

again, we do not know if Lydgate and Hoccleve can be taken as representative of Chaucer's entire readership; nor do details of manuscript ownership indicate how or why Chaucer's works were read, or how they were received. Because of this lack of evidence about Chaucer's actual audience, scholars of Chaucer's work are relatively free to envision Chaucer's audience in almost any manner they please. More importantly for my purposes here, even if studies of Chaucer's audience were able to tell us with absolute certainty its composition, extent, and characteristic traits, still they can only hypothesize about theoretically-pressing questions such as how audiences work, what reading is, and how marks on a page get turned into images and stories in people's minds.

This book, then, studies not only the concept of audience in Chaucer but the ways that critics through the years have envisioned Chaucer's audience. It traces the concepts of Chaucer's audience in the writings of six important Chaucerians of the twentieth century, and assembles a narrative of the ways those ideas changed, both affected by and determining key critical movements in Chaucer studies and English studies as a discipline.[15] This study, therefore, helps make sense of the

---

Princeton University Press, 1993). See also Seth Lerer, "Chaucer's Sons," *University of Toronto Quarterly* 73.3 (Summer 2004) 906–15; Stephanie Trigg, *Congenial Souls: Reading Chaucer from Medieval to Postmodern* (Minneapolis: University of Minnesota Press, 2002), chapter 2; Stephanie Trigg, "Chaucer's Influence and Reception," in Lerer, *Yale Companion,* 297–323; Thomas A. Prendergast and Barbara Kline, eds., *Rewriting Chaucer: Culture, Authority and the Idea of the Authentic Text, 1400–1602* (Columbus: Ohio State University Press, 1999); John J. Thompson, "Reception: fifteenth to seventeeth centuries," *Chaucer: An Oxford Guide*, ed. Steve Ellis (Oxford: Oxford University Press, 2005) 497–511; John M. Bowers, "The *Tale of Beryn* and the *Siege of Thebes*: Alternative Ideas of the *Canterbury Tales*," *Studies in the Age of Chaucer* 7 (1985) 23–50; Paul Strohm, "Chaucer's Fifteenth-Century Audience and the Narrowing of the 'Chaucer Tradition'," *Studies in the Age of Chaucer* 4 (1982) 3–32; A.C. Spearing, "Lydgate's Canterbury Tale: The *Siege of Thebes* and Fifteenth-Century Chaucerianism," *Fifteenth-Century Studies: Recent Essays*, ed. Robert F. Yeager (Hamden: Archon, 1984) 333–64; A.S.G. Edwards, "The Early Reception of Chaucer and Langland," *Florilegium* 15 (1998) 1–22; C. David Benson, "Critic and Poet: What Lydgate and Henryson Did to Chaucer's *Troilus and Criseyde*," *Modern Language Quarterly* 53.1 (March 1992) 23–40; Lerer, *Yale Companion,* 22–5. For collections of references to Chaucer, see Caroline Spurgeon, ed., *Five Hundred Years of Chaucer Criticism and Allusion, 1357–1900,* 3 vols. (London: Cambridge University Press, 1925); Derek Brewer, *Chaucer: The Critical Heritage,* 2 vols. (London: Routledge and Kegan Paul, 1978); Jackson Campbell Boswell and Sylvia Wallace Holton, *Chaucer's Fame in England: STC Chauceriana 1475–1640* (New York: Modern Language Association of America, 2004).

[15] In its historical survey of Chaucer criticism, this book bears some resemblance to the introductory chapters of many anthologies of Chaucer criticism, such as Corinne Saunders's chapter "The Development of Chaucer Criticism" in the Blackwell Guide to Chaucer, or Douglas Gray's introduction to *The Oxford Companion to Chaucer*. Gillian Rudd covers many of the same areas, but mixes together the topics of Chaucer's biography, sources, editing, and imitators with the critical heritage, and hence gives little sense of

Introduction: Chaucer, Audiences and Critics 9

overwhelming diversity of interpretations and readings of Chaucer's works. As definitions of "audience" changed over time, so too did interpretations of Chaucer. For scholars and students trying to navigate their way through the undifferentiated mass of Chaucer criticism, a focus on critics' understanding of audience makes it clear why they read Chaucer the way they do.

Several individual articles have been written studying the course of Chaucer criticism in the twentieth century. Albert Baugh covers the first half of the century; Derek Pearsall provides a more thorough analysis of specific critics, focusing on Kittredge, Chesterton, Lowes, Bronson, Dempster, Speirs, Donaldson, Muscatine, Payne, and Robertson.[16] He updates this survey in his 1986 article, covering especially the debate between the New Critics and the Exegetical Critics.[17] Charles Muscatine focuses on the changing views of Chaucer's religion, but provides a good overview of critical trends as well.[18] Various articles written in the late 1970s and early 1980s by people such as Florence Ridley attempted to deal with the need to move on from the New Criticism/Exegesis debate and the implications of the new critical theories being developed in literary studies, and in doing so these articles often give summaries of the development of Chaucer criticism or the "state of Chaucer studies."[19] Most recently, Ethan Knapp has surveyed the history

---

the chronology or development of Chaucer criticism. The *Riverside Chaucer*, among its copious notes and scholarly apparatus, provides overviews of the critical labyrinth in the introductory notes to each section; again, however, they are meant as surveys rather than in-depth studies of the course of Chaucer criticism. See Corinne Saunders, ed., *Blackwell Guides to Criticism: Chaucer* (Oxford: Blackwell, 2001) 5–21; Douglas Gray, ed., *The Oxford Companion to Chaucer* (Oxford: Oxford University Press, 2003) 117–19; Gillian Rudd, *The Complete Critical Guide to Geoffrey Chaucer* (London: Routledge, 2001) 153–82. For other anthologies of Chaucer criticism, not all of which have introductory chapters but which provide a sense of the trends in criticism because of the selections they make, see Saunders's list on pages 329–30, as well as Derek Pearsall, *Chaucer to Spenser: A Critical Reader* (Oxford: Blackwell, 1999); Piero Boitani and Jill Mann, eds., *Cambridge Companion to Chaucer*, 2nd ed. (Cambridge: Cambridge University Press, 2003); Thomas Stillinger, ed., *Critical Essays on Geoffrey Chaucer* (New York: G.K. Hall & Co, 1998).

[16] Albert C. Baugh, "Fifty Years of Chaucer Scholarship," *Speculum* 26.4 (Fall 1951) 659–72; Derek Pearsall, "The Criticism of Chaucer in the Twentieth Century," *Chaucer's Mind and Art*, ed. A.C. Cawley (Edinburgh: Oliver and Boyd, 1969) 1–25.

[17] Derek Pearsall, "Chaucer's Poetry and Its Modern Commentators: The Necessity of History," *Medieval Literature: Criticism, Ideology, and History*, ed. David Aers (New York: St. Martin's, 1986) 123–47.

[18] Charles Muscatine, "Chaucer's Religion and the Chaucer Religion," *Chaucer Traditions: Studies in Honour of Derek Brewer*, ed. Ruth Morse and Barry Windeatt (Cambridge: Cambridge University Press, 1990) 249–62.

[19] See, among others, Florence Ridley, "The State of Chaucer Studies: A Brief Survey," *Studies in the Age of Chaucer* 1 (1979) 3–16; Florence Ridley, "Questions without Answers—Yet or Ever? New Critical Modes and Chaucer," *Chaucer Review* 16.2 (Fall 1981) 101–6; Morton Bloomfield, "Contemporary Literary Theory and Chaucer," Florence

of Chaucer criticism through to the end of the twentieth century and covering the "theory debates" of the 1980s and 1990s.[20] Most of these articles, like the introductory chapters to collections of criticism, provide good summaries but little analysis. Two scholars who do provide more analysis, Lee Patterson in the first two chapters of *Negotiating the Past* and Anne Middleton in the article "Medieval Studies" (commissioned for a Modern Language Association book surveying literary studies both chronologically and in terms of theoretical fields), do so with explicit ideological goals for mapping out the future of Medieval Studies. Patterson traces the historical roots of the two major schools of criticism in Chaucer studies at the time he was writing (a version of the first chapter was published in 1983, although *Negotiating* was not printed until 1987): New Criticism and Exegetics. To these approaches he adds Marxism, which—unlike both New Criticism and exegetical criticism—takes into account the critic's/historian's own subjectivity and historical situation. Patterson thus undertakes his survey of the theoretical development of Medieval Studies to negotiate between these three competing theories; his stated goal is to discover a historicism that avoids the positivist underpinnings of many of the other theories. Anne Middleton builds on Patterson's work, focusing particularly on the effects of the separation of Medieval Studies programs from literature departments in the 1960s and 1970s.[21] She notes three new directions in which Medieval Studies seems to be moving after the mid-century exegetical debates: rethinking concepts of literacy in less absolute categories, and thinking about the ways in which these affect individuals and society; changing the study of religion to a focus on it as practice rather than doctrine; and returning to the "material and institutional base of medieval literature," the physical and material aspects of textuality, books, and literary production.[22] Middleton closes with a call to return to "literary history," but one that does not envision the Middle Ages as a monolithic "Other," instead focusing on "the multiple material and institutional forms of literacy and textuality, and ... the individual and communal varieties of creative responses to, and assertions of, the power to possess and deploy texts."[23] Her goal is to propose a program for Medieval Studies that will allow it to return from the margin of literary and cultural studies to which it has

---

Ridley, "A Response to 'Contemporary Literary Theory and Chaucer'," and Winthrop Wetherbee, "Convention and Authority: a Comment on Some Recent Critical Approaches to Chaucer," all in *New Perspectives in Chaucer Criticism*, ed. Donald Rose (Norman, OK: Pilgrim, 1981) 23–36, 37–51 and 71–81.

[20] Ethan Knapp, "Chaucer Criticism and its Legacies," in Lerer, *Yale Companion*, 324–56.

[21] Anne Middleton, "Medieval Studies," *Redrawing the Boundaries: The Transformation of English and American Literary Studies*, ed. Stephen Greenblatt and Giles Gunn (New York: Modern Language Association of America, 1992) 12–40.

[22] Middleton, "Medieval Studies," 28–9.

[23] Middleton, "Medieval Studies," 31.

Introduction: Chaucer, Audiences and Critics 11

been consigned, that will capitalize on the advances made in the field without returning to the older absolutisms.

My approach in this book has been slightly different. Rather than surveying the various theories in order to analyze their ideological underpinnings and biases, I have focused on one theoretical question, the concept of audience, and attempted to discern the way in which proponents of various theories deal with this concept. My contention is that ideas about audience, be they implicit or explicit, are fundamental to every literary theory: that the assumptions one makes about audience are inherent to one's theoretical approach, and are crucial in determining the critical conclusions to which one comes. Surveying the course of Chaucer criticism in the twentieth century from this vantage point, from this specific question, has allowed me to discern affinities, trends and developments which are less visible when the question of audience function is omitted from consideration.

This book, then, covers the territory of both a historical survey and a theoretical work. In addition to undertaking a study of twentieth-century Chaucer criticism, by studying the notion of audience in various interpretations of Chaucer's works I am able to propose some conclusions about the way in which notions of audience function in literary criticism. This book thus contributes to the sub-section of the discipline of literary studies which attempts to theorize about the concepts of audience, readership and reception: reader response criticism, reception theory, and narratology.[24] Such theories form the implicit backdrop to my work. Reader response theory has encouraged me to think about the ways in which a text controls or elicits responses in the reader. Reception theory has raised questions regarding the way in which the social, cultural and personal context of an audience influences the reader's participation in the creation of a specific reading or interpretation—the way in which the audience, far from being made up of passive recipients, participates in the creation of a work. Narratology has given me the concepts of "narratee" and "implied reader" as tools with which to consider the ways in which "readers" are already implied or encoded within a text. Yet all of these theories are a step removed from my project. Their focus is on delimiting audiences of various kinds, and studying the way in which those

---

[24] For selected key works in these fields, see Mieke Bal, *Narratology: Introduction to the Theory of Narrative* (Toronto: University of Toronto Press, 1985); Wayne Booth, *The Rhetoric of Fiction* (Chicago: University of Chicago Press, 1961); Seymour Chatman, *Story and Discourse: Narrative Structure in Fiction and Film* (Ithaca: Cornell University Press, 1978); Stanley Fish, *Is There a Text in This Class? The Authority of Interpretive Communities* (Cambridge, Mass.: Harvard University Press, 1980); Gerard Genette, *Narrative Discourse: An Essay in Method*, trans. Jane E. Lewin (Ithaca: Cornell University Press, 1980); Gerard Genette, *Narrative Discourse Revisited*, trans. Jane E. Lewin (Ithaca: Cornell University Press, 1988); James Phelan, *Narrative as Rhetoric: Technique, Audiences, Ethics, Ideology* (Columbus: Ohio State University Press, 1996); Gerald Prince, "Introduction à l'Etude Du Narrataire," *Poétique* 14 (1973) 178–96.

audiences interact with texts. I have taken a theoretical side-step from this: my goal is to consider the way in which the *concept* of audience affects criticism. It is with audience as an idea, a concept, a representation, a theory, that I deal, not with an actual (whether fictional or real) audience. I am interested in critics' *theories* of audience, their pre-established assumptions—how they define the "audience," how they think the audience-text-author dynamic works, how they think texts are communicated and received, and so on. Most importantly, I am interested in the effects that a particular theory of audience has on a critic's literary criticism.

Defining Audiences

It is fairly self-evident that critics can define audiences in different ways, and have done so throughout history. One can define the audience in terms of gender: are the readers of a text male or female? In terms of education: is the audience literate or illiterate? In terms of geography: what nationality or country is the audience assumed to be from? In terms of knowledge: are the members of the audience privy to specialized knowledge that will allow them to understand allusions, genre conventions, etc.? In terms of attitude: do the members of the audience hold particular attitudes or assumptions which will affect their interpretation of the text? All of these definitions, in turn, can be based on research into the actual audience of a particular text, or they can be assumptions in the mind of the critic— and that distinction too is itself a method of audience definition: will the critic limit him/herself to what s/he thinks was the "real" audience of a text, or will s/he work with a vague, ideal, abstract notion of "audience"?

Not all of these choices will have equal effects on the interpretation that results. Whether the audience is from England or the colonies may be less crucial than whether the audience would know about certain conventions of English society, for example. Or whether the audience is assumed to be male or female may be irrelevant to the criticism produced if the men and women in the audience are assumed to share identical attitudes, values and outlooks. On the other hand, some fundamental definitions are nearly prescriptive: if a critic makes a particular assumption about audiences, then s/he is likely to produce a certain kind of interpretation. For example, if a critic assumes a medieval audience is thoroughly religious, and that it is the critic's task to interpret medieval texts historically, he is unlikely to advocate a reading of Chaucer as irreverent or bawdily humourous; if a scholar defines Chaucer's audience as extremely well-educated and well-read, she will probably produce an interpretation of his works which depends heavily upon allusion, literary reference, and inter-textuality.

I begin this study of scholarly understanding of Chaucer's audiences with George Lyman Kittredge for several reasons. Modern Chaucer scholarship in many ways began in the middle of the nineteenth century, with the founding

Introduction: Chaucer, Audiences and Critics 13

of the institutions of the Chaucer Society and the Early English Text Society.[25] Victorian scholars such as F.J. Furnivall and Walter W. Skeat were instrumental in placing Medieval Studies on a "scholarly" footing, finding manuscripts, producing editions, tracing sources, refining questionable line readings, and developing the tools of philology, palaeography, linguistics, and codicology.[26] Skeat produced both a seven-volume edition of Chaucer's Works and a shorter *Student's Chaucer*, which became the standard editions used by literary scholars until the publication of F.N. Robinson's edition of Chaucer in 1933. However, these Victorian scholars were not interpreters or literary critics in the way we would use the words today. They produced little in the way of overarching readings of Chaucer, instead restricting themselves to providing the technical apparatus necessary for other Victorian gentlemen-scholars to produce their own interpretations. The most they might do was to argue the interpretation of a particular line or passage; they would not produce readings of an entire work or poem.

With the growth of English studies in the universities, and the need to provide comprehensive, overarching explanations of texts for undergraduate courses, literary *criticism*, in addition to *scholarship*, began to develop.[27] The generation of scholars around 1900, including George Lyman Kittredge, was the first to produce

---

[25]   Brewer and Gray "conveniently if rather arbitrarily" date the beginnings of "modern" criticism to 1933, the date when F.N. Robinson's edition of Chaucer's works was published; Brewer states that this date marks "roughly the end of the tradition of the generally cultivated amateur critic and reader." English studies had moved into the universities well before that, however, and it seems unfair to call scholars such as Skeat and Furnivall "amateurs" given the extent to which we depend upon their scholarship even today. Brewer, *Critical Heritage*, vol. 1, 1; Gray, ed., *The Oxford Companion to Chaucer*, 117.

[26]   For discussion of Furnivall's and Skeat's contributions, see Donald C. Baker, "Frederick James Furnivall" and A.S.G. Edwards, "Walter Skeat" in *Editing Chaucer: The Great Tradition*, ed. Paul G. Ruggiers (Norman, Oklahoma: Pilgrim Books, 1984) 159–69, 171–89; Charlotte Morse, "Popularizing Chaucer in the Nineteenth Century," *Chaucer Review* 38.2 (2003) 99–125; David O. Matthews, "Speaking to Chaucer: The Poet and the Nineteenth-Century Academy," *Studies in Medievalism* 9 (1997) 5–25; Richard Utz, "Enthusiast or Philologist? Professional Discourse and the Medievalism of Frederick James Furnivall," *Studies in Medievalism* 11 (2001) 189–212; Antonia Ward, "'My Love for Chaucer': F.J. Furnivall and Homosociality in the Chaucer Society," *Studies in Medievalism* 9 (1997) 44–57; Peter Faulkner, "'The Paths of Virtue and Early English': F.J. Furnivall and Victorian Medievalism," *From Medieval to Medievalism*, ed. John Simons (New York: St. Martin's Press, 1992) 27–54; Knapp, "Chaucer Criticism," 329–30 and 334–5; David Matthews, *The Making of Middle English, 1765–1910*, (Minneapolis: University of Minnesota Press, 1999), chapters 6 and 7; James Johnson, "Walter W. Skeat's Canterbury Tale," *Chaucer Review* 36.1 (2001) 16–27; Arthur Sherbo, "More on Walter William Skeat," *Poetica* 36 (1992) 69–89.

[27]   Knapp makes a similar distinction to mine, noting the "segregation of historical scholarship and literary inquiry": Knapp, "Chaucer Criticism," 337. See also L.D. Benson, "A Reader's Guide to Writings on Chaucer," *Geoffrey Chaucer*, ed. Derek Brewer (London: G. Bell & Sons, 1974) 340.

14   *Twentieth-Century Chaucer Criticism*

works recognizable as literary criticism as such. Kittredge straddles both periods. Many of his articles fall into the "old" category of source study or historical reference; however, he also wrote two seminal articles of criticism, arguing for specific interpretations of the Wife of Bath and the Pardoner. Kittredge's book *Chaucer and His Poetry* represents a new era of criticism by offering a general, critical reading of Chaucer's works. *Chaucer and His Poetry* is a good work with which to begin because it was important in other ways too: it founded a school of Chaucer criticism and a method of reading (the so-called dramatic theory); it influenced Chaucer scholarship for at least a generation, if not more;[28] and it became a work which other critics had to "answer" if they were to propose different readings of Chaucer. The works of other scholars studied in this book meet similar criteria. Each either began or can be taken as representative of a school or trend in Chaucer criticism.[29] Each influenced the interpretations of other scholars for many years after publication. Each presented an argument which needed to be "answered" if alternative interpretations were to be proposed.[30] Tracing the changes in these critics' understanding of audience provides a narrative of the changes in Chaucer scholarship since its modern inception. As critics built upon or challenged their predecessors' understanding of Chaucer's audience, they developed new understandings of Chaucer's writings.

Over the course of the twentieth century, the term "audience" was defined in different ways, and for different reasons. Kittredge, whose most important work began its existence as a series of undergraduate lectures, was interested in making Chaucer accessible to students, and so he emphasized the "universal audience,"

---

[28]   See Gray, *Oxford Companion*, 117.

[29]   Ethan Knapp focuses on many of the same scholars as I have chosen, with the exception of choosing John Spiers rather than C.S. Lewis. See Knapp, "Chaucer Criticism."

[30]   Critically, all of these scholars developed reputations as good teachers, as well as leading researchers; this may in part explain their far-reaching influence, as their ideas were disseminated through undergraduate teaching and doctoral supervisions. See the introductory chapter in George Lyman Kittredge, *Chaucer and His Poetry* (Cambridge, Mass.: Harvard University Press, 1970); Elizabeth Jackson, "The Kittredge Way," *College English* 4.8 (May 1943) 483–7; Stuart P. Sherman, "Professor Kittredge and the Teaching of English," *The Origins of Literary Studies in America: A Documentary Anthology*, ed. Gerald Graff and Michael Warner (New York: Routledge, 1989) 148–9; Derek Brewer, "The Tutor: A Portrait," *C.S. Lewis at the Breakfast Table and Other Reminiscences*, ed. James T. Como (London: Collins, 1980) 41–67; Walter Hooper, *C.S. Lewis: A Companion & Guide* (New York: Harper Collins, 1996) 18–21; Mary J. Carruthers, "Speaking of Donaldson," *Acts of Interpretation: The Text in Its Context: Essays in Honor of E. Talbot Donaldson*, ed. Mary J. Carruthers (Norman: Pilgrim Books, 1982) 375–80; Elizabeth D. Kirk, "Donaldson Teaching and Learning," *Chaucer Review* 41.3 (2007) 279–88; Ralph Hanna, "Donaldson and Robertson: An Obligatory Conjunction," *Chaucer Review* 41.3 (2007) 240–49; Wood, Chauncey, "In Memoriam: D.W. Robertson Jr., 1914–1992," *Chaucer Review* 28.1 (1993) 1–4.

Introduction: Chaucer, Audiences and Critics   15

the way in which people, both medieval and modern, connect to Chaucer's poetry. C.S. Lewis, in the following generation, reacting in part against the distorting generalizations Kittredge's approach entailed, wished to emphasize the difference between Chaucer's time and now, and focused on Chaucer's medieval readers. D.W. Robertson and his exegetical followers carried Lewis's historical approach further, and fit Chaucer's poetry into the highly-specialized discourse of medieval exegetical readers. E. Talbot Donaldson, a contemporary of Robertson's, reacted against the elitism and extensive scholarship required for Robertson's approach, and developed interpretations of Chaucer's poetry on the basis of his own close reading and his personal responses to it. Carolyn Dinshaw, a student of Robertson's but in many ways closer to Donaldson in her approach, combined historicism with a deeply personal and political approach to criticism. Lee Patterson, also in the post-exegetical debate period, is representative of a recent group of scholars who have attempted to negotiate between the perils of subjectivity and the lure of a false sense of objectivity, and thus searched for medieval individuals who have left some historical trace of a response to Chaucer's works.

Within the different definitions of the term "audience" are some commonalities which are helpful in sorting through these critics and their approaches. Several abstract categories of audience definition seem fundamental in limiting and conditioning a critic's interpretation, and best explain the diversity in interpretation in Chaucer criticism. First, one of the most fundamental criteria for audience definition facing a critic of Chaucer's works is historicity: that is, whether the critic will limit Chaucer's audience historically or not. Some scholars believe that interpretations of Chaucer's works should be limited to the way in which a medieval audience (however that, in turn, is envisioned) would have read the texts. Others have a more cross-historical definition of audience, and include twentieth-century readers of Chaucer in their concept of "audience."[31] These latter scholars therefore have few compunctions about proffering twentieth-century interpretations of Chaucer's works as well as, or instead of, "medieval" interpretations. This decision, obviously, has a major impact on the kinds of scholarship each critic does, as well as the readings of Chaucer they produce. I argue that scholars from the first category, such as C.S. Lewis, D.W. Robertson, and Lee Patterson, tend to assume not only that Chaucer's "audience" proper includes only his medieval listeners and readers, but that as a result modern readers should do their utmost to read Chaucer's works in the way that first audience would have read them. On the other hand, scholars from the second category, such as George Lyman Kittredge and E. Talbot Donaldson, tend to assume that human nature is consistent or uniform, and thus universalize their own responses, their own "careful readings" of Chaucer's works, to Chaucer's audience throughout time. Carolyn Dinshaw, who also belongs

---

[31]   Thomas Stillinger writes, "For centuries now, it has been possible to think about Chaucer in two quite different ways. He is an ancient writer, his texts silent monuments of a lost world; and, at the same time, he is a living poetic voice." *Critical Essays on Geoffrey Chaucer*, 2.

to this second category, maintains the distinction between medieval and modern responses; nonetheless, she advocates cross-historical readings which take both medieval and modern interpretations into account.

Another way in which one can define the audience is in terms of irony: is the audience situated relatively "closely" to the characters and narrator, sharing their perspective, sympathies, and assumptions; or is the audience assumed to be at some distance from the characters and the narrator, aware of a gap between the characters' perspectives and their own, and thus alive to irony, mockery, and satire? If one believes that the members of Chaucer's audience are "close," in sympathetic terms, to the text—that they identify closely with the characters, narrator, or message of the work—then one will advocate relatively unironic, "straight" readings of Chaucer. If, however, one posits a sceptical, slightly distrustful audience open to double meanings and innuendo, and situated at a distance from the characters or narrator, then one will tend to argue for highly ironic readings of Chaucer. Early in the twentieth century, critics tended to hold an image of "audience" as relatively unsuspicious and sympathetic, and therefore read Chaucer's works relatively "straight," allowing for momentary dramatic ironies but for the most part taking the surface meaning of the text literally. With the advent of New Criticism and exegetical criticism, as diametrically opposed as those two schools of thought were, came more ironic readings of Chaucer, and critics who posited audiences that were suspicious and sceptical, and at times took the text to mean exactly the opposite of what it means literally.

A third, crucial category of audience definition is homogeneity: is the audience assumed to be relatively homogeneous in its composition, or is it heterogeneous? Will most members of the audience react to the text in more-or-less the same ways, or will there be a diversity of response? This division seems to be the one that has undergone the most evident chronological development over the course of the century: early in the century, critics almost always assumed a relatively homogeneous audience. (Indeed, C.S. Lewis explicitly dismissed from consideration marginal and aberrant responses.) By the middle of the century, people were acknowledging the possibility of other responses—E. Talbot Donaldson briefly envisioned a female reader, while D.W. Robertson entertained the idea of "bad" readers who would not conform to the religious dictates of the Middle Ages—but this possibility of heterogeneity did not significantly affect their interpretations of Chaucer. In the last quarter of the twentieth century, however, critics began to give serious consideration to the possibility of a diverse audience and a multiplicity of interpretation. As a result, criticism today is markedly different from its predecessors, and has opened up new fields for Chaucer studies, especially studies of Chaucer's variety of audiences.

The "audience function" took many forms over the course of the twentieth century, and as a result, an almost overwhelming variety of Chaucer criticism was produced. As different literary theories and approaches developed in English studies as a whole, these were applied to Chaucer's works, and brought with them inherent, often unstated, ideas about audiences and readers. At the same time, as more studies of Chaucer's contemporary listeners and readers were done, these new ideas about Chaucer's audience led to different critical approaches and prompted rethinkings of the underlying theories. This book will attempt to make sense of the changes in ideas about Chaucer's audience and in Chaucer criticism as a whole, both in terms of chronological development and in terms of underlying theoretical assumptions.

Chapter 1
George Lyman Kittredge (1860–1941): The Dramatic Reader

The turn of the twentieth century was, in many ways, a crucial time in the history of English studies. English literary studies were moving from the realm of the gentleman scholar into the universities. No longer simply the purview of gentlemen with time on their hands, by moving into academia and becoming specialized and professionalized, English literary study, paradoxically, became open to all classes. English, and especially Medieval Studies, had already been made "scholarly" with developments and improvements in philology, palaeography, manuscript studies, codicology, and editorial techniques by nineteenth-century scholars. For medieval English literature, these included Frederick James Furnivall, Walter W. Skeat, and other members of the Chaucer Society, who had printed transcripts of the important Chaucer manuscripts, re-edited Chaucer's works, and begun the invaluable Early English Text Society, dedicated to editing and printing medieval and early Renaissance works.[1] George Lyman Kittredge, one of the most important Chaucerians in the early decades of the twentieth century, in many ways exemplified the spread of English studies beyond the realm of Victorian "gentlemen scholars," since he was the son of a merchant. After taking a degree in Classics at Harvard, as a young man Kittredge taught Latin for several years at Phillips Exeter School in Exeter, New Hampshire. He had met Francis Child at Harvard, and on Child's advice he studied in Germany for a year, from 1886–1887, returning to teach English at Harvard in 1888. Over the course of his long career at Harvard, Kittredge taught Old Norse, Old English, Middle English, romances, Chaucer, Spenser, Shakespeare, Bacon, Milton, and the Bible; he also worked with the man who was to produce a lasting edition of Chaucer's works, Fred N. Robinson.

---

[1] For discussion of Furnivall's and Skeat's contributions to Chaucer scholarship, see fn. 25 in the Introduction. For nineteenth–century scholarship in medieval studies, see Lee Patterson, *Negotiating the Past: The Historical Understanding of Medieval Literature* (Madison: University of Wisconsin Press, 1987) 9–18. For the Victorian scholars and societies, see Harrison Ross Steeves, *Learned Societies and English Literary Scholarship* (New York: Columbia University Press, 1913); John Gross, *The Rise and Fall of the Man of Letters* (London: Macmillan, 1969); Richard D. Altick, *The Scholar Adventurers* (New York: Macmillan, 1960); Martin Hewitt, ed., *Scholarship in Victorian Britain* (Leeds: Centre for Victorian Studies, 1998). For the movement of literary studies into the universities, see, among others, Jo McMurty, *English Language, English Literature: The Creation of an Academic Discipline* (Hamden: Archon, 1985).

20   *Twentieth-Century Chaucer Criticism*

Kittredge was chair of the Division of Modern Languages from 1894–1924 and of Comparative Literature from 1917–1936. In 1917 Harvard named him the first Gurney Professor of English literature. Kittredge was granted honorary doctorates from Harvard (1907), Johns Hopkins (1915), McGill (1921), and Oxford (1932), among others.[2]

In his career, Kittredge brought together two strands of scholarship from the previous century. Having studied at German universities, he was well-versed in the techniques of philology and source-study; his mentor, however, was Francis J. Child, and from Child he developed an interest in oral literature, folklore, and popular ballads.[3] The two traditions were complementary, rather than mutually exclusive: by studying oral and popular stories and ballads from Scotland, Wales, and the American Appalachians, one could gain insight into older oral or semi-oral cultures and literatures, such as early medieval literature. Conversely, when "scholarly" techniques of philology, etymology, source-study, and comparative analysis were applied to the "unliterary" genres of folklore and ballad, these genres moved into the universities. Studying them became respectable and "scientific," and contributed to the professionalization of English studies.[4] As well, Kittredge was at Harvard during the formative years of George Pierce Baker's "English 47" workshop, which was the first course in America to teach playwriting, and was instrumental in making the study of modern drama and dramatic writing a "respectable" field of study in universities across the country. Harvard was also emerging from its conversion from a clerically-oriented curriculum to a secular institution under the leadership of Charles W. Eliot, President of Harvard from 1869–1909. It is interesting to speculate what role this increased interest in drama

---

[2]   For biography, see Clyde Kenneth Hyder, *George Lyman Kittredge: Teacher and Scholar* (Lawrence: University of Kansas Press, 1962); Alice Robertson, *A Biographical Study of George Lyman Kittredge*, unpublished MA diss. University of Maine, June 1947; Rosalyn Rossignol, "Kittredge, George Lyman," *Chaucer: A Literary Reference to His Life and Work* (New York: Infobase Publishing, 2007) 480; Derek Pearsall, "Kittredge, George Lyman," *Dictionary of American National Biography* (New York: OUP 1999) 781–2.

[3]   For Kittredge's knowledge of German philology, see Hyder, *George Lyman Kittredge,* 39–40; A. Robertson, *A Biographical Study,* 21. For the influence of German philologists on English academics, see Richard Utz, *Chaucer and the Discourse of German Philology: A History of Reception and an Annotated Bibliography of Studies, 1793–1948* (Turnhout, Belgium: Brepols, 2002), especially 103–26; Richard Utz, "When Dinosaurs Ruled the Earth: A Short History of German *Chaucerphilologie* in the Nineteenth and Early Twentieth Century," *PhiN: Philologie im Netz* 21 (2002) 56–62; Bliss Perry, "And Gladly Teach," *The Origins of Literary Studies in America: A Documentary Anthology*, eds. Gerald Graff and Michael Warner (New York: Routledge, 1989) 139. For Kittredge's debt to Child, see Hyder, *George Lyman Kittredge*, 78–82; A. Robertson, *A Biographical Study*, 17.

[4]   For a strangely disapproving account of Child's and Kittredge's contribution to the professionalization of English literature, see Jill Terry Rudy, "Transforming Audiences for Oral Tradition: Child, Kittredge, Thompson, and Connections of Folklore and English Studies," *College English* 66.5 (May 2004) 524–45.

George Lyman Kittredge (1860–1941): The Dramatic Reader 21

and emphasis on secularization might have played in the formation of Kittredge's theory of the "roadside drama" and his decidedly secular readings of Chaucer's works.[5]

As well as being situated at an important time in the history of English studies, Kittredge marks a turning point in Chaucer studies, and hence is appropriate as a starting point in this study.[6] Scholars such as Skeat, Furnivall, and Child were concerned primarily with editing and publishing: they wanted to make accurate and scholarly editions of Chaucer, other poets, and popular ballads available to a broader readership. They were also concerned with source-study, seeking to discover Chaucer's relationship to his French, English or Italian predecessors and to trace the various themes and motifs in folklore and ballads. In a way that seems slightly alien to a modern academic of English, they did not provide much analysis or interpretation of the works. To put it another way, they were *scholars*, but they were not also *critics*. Skeat's compendious notes to his edition of Chaucer, for example, include philological points, manuscript variants, Middle English spelling and pronunciation, source identification, and historical reference, but—when one compares them to the pages and pages of discussion in the *Riverside Chaucer* of various interpretations of Chaucer—virtually no analysis or interpretation.[7] Kittredge's first articles fall within this tradition. Most of the articles Kittredge printed in *Modern Philology*, *Modern Language Notes* or *PMLA* during the first two decades of the twentieth century are either source studies that trace passages in Chaucer back to Deschamps, Machaut or others, or historical studies that attempt to identify individuals mentioned in Chaucer with real historical figures.[8] Only two are substantially different in their approach: "Chaucer's Pardoner" attempts to

---

[5]   Thank you to the anonymous reader of this manuscript for this suggestion. For the development of "English 47" at Harvard, see Cecil Ellsworth Hinkel, *An Analysis and Evaluation of the 47 Workshop of George Pierce Baker*, unpublished PhD diss., Ohio State University, 1959; Lafayette McLaws, "A Master of Playwrights," *North American Review* 200.706 (September 1914) 459–67.

[6]   D.S. Brewer, too, sees Kittredge as a "bridge" between nineteenth- and twentieth-century criticism: see D.S. Brewer, "The Criticism of Chaucer in the Twentieth Century," *Chaucer's Mind and Art*, ed. A.C. Cawley (Edinburgh: Oliver and Boyd, 1969) 5.

[7]   Walter W. Skeat, ed., *The Complete Works of Geoffrey Chaucer*, 6 vols. (Oxford: Clarendon Press, 1894).

[8]   See G.L. Kittredge, "Chaucer and the *Roman de Carité*," *Modern Language Notes* 12.2 (February 1897) 57–8; G.L. Kittredge, "Coryat and the Pardoner's Tale," *Modern Language Notes* 15.7 (November 1900) 193–4; G.L. Kittredge, "A Friend of Chaucer's," *PMLA* 16.3 (1901) 450–52; G.L. Kittredge, "Chaucer's Alceste," *Modern Philology* 6.4 (Spring 1909) 435–9; G.L. Kittredge, "Chaucer's Envoy to Bukton," *Modern Language Notes* 24.1 (Winter 1909) 14–15; G.L. Kittredge, "Chaucer's Medea and the Date of the *Legend of Good Women*," *PMLA* 24.2 (1909) 343–63; G.L. Kittredge, "Chauceriana," *Modern Philology* 7.4 (Spring 1910) 465–83; G.L. Kittredge, "Chaucer's *Troilus* and Guillaume de Machaut," *Modern Language Notes* 30.3 (March 1915) 69; G.L. Kittredge, "Guillaume de Machaut and the *Book of the Duchess*," *PMLA* 30.1 (1915) 1–24; G.L.

analyze the psychology of the Pardoner and explain his contradictory actions, while "Chaucer's Discussion of Marriage" introduces Kittredge's famous "marriage group" theory, which maintains that the Wife of Bath initiates a discussion on marriage to which the Clerk, Merchant, and Franklin respond.[9] Both of these arguments would be incorporated into Kittredge's later work, *Chaucer and His Poetry*.[10] It is this work that really marks a new direction in Chaucer studies. In *Chaucer and His Poetry*, Kittredge offers a full-blown *interpretation* of Chaucer and analyzes the characters, development, structures, and themes, rather than solely carrying out source-study, philological explication, or historical exploration.[11]

Chaucer and His Poetry is important for other reasons. Essentially a series of lectures given at the Johns Hopkins University in the spring of 1914, *Chaucer and His Poetry* made claims about Chaucer's writing that were to influence Chaucer studies, in various ways, for most of the twentieth century.[12] While few scholars today would advocate a wholehearted adoption of Kittredge's dramatic principle, such as that used by Lumiansky in his work *Of Sondry Folk,* some are still attempting to rework the dramatic theory in ways which complement more recent

---

Kittredge, "Lewis Chaucer or Lewis Clifford?" *Modern Philology* 14.9 (January 1917) 513–18.

[9] G.L. Kittredge, "Chaucer's Pardoner," *Atlantic Monthly* 72 (December 1893) 829–33; G.L. Kittredge, "Chaucer's Discussion of Marriage," *Modern Philology* 9.4 (Spring 1912) 435–67.

[10] George Lyman Kittredge, *Chaucer and His Poetry* (Cambridge, Mass.: Harvard University Press, 1970).

[11] Ethan Knapp gives a similar division between "fundamental historical research" and "descriptive literary criticism" and agrees with my identification of Kittredge as among the first to practice this kind of criticism: Ethan Knapp, "Chaucer Criticism and its Legacies," Seth Lerer, ed., *The Yale Companion to Chaucer* (New Haven: Yale University Press, 2006) 337. This choice is, of course, open to contention. The move was happening all across English studies, and Kittredge's contemporaries were performing similar analyses. Few of these early efforts were thorough-going, however, and Kittredge seems in the forefront of a new trend in English Studies. Thomas Lounsbury, W.P. Ker, and G.K. Chesterton, among others, could also be nominated as pioneers in "literary criticism" as opposed to "scholarship"; none of these, however, wrote criticism on Chaucer as far-reaching or influential on later decades of Chaucer scholarship as Kittredge's, though Lounsbury and Chesterton, at least, were influential in shaping the popular reception of Chaucer. Many scholars agree with me in highlighting the importance of Kittredge: see, among others, Thomas Stillinger's introduction in *Critical Essays on Geoffrey Chaucer*, ed. Thomas Stillinger (New York: G.K. Hall & Co, 1998) 1.

[12] It is important to note that despite the printing date of 1915, the lectures were given in April and May of 1914 and were probably developed over the preceding years; hence the remarkably optimistic tone of some passages, which belongs to the heyday mood of turn-of-the-century America and feels out of place, almost offensive, at the beginning of the Great War.

George Lyman Kittredge (1860–1941): The Dramatic Reader 23

theoretical developments.[13] Likewise, although the heyday of the "marriage group" controversy has passed, people are still writing articles on Kittredge's "marriage group."[14] Other scholars reject the depiction of the "marriage group" in its limited sense as a "discussion" between the Wife of Bath, the Clerk, the Merchant and the Franklin, but nonetheless acknowledge that themes raised by these tales, such as marriage, women's sovereignty, and *gentillesse,* run throughout the *Canterbury Tales.*[15] Kittredge's concept of Chaucer's audience has been challenged many times, most notably by critics such as C.S. Lewis and D.W. Robertson, who

---

[13] R.M. Lumiansky, *Of Sondry Folk: The Dramatic Principle in the* Canterbury Tales (Austin: University of Texas Press, 1955); for modern "revivals" and revisions of the dramatic theory, see, for example, Jeff Henderson, "Chaucer's Experiment in Narrative Metadrama: The General Prologue as Dramatis Personae," *Publications of the Arkansas Philological Association* 14.1 (Spring 1988) 13–24; H. Marshall Leicester, *The Disenchanted Self* (Berkeley: University of California Press, 1990); John M. Ganim, "Drama, Theatricality and Performance: Radicals of Presentation in the *Canterbury Tales,*" *Drama, Narrative and Poetry in the* Canterbury Tales, ed. Wendy Harding (Toulouse: Presse Université du Mirail, 2003) 66–82.

[14] For the major controversy, see, among others, W.W. Lawrence, "The Marriage Group in the *Canterbury Tales,*" *Modern Philology* 11 (1912–1913) 247–58; John Kenyon, "Further Notes on the Marriage Group in the *Canterbury Tales,*" *Journal of English and German Philology* 15 (1916) 282–8; Carleton Brown, "The Evolution of the Canterbury 'Marriage Group'," *PMLA* 48 (1933) 1041–59; Sister Mariella, "The Parson's Tale and the Marriage Group," *Modern Language Notes* 53.4 (Spring 1938) 251–6; Germaine Dempster, "A Period in the Development of the *Canterbury Tales* Marriage Group and of Blocks B2 and C," *PMLA* 68 (1953) 1142–59; for disagreement with Kittredge see Henry Barrett Hinckley, "The Debate on Marriage in the *Canterbury Tales,*" *PMLA* 32.2 (1917) 292–305; C.P. Lyons, "The Marriage Debate in the *Canterbury Tales,*" *English Literary History* 2 (1935) 252–62. References are made to the Marriage Group throughout the century and to the present day: see R.E. Kaske, "Chaucer's Marriage Group," *Chaucer the Love Poet,* ed. Jerome Provost *et al.* (Athens: University of Georgia Press, 1973) 45–65; Clair C. Olson, "The Interludes of the Marriage Group in the *Canterbury Tales,*" *Chaucer and Middle English Studies in Honour of Rossell Hope Robbins,* eds. Beryl Rowland and Lloyd A. Duchemin (London: Allen and Unwin, 1974) 164–72; Ruth Berggren, "Who Really Is the Advocate of Equality in the Marriage Group?" *Massachusetts Studies in English* 6.1 (1977) 25–36; Warren Ginsberg, "The Lineaments of Desire: Wish-Fulfillment in Chaucer's Marriage Group," *Criticism* 25.3 (Summer 1983) 197–210; Joan G. Haahr, "Chaucer's 'Marriage Group' Revisited: The Wife of Bath and Merchant in Debate," *Acta* 14 (1990) 105–20; Zong-Qi Cai, "Fragments I–II and III–IV in *The Canterbury Tales*: A Re-Examination of the Idea of the 'Marriage Group'," *Comitatus* 19 (1988) 80–98; Susan Yager, "Boethius, Philosophy and Chaucer's 'Marriage Group'," *Carmina Philosophiae* 4 (1995) 77–89; Mari Pakkala-Weckström, "Discourse Strategies in the Marriage Dialogue of Chaucer's *Canterbury Tales,*" *Neuphilologische Mitteilungen* 105.2 (2004) 153–75.

[15] See, to cite only one example among many, Helen Cooper's discussion of "The Woman Question" in Helen Cooper, *The Structure of the* Canterbury Tales (London: Duckworth, 2001) 221.

24   *Twentieth-Century Chaucer Criticism*

object to Kittredge's ahistoricity; nonetheless, Kittredge's main assumption, that Chaucer's audience was much like a theatrical audience, watching characters in a play, still has some appeal today—if only because of the vividness of the characters and the drama between them. Most Chaucerians, I suspect, would find it difficult to teach an undergraduate course on Chaucer without considering the psychology of the Pardoner, or the relationship of the Wife of Bath's Prologue to her Tale, or the dynamic interactions between the various pilgrims.[16] As C. David Benson writes, "[Kittredge's] central assumption—that the Canterbury pilgrims have complex, believable personalities that intimately inform their individual tales—is still widely, if unsystematically, accepted today, with few feeling the need to justify its validity."[17]

The Author and the Audience

Kittredge's fundamental rule as a critic, and that of many of his contemporaries, is that the author is always right—at least when it comes to Chaucer. Whether this held true for lesser authors than Chaucer is unclear, but when it comes to the medieval master, Kittredge works on the assumption that Chaucer made no mistakes, that everything in his works and writing is *meant* to be there. He writes emphatically, "*Chaucer always knew what he was about.*"[18] For the critic, this means that if anything doesn't seem to fit, or if anything seems to be a mistake, the critic must re-work his theory to accommodate the extraneous parts, rather than ignoring or dismissing the oddities in favour of the over-arching theory. This has a major implication with regard to Kittredge's theory of audience. If modern readers do not understand an aspect of Chaucer's work, the problem is with them, and not with the text or author. Even the most extraneous details, then, must be accounted for and explained: this is a theory that does not allow for laziness or superiority on the part of the audience. The author is always superior to the audience, and therefore the reader must continue to analyze the text until he understands the

---

[16]   Carolyn Dinshaw, among others, maintains that Kittredge's dramatic theory is still prevalent in undergraduate teaching: see Carolyn Dinshaw, *Getting Medieval: Sexualities and Communities, Pre- and Postmodern* (Durham: Duke University Press, 1999) 123; Carolyn Dinshaw, "Chaucer's Queer Touches/A Queer Touches Chaucer," *Exemplaria* 7.1 (1995) 83. Peter Beidler, although he does not advocate Kittredge's dramatic theory, nonetheless suggests teaching Chaucer as drama: Peter G. Beidler, "Teaching Chaucer as Drama: The Garden Scene in the Shipman's Tale," *Exemplaria* 8.2 (1996) 485–93.

[17]   C. David Benson, "The *Canterbury Tales*: Personal Drama or Experiments in Poetic Variety?" *The Cambridge Chaucer Companion*, eds. Piero Boitani and Jill Mann (Cambridge: Cambridge University Press, 1986) 94.

[18]   Kittredge, *Chaucer and His Poetry*, 151; *his italics*.

author's purpose to its fullest.[19] Alongside this assumption, however, Kittredge makes another claim, more implicit but further-reaching in terms of his criticism: he maintains that "what Chaucer was about" was creating life-like characters in dramatic situations. Situated at the turning of the twentieth century, schooled in the values of unity, psychological realism and character development which underlay genres such as the Victorian novel or, in poetry, dramatic monologues such as Robert Browning's "My Last Duchess," Kittredge shared the aesthetic ideals of many of his contemporaries. Far from worrying that he might be imposing nineteenth- or twentieth-century values on works of a different era, Kittredge fully believed that a medieval audience would have looked for the same characteristics in Chaucer's writing. Medieval readers or listeners would have been alive to the psychological drama of Chaucer's characters, and they would have perceived the "realism" in Chaucer *as* realism.[20] We can see, in Kittredge's analysis, the "author function" and the "audience function" working in tandem. Interpretations of the text are limited by the "author function"—the image of Chaucer as a realistic, dramatic writer. These limitations are then supported by the "audience function"— the claim that a medieval audience would have appreciated drama and realism.

Because of these two overall operating assumptions, that Chaucer always knew what he was about and that "what he was about" was dramatic characterization, Kittredge takes as his main goal "to illustrate Chaucer's art in the two main points of character and dramatic method."[21] This goal underlies not only Kittredge's method and analysis, but his reasons for choosing to discuss particular fragments or groups of tales rather than others. One gets the sense, however, that Kittredge could explain any part of the *Canterbury Tales* with his dramatic theory: he could equally have chosen other sections, which would have proven his point almost as effectively. Because Chaucer is always right, when it seems at first glance that he seems to be "violating dramatic fitness," we as readers "must look to our steps"—in other words, we must find ways of explaining the text that remain consistent with dramatic fitness.[22] Indeed, much of Kittredge's book is spent doing just that, and rather than avoiding the "problem spots" he often seeks them out: the Clerk's "Envoy," for example, or the Pardoner's self-revelatory confessions— sections which seem to break the dramatic realism of the text. Once one accepts Kittredge's two basic premises, that Chaucer knew what he was doing, and that he was creating situations of realistic dramatic characterization, the critic's job is relatively straightforward: every detail in the text must be explained in terms of a

---

[19]   Throughout this book, I will use the pronoun that corresponds with the assumptions about the gender of the reader of the scholar being discussed; thus since Kittredge tends to assume the reader was male, I will use the pronoun "he".

[20]   See Kittredge, *Chaucer and His Poetry*: for example, the comments on the drama of the pilgrims, 156–7; the reception of the Wife of Bath, 34; the realism of the walls in the Temple of Venus, 81–2; the realism of science, 93.

[21]   Ibid., 147.

[22]   Ibid., 151.

26   *Twentieth-Century Chaucer Criticism*

character's motivations and the dramatic situation, and if a detail does not seem to fit, the critic must reconsider his understanding of the character until it does.

A Universal Audience

This straightforward approach betrays a basic assumption about the nature of audiences. Kittredge, despite being compelled to acknowledge scholars who disagree with him, tends to assume that most readers—at least most sensible ones—will share his readings. Kittredge at once universalizes his own response and assumes a universality of readers. Thus, when he states that the *Book of the Duchess* is very like a real dream, he writes that "every reader must instantly admit" this effect.[23] He allows that not all readers actually approach the *Canterbury Tales* in the same manner, but cannot believe that they do not instinctively share the same *feeling*: "Most readers, I am aware, treat this great masterpiece simply as a storehouse of fiction, and so do many critics. Yet everybody feels, I am sure, that Chaucer was quite as much interested in the Pilgrims themselves as in their several narratives."[24] Clearly, Kittredge assumes a universal audience and a universal response, which, for the most part, coincides with his own response and reading of Chaucer. Unlike Donaldson, Kittredge rarely indicates his universalization with the use of first person plural—he doesn't talk about "our" response or how "we" feel. Instead, he simply offers his reading as definitive.[25] Kittredge is certain his reading accords not only with the experience of most of the readers of Chaucer, but with Chaucer's own intentions: "From this point of view, which surely accords with Chaucer's intention, the Pilgrims do not exist for the sake of the stories, but *vice versa*."[26] Kittredge's tendency to offer his own reading as "fact" is evident in the form of *Chaucer and His Poetry*: several multi-page-length paraphrases of Chaucer's Works are given in modern English, as though the only impediment to the modern reader in understanding Chaucer the way Kittredge understands him were the difficulty of the Middle English.

This universal audience extends beyond the "academic scholars" of Kittredge's day. Kittredge minimizes the distance between medieval and modern readers rather than emphasizing it. He believes that, for the most part, medieval people and medieval times were very like modern people and modern times, and thus he believes that medieval readers would have approached Chaucer in much the same way modern readers do.[27] Indeed, medieval times were more like modern times than were the seventeenth or eighteenth centuries; the later Middle Ages

---

23   Ibid., 68.

24   Ibid., 153.

25   See, for example, Kittredge's comments on the "drama" of the *Tales:* ibid., 155.

26   Ibid., 155.

27   L.D. Benson, "A Reader's Guide to Writings on Chaucer," *Geoffrey Chaucer*, ed. Derek Brewer (London: G. Bell & Sons, 1974) 342.

George Lyman Kittredge (1860–1941): The Dramatic Reader 27

was "a singularly 'modern time'" and Chaucer was the "most modern of English poets."[28] Like the early twentieth century—at least in Kittredge's eyes—the medieval era was "a hard, practical, bustling, struggling, delightful age," and all of the social and political problems of Chaucer's day are echoed in conflicts from our own day.[29] Far from having to bridge the gap between medieval times and now, or having to explain an alien medieval mindset or mentality to modern readers, Kittredge writes, "What strikes me when I try to comprehend the second half of the fourteenth century, is not the strangeness, but the familiarity."[30] Thus, in response to those who find medieval works overly digressive, Kittredge says, "some digress, and some do not, precisely as in modern times"; to those who deplore the overly-conventional structures of medieval literature and society, Kittredge admits, "[the medieval age] had its conventional rules, in art, in literature, in science, in religion," but adds in parentheses, "even as you and I!"[31] Many things which at first seem alien or foreign in medieval times are simply familiar creatures in strange clothing: the superficially-surprising intimacy of the socially-diverse pilgrims in the *Canterbury Tales* is like the intimacy of travellers in the smoking-room of a steamship; the Host, in his inability to interrupt the Monk's tiresome, over-long litany of tragedies is similar to a "helpless toastmaster" faced with the droning after-dinner oration of a self-involved speaker at a modern formal dinner. Chaucer is very modern, Kittredge writes, "You can translate his situations into our own at any given moment."[32] Kittredge also reacts against those who perceive the Middle Ages as blindly submissive to church strictures and feudal hierarchies—medieval times, just as our own, had their "spirit of radicalism," and "to describe as an era of dumb submissiveness the age of Wyclif, and John Huss, and the Great Schism, of the Jacquerie in France and Tyler and Ball in England, is to read both literature and history with one's eyes shut."[33] Likewise, medieval people were no more or less scientific than modern people: we, like them, develop generalities based on observation, and their alchemy was as dependent upon empirical experimentation as our chemistry. Even the most radically inaccessible conventions of medieval writing and society, such as the dogmas of courtly love, are really just "expressions, in language different from ours, of facts that no one challenges when couched in modern terms."[34] So the medieval symptoms of love-sickness, such as Troilus's weeping and wailing and Arcite's deathly pallor, are based on sentiments we ourselves share; the emotions are simply expressed in different forms. "Give me forty-eight hours," Kittredge declares, "and I will

---

[28] Ibid., 2.

[29] Ibid., 30, 2. Again, it is important to remember that this would have been written before the advent of the Great War.

[30] Ibid., 8–9.

[31] Ibid., 23, 30.

[32] Ibid., 165.

[33] Ibid., 8.

[34] Ibid., 124.

28 *Twentieth-Century Chaucer Criticism*

translate every mediaeval symptom into modern journalese, and my version shall keep step with the daily records [in gossip columns and newspapers]."[35]

Kittredge develops this premise, that medieval times were relatively similar to our own, in part because he believes that human nature remains the same throughout all eras. Chaucer was principally a student of that human nature, and thus what was true or realistic in his works in medieval times remains true and realistic today. Chaucer's "speciality was mankind," Kittredge writes, and when we perceive Chaucer as modern, we are really perceiving "the everlasting truth, the enduring quality that consists in conformity to changeless human nature." Chaucer portrayed not only the everyday life and people of the fourteenth century, but also the "immemorial habit of mankind."[36] Kittredge's frequent description of the *Canterbury Tales* as a "Human Comedy" likewise demonstrates this belief that human nature is constant: it is not a fourteenth-century comedy but a "Human" one, and the capitalizations indicate the essentialism and uniformity of that idea of humanity. This belief in the consistency of human nature means that Kittredge need trouble himself little about the differences between a medieval audience and a modern one: there may be superficial differences, but, fundamentally, both audiences will read Chaucer's works in largely the same way.

Chaucer's Contemporary Audience

Despite this underlying belief in the uniformity of human nature, and despite an attendant inclination to "universalize" and unify Chaucer's audience, Kittredge is not so unsubtle as to admit no difference whatsoever between medieval and modern times. As a result, he usually justifies his "universal" interpretations with reference to Chaucer's contemporary readers. The two aspects of his criticism, his tendency to universalize and his recognition of the need to ground interpretation in contemporary response, are clear:

> Manifestly, we are bound to take account of the readers whom Chaucer had in mind. ... Great poets, no doubt, address themselves to posterity; and posterity is free to interpret them, for its own comfort and inspiration, in any terms that it finds useful. But they address themselves, in the first instance, to their immediate contemporaries. They may be for all time ultimately, but that is by virtue of the eternal nature of the things that really matter in human life. What Chaucer meant to his contemporaries is, then, a pertinent question.[37]

Kittredge's image of Chaucer's audience, therefore, is universalized. The responses of both modern and medieval readers are considered in developing the "audience

---

[35]   Ibid., 124.

[36]   Ibid., 1, 148.

[37]   Ibid., 80–81.

function" which Kittredge uses—but for the most part, he believes, medieval and modern people will have approximately the same response. Kittredge thus insists upon the validity of a modern response, "posterity's" freedom to interpret poets "in any terms it finds useful." In Kittredge's terms, however, just as the medieval response does not invalidate the modern one, so the modern one does not displace the medieval response. Modern readers will appreciate the "eternals" in Chaucer's writings, the fundamental concepts which relate to human nature, but Chaucer's immediate readers can teach us about the details which had a contemporary appeal. So, for example, "however you and I may feel about it," for medieval readers the story of Griselda was "infinitely pathetic"—one of Petrarch's friends wept while reading it—and we need to bear this response in mind when reading the Clerk's Tale.[38]

Chaucer's first readers, according to Kittredge, were the knights and ladies of the court. The audience for *Book of the Duchess* is clearly John of Gaunt, who was of Chaucer's generation and was a similar age. The audience for the rest of Chaucer's works may have been slightly less noble, but was almost certainly courtly and upper-class. This audience knew Chaucer as a "learned" writer, and Kittredge says they must also have ranked him highly as a religious writer (although Kittredge himself, frankly, pays little attention to this perception in the rest of his criticism). More importantly, Chaucer's educated contemporaries would have been familiar with the conventions and genres within which Chaucer writes, especially the conventions of courtly love. As a result, Kittredge believes, medieval readers would have liked and expected psychologically-developed characters, "or what passed for psychology in the mediaeval love-poets, the analysis of emotion in terms of Chrétien de Troyes and the Roman de la Rose."[39] Kittredge does not develop this theory of the psychology of courtly love in the way that C.S. Lewis later does, and, in fact, he uses it to take his criticism in a radically different direction from Lewis. While Lewis uses the psychological nature of courtly love poetry to analyze *Troilus and Criseyde* to great effect, Kittredge turns from *Troilus and Criseyde* to the *Canterbury Tales*, and provides a psychological, dramatic reading of the pilgrims. Like Lewis, he grounds his reading in surviving responses from medieval readers; but the two critics, using different evidence in a similar manner, reach vastly different conclusions. Lewis uses writers such as Lydgate and Hoccleve to prove that Chaucer was regarded as a courtly love poet and master rhetorician. Kittredge, by contrast, uses different medieval responses to show that Chaucer was regarded as a great comedian and dramatizer of character. The "Envoy to Bukton," for example, proves that the Wife of Bath, whom Kittredge calls a "great comic character," had become "almost proverbial among Chaucer's friends and readers."[40] She was so life-like that she could be referred to as though she were alive. Kittredge enlists the anonymous *Tale of Beryn* to provide his most

---

[38] Ibid., 195.

[39] Ibid., 109.

[40] Ibid., 34.

convincing argument in favour of a dramatic reading of the *Canterbury Tales*. The author of *Beryn*, he argues, evidently read the *Canterbury Tales* dramatically and psychologically, for he was far more interested in the pilgrims themselves than in their tales. The *Beryn* author devotes much of his energy to the actions of the pilgrims at the Checker Inn in Canterbury and their interactions before they return to London, rather than to the Tale of Beryn itself. "The author of *Beryn* did not mistake the Canterbury Tales for a volume of disconnected stories," Kittredge states. "He recognized the work for what it really is—a micro-cosmography, a little image of the great world." Based on evidence such as this, Kittredge concludes that "Chaucer's contemporaries were quite aware of the dramatic nature of the Pilgrimage and the significance of the Pilgrims as characters in the comedy."[41] In other words, medieval readers read the *Canterbury Tales* and *Troilus and Criseyde* in much the same way that twentieth-century readers read Victorian novels: they were interested in individual characters, open to psychological explanations for the characters' actions or traits, alive to character development, and expectant of a unity of character and personality from which the characters would speak and interact. Indeed, Kittredge calls *Troilus* the "first novel."[42]

Alongside this dramatic characterization and realism, and in accordance with his emphasis on the "courtly" nature of Chaucer's writing and audience (as opposed to his religious or "learned" writings), Kittredge believes Chaucer's audience would have had an appreciation of his humour and irony. He does not elaborate on this assumption explicitly, but implicitly it underlies much of his criticism. The *House of Fame* is written in a spirit of "riotous humor"; Pandarus is not only "a servant of the god of love with all his heart" but "a humorist and a man of action," an "arch-humorist"; while Chaucer himself is described as "sympathetic and ironic," the "supreme ironist, the kindly man of humor."[43] However, Kittredge does not seem to uphold a definition of irony as pervasive or multi-layered; Chaucer's humour is relatively straightforward, and not used for some deeper moral purpose or didactic goal. So, for example, in contrast with later critics such as E. Talbot Donaldson, Kittredge does not perceive a great ironic distance between Chaucer and his narrator. The audience is to take Chaucer more-or-less at his word, and does not need to approach his statements suspiciously or warily. The narrator's enthusiastic superlatives in the General Prologue are not taken as markers or indications of irony, but as serious, if good-humoured, statements: "Chaucer had an immense enthusiasm for life in this world; for the society of his fellow-creatures, high and low, good and bad. ... Whatever was good of its kind was a delight to him. And he had such stupendous luck in always meeting nonpareils! There was no better priest than the Parson anywhere; no such Pardoner from one end of England to another;

---

[41] Ibid., 156–7.

[42] See Steve Ellis, *Chaucer at Large: The Poet in the Modern Imagination* (Minneapolis: University of Minnesota Press, 2000) 25.

[43] Kittredge, *Chaucer and His Poetry*, 101, 137–8, 125.

never so great a purchaser as the Man of Law."[44] Kittredge notes momentary, tongue-in-cheek irony in Chaucer, as when the author protests that his wit is poor or that he is not a good writer, and some ironies of circumstance, such as the ending of the Pardoner's Tale. However, he does not posit the distance between audience and character, or poet and narrator, that later twentieth-century critics would. So, for example, when Chaucer apologizes for disregarding the "proper" arrangement of subjects, Kittredge assumes the apology is serious, and that Chaucer's readers really would have been perturbed by disruptions to the conventional order. Likewise, when it comes to the Prioress, Kittredge rejects a mocking, satirical or ironic interpretation of the kind given by almost all later twentieth-century critics. "Of all the Canterbury Pilgrims none is more sympathetically conceived or more delicately portrayed than Madame Eglantine, the prioress," Kittredge writes, and without offering supporting evidence or proof, declares, "Nothing is farther from Chaucer's thought than to poke fun at [her]."[45] Likewise, Chaucer's descriptions of the other clerics are to be taken as "straight": it is a "gross error" to suppose that Chaucer might have satirized the Church.[46] Chaucer might be mildly amused by some of his characters, but for the most part he is sympathetic to them, and the audience is to adopt a position of similar sympathy. The distance between poet, narrator, characters and audience, therefore, is much smaller in Kittredge's criticism than for later critics: the audience is "close" to the characters in terms of sympathy, perspectives, and assumptions, and Kittredge assumes that the audience would not seriously disagree with the narrator.[47] For the most part Chaucer says what he means, means what he says, and we as an audience can share in his amusement at some of the characters without losing our essential sympathy for them, or interpreting Chaucer's affectionate amusement as condemnation or satire.

Kittredge envisions an audience for Chaucer which was not particularly bookish. Chaucer's readers would have been educated, but not overly so, and certainly would not have had at their fingertips the wealth of reference and allusion that later exegetical critics such as D.W. Robertson assumed for Chaucer's readers. So, for example, Kittredge attributes the inclusion of digression and exempla in many medieval works not to the possibility that medieval people "enjoyed books

---

[44] Ibid., 32; cf. 184: "Chaucer was a guest at the Tabard when the Pilgrims arrived, and he at once made himself so agreeable that they invited him to join the party. He circulated among them, and actually spoke to every one of the nine-and-twenty. This, beyond question, is the real Chaucer."

[45] Ibid., 175, 177.

[46] Ibid., 33.

[47] Geoffrey Gust points out the seeming contradiction between Kittredge's insistence that we take the pilgrims as dramatic characters but his tendency to take the narrator "straight," as the author himself speaking: Geoffrey Gust, *Constructing Chaucer: Author and Autofiction in the Critical Tradition* (New York: Palgrave Macmillan, 2009) 29.

which told them what they already knew,"[48] which is C.S. Lewis's conclusion, but to the possibility that a medieval audience *wouldn't*, in fact, have already known the story: a medieval author "tells the tale, instead of merely citing the incident, because he cannot assume, as a modern may, that his readers are familiar with it."[49] When speculating on the nature of the tidings told by the man of authority at the end of the *House of Fame*, Kittredge states that it cannot be a "story out of a book," because neither Chaucer nor his audience would be excited by that; instead, it must be some "first-rate piece of news concerning love ... most likely it is a contemporary affair, which would be of interest to the English court."[50] Kittredge projects this image of Chaucer's reader onto the Eagle of the *House of Fame* in the same way, saying that his knowledge about the transmission of sound comes not from books, but from observation; the audience would be convinced by the Eagle's theories not because the Eagle drew on authoritative works, but because they themselves had made similar observations.[51] Likewise, the description of Blanche in the *Book of the Duchess* does not come solely from literary convention but from her real appearance: "we cannot doubt that it was true to the life in the case of the Duchess Blanche"; the House of Rumour, too, is a "transcript from actual life," a "Celtic" building like one that Chaucer and his readers might have actually seen in Scotland or Wales.[52]

In one respect, however, Kittredge envisions the medieval reader to have been at least somewhat "bookish," and to have cultural competencies not shared by modern readers. Kittredge believes that most medieval readers would know the "code" and understand the conventions of courtly love. Courtly love was a codified "system," rather than a random assemblage of motifs, and Kittredge uses words like "doctrines," "dogmas," "chivalric system" and "articles of the code" to describe it.[53] The conventions of courtly love literature would have been well-understood, and on the basis of this Kittredge argues against scholars such as Bernhard ten Brink who interpret works such as the *House of Fame* as autobiographical allegory. The *House of Fame* uses the "traditional machinery of the visions of love," and thus Chaucer's readers would not have assumed it somehow described or referred to events in the author's own life.[54] The influence of courtly love conventions comes through most strongly in *Troilus and Criseyde*, of course, and while Kittredge again stresses that the underlying emotions have

---

[48] C.S. Lewis, *The Discarded Image: An Introduction to Medieval and Renaissance Literature* (Cambridge: Cambridge University Press, 1967) 200.

[49] Kittredge, *Chaucer and His Poetry*, 24.

[50] Ibid., 103.

[51] Ibid., 88. Kittredge is almost certainly wrong here, for the Eagle's theories seem to come straight out of medieval textbooks on sound: see Martin Irvine, "Medieval Grammatical Theory and Chaucer's *House of Fame*," *Speculum* 60.4 (October 1985) 850–76.

[52] Ibid., 65, 105.

[53] Ibid., 63, 123, 124, 125.

[54] Ibid., 99.

George Lyman Kittredge (1860–1941): The Dramatic Reader 33

not changed since medieval times, it is nonetheless here that the distance between the medieval and modern reader is most apparent. Kittredge argues that modern readers must accept and understand the conventions of courtly love before they attempt to interpret Troilus's and Criseyde's characters or behaviour. Within this system there was nothing wrong in Criseyde's loving Troilus; her sin was in her unfaithfulness.[55] He is perhaps less sanguine than some later critics about the compatibility of courtly love ethics and Christian ethics, but nonetheless declares that the readers would have known which ethical system to apply, and again shows that such "double standards" are not unique to medieval times: "The theories of the chivalric code were known to Chaucer's readers, and they were immediately taken for granted on his announcement ... that the *Troilus* is dedicated to love's servants. However correct their personal code of morals, they accepted the ethics of chivalric love for the purposes of this poem without demur, precisely as we in modern times accept the barbarous and outworn code of revenge when we read Hamlet."[56] However, Kittredge suspects that Chaucer's readers would know that they must eventually turn from the courtly love earth-bound morality to the Christian morality of eternity. By the ending of *Troilus and Criseyde*, he writes, we come to suspect that "the principles of the code are somehow unsound; that the god of love is not a master whom his servants can trust."[57]

The Human Comedy

These assumptions about Chaucer's first readers—that they would perceive characters dramatically and psychologically; that they were conversant in literary conventions such as that of courtly love, but would not have been overly bookish; that they would have appreciated gentle irony and humour but would not have interpreted it as radical satire; and, most importantly, that their response would not have been very different from a modern reader's response—have major consequences for Kittredge's reading of Chaucer, especially the *Canterbury Tales*. The first major premise upon which Kittredge's criticism is based is that the audience would perceive Chaucer's characters as being psychologically realistic and developed. So, for example, Kittredge believes a medieval audience would enjoy *Troilus and Criseyde* not because of its artistry or plot, but because of the details of characterization: it is this point he is emphasizing when he calls *Troilus* an "elaborate psychological novel."[58] Kittredge is quick to point out that the realism in *Troilus and Criseyde* is psychological, not actual—Troilus behaves like a medieval, not an ancient Greek, knight. Likewise, it is this psychological realism Kittredge means when he calls the *Canterbury Tales* "true to life." He

---

[55]   Ibid., 130, 134.

[56]   Ibid., 131.

[57]   Ibid., 143.

[58]   Ibid., 112; cf. 109.

34   *Twentieth-Century Chaucer Criticism*

is not concerned with the realism of the timing of the journey to Canterbury, or the realism of giving lengthy stories in poetry, but with the way the pilgrims, as characters and individuals, would have seemed lifelike to the medieval audience. One of the indications of such realism, Kittredge argues, is the way in which Chaucer includes himself as a character in the *Canterbury Tales*. This indicates that the reader is to take the other characters as being as "real" as Chaucer himself is. Chaucer exists, the reasoning goes, and "therefore the Prioress existed, and the Reeve, and the Manciple. ...."[59] Even without this prompt, however, Kittredge believes that readers would have perceived the characters as psychologically realistic because they reflect human nature so well. Therefore the *Troilus* is "instinct with humour, and pathos, and passion, and human nature" while the character of Pandarus is "a rare but perfectly human compound of enthusiasm and critical acumen." Criseyde's inconsistencies "are those of human nature."[60] For those critics who do not perceive the psychological realism of Chaucer's characters, Kittredge advises them not to read more, or to do more historical study, "but to mingle for a day or two with their fellow-creatures."[61] If they do not recognize the psychological realism of Chaucer's writing, it is not because they have not studied Chaucer enough, but because they do not understand human nature well enough. Even the dream-poems, which most critics would consider more fantastic than realistic, Kittredge insists are realism: a realistic portrayal of the way dreams really function.

Alongside this psychological realism is an assumption of psychological *consistency*: because the characters are psychologically true-to-life, they always behave in ways consistent with the composition of their personality. If a character does not seem to be consistent, then the audience is not doing its job properly, and must reconsider its image of the character until there are no more inconsistencies. This can occasionally prompt some rather convoluted readings, as in Kittredge's reading of the Pardoner. Kittredge, to fulfil the requirement of psychological realism and consistency, must account for the Pardoner's astonishing self-revelations to the assembled pilgrims, and the Pardoner's later attempt to sell the pilgrims relics he has already admitted to being false. He rejects the explanation that the Pardoner was drunk, finding it inadequate to explain the excess of the Pardoner's self-disclosure. Instead, he suggests that the Pardoner's cynicism and frankness is a pre-emptive move which forestalls the condemnation of the other pilgrims: "the Pardoner is willing to pass for a knave, but objects to being taken for a fool."[62] At the end of his tale, the Pardoner gets carried away in the excess of his own rhetoric, and "under the spell of the wonderful story he has told and of the recollections that stir within him, he suffers a very paroxysm of agonized sincerity," and admits to the pilgrims that Christ's pardon is the only true pardon.

---

[59]   Ibid., 161.

[60]   Ibid., 112, 139, 135.

[61]   Ibid., 29.

[62]   Ibid., 214.

George Lyman Kittredge (1860–1941): The Dramatic Reader   35

Appalled at his own sincerity, the Pardoner then takes refuge in "a wild orgy of reckless jesting," jokingly attempting to sell his fake relics to the pilgrims, who do not realize the Pardoner is joking, and react negatively.[63] In order to account for the facts of the text, therefore, within the "audience function's" limiting presupposition of unity and consistency of character, Kittredge posits an entire inner psychological drama for the Pardoner, from his getting caught up in the power of his own story, to the "falling away" of his cynicism, to the "paroxysm of agonized sincerity," to his "emotional crisis," to his "revulsion of feeling"[64]—none of which is explicitly described in Chaucer's text. The audience of the *Canterbury Tales*, like the audience of a play, is required to "fill in the blanks" of a character's motivations and psychological states to account for the action explicitly depicted "on stage."

Kittredge also believes Chaucer's writing is "realistic" in ways that go beyond psychological realism. He argues that Chaucer's works accurately reflect the social dynamics and situations of the late fourteenth-century. Again, it should be emphasized that this is not a realism that concerns itself with accuracy in every detail. Within these qualifications, however, Kittredge stresses the realistic quality of Chaucer's works, especially the *Canterbury Tales*, and believes that Chaucer's contemporary audience would have recognized themselves, their fellow-citizens, and their society in his work. So, for example, the discord between the Friar and the Summoner reflects an actual social reality in which friars and summoners rarely got along: "Details like this needed no footnotes for Chaucer's contemporary readers. They are, indeed, to be taken for granted as part of the setting or background."[65] Other details reflect medieval reality, rather than literary conventions or bookish allusion. From the way sound is described as travelling in the *House of Fame*, to the wicker-work structure of the House of Rumour, Kittredge insists the descriptions come not from literature but from lived experience. When Pandarus declares to Troilus that he will stand with him if he fights for Criseyde, though he should die "in a strete as dogges liggen dede," Kittredge comments, "This is not rhetoric; it is stark realism. Chaucer and all of his readers had seen slain men lying in the street like dead dogs."[66] Likewise, medieval readers, unlike modern critics, would not look from the framing conceit of the *Canterbury Tales* to other medieval frame tales, but to actualities of medieval life. The fact that Chaucer's frame tale resembles other frame tales is insignificant. Rather, the frame tale of pilgrims telling stories while travelling comes from Chaucer's own observations of real pilgrims travelling to Canterbury. "Newton did not learn that apples fall by reading treatises on pomology," Kittredge comments wryly.[67] Chaucer, like Newton, was an empiricist and an observer. The *Canterbury Tales* depicts the

---

[63] Ibid., 217.

[64] Ibid., 216–17.

[65] Ibid., 29.

[66] Ibid., 142.

[67] Ibid., 149.

"life of the time"; it records "the age, in its habit as it lived."[68] There is no need for a modern audience to posit far-fetched literary or folkloric explanations for the details in Chaucer's text.

Kittredge's emphasis on the psychological nature of Chaucer's characters, the realism of their interactions, and the reflection of fourteenth-century society in the situations and settings, means that he believes that Chaucer's works should be approached as if they were a drama. The audience, he believes, would have visualized the stories as though the events were taking place in front of their eyes. In this, modern audiences should take their cue from the medieval audience: "One thing is certain: we should not read this outburst of raillery [from the Host] without an attempt to visualize the scene and imagine the action. ... We must not only listen, but look. In our mind's eye, we must see the Pilgrims, and watch their demeanor."[69] He describes the *Canterbury Tales* with terms drawn from drama: he calls it a "Human Comedy," a "play"; the pilgrims are the "*dramatis personae*"; the General Prologue is "the first act, which sets the personages in motion"; the tales of the pilgrims are "speeches," "soliloquies," "conversation."[70] The pilgrims always speak "in character"; none of the narratives of the *Canterbury Tales* has the author breaking through or Chaucer speaking in his own voice. The tales exist primarily for the purpose of the self-revelation of character and personality on the part of the pilgrims telling them: "The Pilgrims do not exist for the sake of the stories, but *vice versa*. Structurally regarded, the stories are merely long speeches expressing, directly or indirectly, the characters of the several persons. They are more or less comparable, in this regard, to the soliloquies of Hamlet or Iago or Macbeth."[71]

The stories of the *Canterbury Tales* do not spring fully-born from nothingness, but grow out of the dramatic exigencies of the situation. Thus the Clerk's Tale is not interesting to Kittredge because of its reworking of Petrarch's story, nor because of its poetic or narrative form, but because of the things it reveals about the Clerk himself, and the way it participates in an extended dialogue, a discussion of marriage, with the Wife of Bath. The envoy at the end of the Clerk's Tale, rather than being the problem many critics perceive it to be, is actually an extension of and elaboration on the aspects of the Clerk's character already revealed during the telling of his tale. Kittredge calls it "completely dramatic," saying, "It is not Chaucer who speaks, but the Clerk of Oxenford, and every word is in perfect character." The envoy does not violate dramatic propriety, but, "on the contrary, as we have seen, it is adjusted, with the nicest art, not only to his character, but also to the situation and the relations among the *dramatis personae*."[72] Likewise, the Wife of Bath does not exist in order for Chaucer to comment upon the role of women, or

---

[68] Ibid., 6–7.

[69] Ibid., 182, 194.

[70] Ibid., 154–5; cf. 161, 167, 192.

[71] Ibid., 154.

[72] Ibid., 199–200.

to satirize the church. She exists as a character, not a treatise or commentary: "The Wife of Bath is an individual expressing herself in character, not a stalking horse for a satirist's poisoned arrows. Her revelations apply to herself. To extend them to wives or women in general, is as ludicrous as it would be to interpret Iago's cynical speeches as Shakspere's [*sic*] satire on men and husbands."[73] As in this example, Kittredge often turns to Shakespearean studies as a model for reading Chaucer's works, following the critical techniques developed in the analysis of drama.[74] The linking sections between the tales function not only as crucial parts in the drama itself, but work as "stage-directions" for the "play," setting the scene for us and putting the "dialogue" (i.e., the tales) in context. Kittredge's dramatic emphasis means that his criticism focuses much more on the interactions between characters than on other possible areas of critical study, such as Chaucer's poetic techniques, use of genre, and so on. This emphasis on drama, especially in the *Canterbury Tales*, was Kittredge's most influential contribution to Chaucer studies. He insisted that the study of the pilgrims and their interactions was as important, if not more important, than the study of the individual tales.

Out of this contention that readers of the *Canterbury Tales* should perceive the work as a drama grew Kittredge's most controversial contribution to Chaucer studies: the theory of the "marriage group." If the audience is "watching" the characters as though they were in a play, they will not perceive the tales as discrete units, but as inter-related "speeches" which create the "action" of the drama. A drama must have tension, conflict, dynamism: thus Kittredge sees in the tales of the Wife of Bath, the Clerk, the Merchant and the Franklin, a conflict over the nature and importance of marriage. A proposition or argument which the Wife sets forth about the "Tribulation in Marriage" is, after an intermediary, unrelated "act" about the Friar and the Summoner, answered by the Clerk, recast by the Merchant, and finally resolved by the Franklin, who "summariz[es] the whole debate and bring[s] it to a definitive conclusion." This whole interaction creates a completed "act" in Chaucer's "Human Comedy."[75] Kittredge bases his "marriage group" theory on the comments the Wife makes about clerks, which the Clerk responds to in his "Envoy" about the Wife of Bath; and upon the thematic threads about marriage and the nature of women which run through all four tales. This theory of the "marriage group," is intimately related to Kittredge's ideas of audience: if the audience were not envisioned as a theatrical audience, with the expectations and assumptions of such an audience, there would have been less need for an interpretation which stresses the dynamism and conflict in the *Canterbury Tales*. Likewise, if Kittredge did not believe that the tales would be perceived at least in part as "speeches" spoken by the various pilgrim characters, their role as aspects

---

[73] Ibid., 200.

[74] Kittredge was well known as a scholar and teacher of Shakespeare, as well as Chaucer and other medieval authors, and his interest in Shakespeare may have influenced his development of dramatic theory for the *Canterbury Tales*.

[75] Kittredge, *Chaucer and His Poetry*, 185.

of an ongoing argument or discussion would have been less evident. Kittredge's insistence upon the *Canterbury Tales'* dramatic qualities encourages the modern reader of Chaucer to consider the *Tales* as a whole, and to perceive the thematic inter-relationships between the tales and among the characters.

George Lyman Kittredge, then, is one of the first critics in the twentieth century to offer thorough-going literary criticism of Chaucer's works, rather than just source-study, philological work, or editorial scholarship. Kittredge's humane, optimistic confidence in the universality of human nature would be starkly challenged by some later scholars, and robustly upheld by others. His perception of the essentially dramatic nature of the pilgrims, who inadvertently reveal their own character through their speeches and tales, would be transferred to the narrator, who would come to be perceived as one character among others. In his theories about Chaucer as a supreme realist and the *Canterbury Tales* as a psychological drama, Kittredge would set the stage for the next decades—indeed, in some ways the next century—of Chaucerian criticism, as scholars developed, challenged, or reinterpreted his ideas. C.S. Lewis, the focus of the next chapter, would continue the idea of Chaucer's characters as psychological entities, but would emphatically reject Kittredge's emphasis on drama. He would also contest Kittredge's focus on the *Canterbury Tales*, turning instead to Chaucer's allegorical works and to *Troilus and Criseyde*. Most importantly, he would object to Kittredge's claim that medieval times were much like our own, arguing instead that the medieval world was a "foreign land" which readers needed to understand in order to read medieval literature properly.

Chapter 2

C.S. Lewis (1894–1963):
The Psychological Reader

There are two kinds of travellers, C.S. Lewis writes in his essay "De Audiendis Poetis." There is the Englishman who "carries his Englishry abroad with him," meeting other English tourists, drinking English tea, staying in English-style hotels. Then there is the traveller who eats the local food, drinks the local wines, and begins "to see the foreign country as it looks, not to the tourist, but to its inhabitants," who comes home "thinking and feeling as [he] did not think and feel before."[1] In the same way, he declares, there are two kinds of readers: those who bring their modern preconceptions to ancient literature, enjoying only the sections or aspects which appeal to a modern aesthetic, and those who immerse themselves as fully as possible in the mindset of the time, reading the literature as a contemporary would.

In the 1920s and 30s, literary critics and theorists I.A. Richards and F.R. Leavis and their followers developed a kind of literary criticism which treated texts as self-contained ahistorical aesthetic objects, studied without reference to a historical context and valued instead for their "timeless" qualities such as poetic form or irony. C.S. Lewis, in many ways, was a lone, but highly influential voice opposing this method of reading. In this anti-historicist context, Lewis aimed to promote the second kind of "tourism" he delineates, wherein "travellers" to medieval texts appreciate those texts on medieval, not modern, terms. Against the approach of many of his contemporaries, and against the previous generation of scholars such as George Lyman Kittredge, C.S. Lewis promoted a style of reading which, rather than valuing the texts in terms of modern aesthetic values such as realism, dramatic conflict or modernist irony, attempted to read medieval texts according to a medieval "mindset." To aid in this kind of reading, in books such as *The Discarded Image* and *The Allegory of Love* Lewis tries to provide the modern Englishman with a "map" to the "foreign lands" of medieval literature. His goal is to recreate the medieval "mindset" which readers are to adopt before they immerse themselves in medieval literature. Unlike George Lyman Kittredge, Lewis does not believe that a sympathetic understanding of medieval literature will come naturally after a basic grasp of Old or Middle English is attained. Instead, sympathy and understanding for medieval ways of thinking must come gradually, through extensive reading of medieval literature, imaginative engagement with the

---

[1] C.S. Lewis, *Studies in Medieval and Renaissance Literature* (Cambridge: Cambridge University Press, 1966) 2–3.

40   *Twentieth-Century Chaucer Criticism*

past, and broad learning about medieval customs and culture. The job of a scholar of English literature is to act as an interpreter for this traveler to the past: to map out the medieval mind and culture in detail and breadth so the modern reader can slide as easily as possible into the medieval way of reading.[2]

C.S. Lewis spent most of his life at Oxford, but he felt himself out of step with many of the individuals at his college, Magdalen, and at Oxford more broadly. (It was Cambridge, and not Oxford, that distinguished Lewis with a Chair especially created for him, the Professorship of Medieval and Renaissance Literature.) Instead, the most important intellectual influence on Lewis was the informal group of scholars and writers at Oxford dubbed the "Inklings," especially J.R.R. Tolkien. To Tolkien Lewis credited his conversion from atheism to Christianity, and with Tolkien Lewis shared a belief in the importance of myth-making and fantasy. Meredith Veldman argues that Lewis and Tolkien spearheaded a fantasy-writing movement fundamentally romantic in its values, which looked back to a community-based, Christian, pastoral, Northern European past as a protest against an industrial, impersonal, materialistic present.[3] Both saw themselves as outsiders,

---

[2]   See C.S. Lewis, *An Experiment in Criticism* (Cambridge: Cambridge University Press, 1961) 121–2. The scholarship on Lewis's academic contributions is paltry compared with the amount of study devoted to his Christian writings or his fiction. See Kathryn Kerby-Fulton, "'Standing on Lewis's Shoulders': C.S. Lewis as Critic of Medieval Literature," *Studies in Medievalism* 3.3 (Winter 1991) 257–78; George Watson, *Critical Essays on C.S. Lewis* (London: Scolar Press, 1992); Carolyn Keefe, ed., *C.S. Lewis: Speaker and Teacher* (London: Hodder and Stoughton, 1971); Chad Walsh, *The Literary Legacy of C.S. Lewis* (London: Sheldon Press, 1979), chapter 8; Joerg O. Fichte, "The Reception of C.S. Lewis' Scholarly Works in Germany," *Man's "Natural Powers": Essays For and About C.S. Lewis*, ed. Raymond P. Tripp, Jr. (Church Stretton: Society for New Language Study, 1975) 17–22; Colin Burrow, "C.S. Lewis and *The Allegory of Love*," *Essays in Criticism* 53.3 (2003) 284–94; William Calin, "C.S. Lewis, Literary Critic: A Reassessment," *Mythlore* 23.3 (Summer 2001) 4–20; William Calin, *The Twentieth-Century Humanist Critics: From Spitzer to Frye* (Toronto: University of Toronto Press, 2007) 85–100; Thomas L. Martin, "Is C.S. Lewis Still Relevant to Literary Studies Today?" *Journal of the Wooden O Symposium* 1 (2001) 26–35; Douglas McMillan, "Discarded and Reclaimed Images, Natives, and Dinosaurs: C.S. Lewis as Teacher and Literary Historian," *Lamp-Post* 21.3 (Fall 1977) 17–25; Charles F. Beach, "C.S. Lewis, Courtly Love, and Chaucer's *Troilus and Criseyde*," *C.S. Lewis* 26.4 (February 1995) 1–10; Linda Lusk, "C.S. Lewis as a Critic 'At the Present Time'," *C.S. Lewis* 22.6 (Spring 1991) 1–9; Bruce L. Edwards, ed., *The Taste of the Pineapple: Essays on C.S. Lewis as Reader, Critic and Imaginative Writer* (Bowling Green, Ohio: Popular, 1988); Bruce L. Edwards, Jr., "Deconstruction and Rehabilitation: C.S. Lewis and Critical Theory," *C.S. Lewis* 13.11 (September 1982) 1–7; Judith Kollman, "C.S. Lewis as Medievalist," *C.S. Lewis* 10.7 (1979) 1–5; Rosalyn Rossignol, "Lewis, C(live) S(taples)," *Chaucer: A Literary Reference to His Life and Work* (New York: Infobase Publishing, 2007) 488. Several periodicals are devoted to Lewis, but they tend to focus on his fictional or devotional writings.

[3]   Meredith Veldman, *Fantasy, the Bomb, and the Greening of Britain: Romantic Protest, 1945–1980* (Cambridge: Cambridge University Press, 1994) 3, 37–114. See also

C.S. Lewis (1894–1963): The Psychological Reader

fighting a rearguard action against a society whose values they did not share. Lewis calls himself a "dinosaur," who holds the values, beliefs and aesthetic sensibilities of a bygone era. It is not surprising, then, that Lewis's scholarship paralleled his fictional and Christian writing: all three reflect a backward-looking and nostalgic longing for the values of a past which could address the ills of the present.[4]

More than most scholars of his generation, C.S. Lewis demonstrates a clearly-defined, thoroughly-developed imaginative vision of a medieval audience. The assumptions he makes about this audience are implicit in places, but for the most part they are explicit and forcefully stated. Reacting against the kind of criticism George Lyman Kittredge represented, which considered Chaucer's age as "vastly like our own" and troubled itself little with the differences between a medieval and a modern audience, C.S. Lewis spent his career building up an image of the medieval audience, and arguing that modern people have to immerse themselves as much as they can in the mindset of medieval times to read medieval literature properly. He turned away from Kittredge's character-based criticism to study broader patterns, symbols, and structures in literature. Likewise, he disapproved of the "biographical" emphasis in much literary criticism, which tended to consider all literature as an expression of the personality of the author.[5] Lewis also fought against the kind of criticism championed by followers of I.A. Richards and F.R. Leavis, which he considered overly personal and judgmental: "to them criticism is a form of social and ethical hygiene," he writes in *An Experiment in Criticism*.[6] Literature, he believed, should be judged on its formal, literary and aesthetic qualities, and such an assessment should be informed by a thorough knowledge of the era in question. It should not be subjected to a judgment based on its social merit or a critic's personal response to it. Later in his career, Lewis reacted against new trends in criticism, such as the anthropological approach adopted by scholars

---

Norman Cantor, *Inventing the Middle Ages* (New York: William Morris, 1991) 209–10.

[4] For biographies and personal reminiscences, see George Sayer, *Jack: A Life of C.S. Lewis* (London: Hodder and Stoughton, 1997); Roger Lancelyn Green and Walter Hooper, *C.S. Lewis: A Biography* (London: HarperCollins, 2002); Keefe, *C.S. Lewis*; James T. Como, ed., *C.S. Lewis at the Breakfast Table and Other Reminiscences* (London: Collins, 1980); A.N. Wilson, *C.S. Lewis: A Biography* (London: Collins, 1990); Cantor, *Inventing*, chapter 6; Walter Hooper, *C. S. Lewis: A Companion & Guide* (New York: Harper Collins, 1996), 3–136.

[5] Lewis's foremost opponent on this point was E.M.W. Tillyard. The controversy between Lewis and Tillyard took place over several years in *Essays and Studies*, and is reprinted in C.S. Lewis and E.M.W. Tillyard, *The Personal Heresy: A Controversy* (Oxford: Oxford University Press, 1939).

[6] Lewis, *Experiment*, 10. Quoted in Green and Hooper, *C.S. Lewis: A Biography*, 415. For accounts of the dispute between Lewis and the followers of Leavis, see Green and Hooper, *C.S. Lewis*, 408–17; Brian Barbour, "Lewis and Cambridge," *Modern Philology* 96.4 (May 1999) 440–59.

R.S. Loomis and John Speirs.[7] This school of criticism had its roots in Victorian folklore studies, but drew new life from a revived interest in anthropological studies of contemporary primitive societies. Lewis believed that while literature might be useful to anthropology, the process rarely went the other way: knowing that Gawain might somehow be culturally or mythically descended from a sun god does not help the reader understand *Le Morte Darthur*. The only potentially useful aspect of the anthropological approach, the "reverence and a sense of mystery" some followers of the anthropological school derived from their studies, was just as easily acquired, Lewis thought, from the medieval books themselves, helped with some historical knowledge, a bit of scholarship, "health, quiet, an easy chair, [and] a full, but not too full, stomach."[8]

C.S. Lewis's most influential contribution to medieval literary studies in general and Chaucer studies in particular was *The Allegory of Love*.[9] First published in 1936, this book traces the development of allegorical poetry and the courtly love tradition from the Provençal troubadours, through the later French poetry of Chrétien de Troyes and the *Roman de la Rose*, to the fourteenth-century English writers Chaucer, Gower, and Usk, finishing, finally, with Spenser's *Faerie Queene*. It suggests that the two traditions, allegory and courtly love, are linked in development, and that later medieval poetry can be read through the conventions developed in earlier courtly love and allegorical modes. Lewis's analysis of the "theory" of courtly love, although it later drew much criticism and would be advocated in its entirety by few scholars today, nonetheless inspired a generation and made contributions to our reading of Chaucer in general, and *Troilus and Criseyde* in particular, which we now take for granted.[10]

Courtly Love

The four aspects of the medieval mindset which Lewis outlines in *The Allegory of Love*, and which became his most important contribution to Chaucer studies, are his understanding of courtly love, his rejection of irony as a ruling mode in Chaucer,

---

[7]   See especially the articles "The Anthropological Approach," *English and Medieval Studies*, ed. Norman Davis and C.L. Wrenn (London: Allen and Unwin, 1962) 219–30, and "'De Audiendis Poetis'" in Lewis, *Studies*, 1–17. The works Lewis is attacking are J. Speirs, *Medieval English Poetry: The Non-Chaucerian Tradition* (London: Penguin, 1957); R.S. Loomis, "The Origin of the Grail Legends," *Arthurian Literature in the Middle Ages* (Oxford: Clarendon, 1959) 274–94. For an assessment of this controversy, see Francis Lee Utley, "Anglicanism and Anthropology: C.S. Lewis and John Speirs," *Southern Folklore Quarterly* 31.1 (March 1967) 1–11.

[8]   Lewis, "Anthropological Approach," 223–4, 226.

[9]   See Roger Sharrock, "Second Thoughts: C.S. Lewis on Chaucer's *Troilus*," *Essays in Criticism* 8.2 (April 1958) 125.

[10]   Calin, *Humanist Critics*, 91.

his theory of allegory, and his emphasis on the psychology of medieval works. The first chapter of *The Allegory of Love* traces the development of what Lewis calls the "courtly love code" from eleventh-century troubadour poetry to later writers such as Chrétien de Troyes. Lewis argues that the love depicted in Provençal troubadour poetry marked a major turning point in the history of literature. According to Lewis, it was then that love between a man and a woman became the central subject of literature, and was defined as the most meaningful experience in a person's life. Lewis believes that courtly love, by the time it reached England, was a coherently developed "code" of love (rather than a random assemblage of trends or impulses). This theory of love had rules: the key characteristics of the code, as first set out by the troubadours, were "Humility, Courtesy, Adultery and the Religion of Love."[11] Whether or not people actually lived by these rules is irrelevant: Lewis argues that what is important is that the rules were operative in the literature of the time. The lovers in these books were noble and courteous, for the tradition developed in the aristocratic courts of the Aquitaine, and the audience of the works, for the most part, would have been courtly. They were humble, approaching Love and the beloved as supplicants, not conquerors. They were followers of a "religion" of love, in that they paid metaphorical homage to the God of Love and were obedient to his commands. Finally, at least according to Lewis, the courtly lovers described in the literary tradition were predominantly adulterous, since the tradition was modeled on a knight's devotion to his feudal lord's wife. Importantly, Lewis assumes that the theory of courtly love remained consistent in its broad outlines, from eleventh-century Provence through twelfth-century northern France to fourteenth-century England.[12] Its "rules" stayed more

---

[11] C.S. Lewis, *The Allegory of Love* (Oxford: Clarendon Press, 1936) 12, *his capitals*. Both the idea of courtly love as a whole and Lewis's defining characteristics, particularly the emphasis on adultery, have been challenged by later scholars; but what concerns me here is less the actual elements of the theory of courtly love, as the effect that this theory has on his image of Chaucer's audience. Two major critics of Lewis's theory, albeit from completely different critical stances, were Donaldson and Robertson: see "The Myth of Courtly Love" in E. Talbot Donaldson, *Speaking of Chaucer* (London: Athlone Press, 1970) 154–63; D.W. Robertson, Jr., *A Preface to Chaucer: Studies in Medieval Perspectives* (Princeton: Princeton University Press, 1962) 391–503. For a more subdued criticism, see N.K. Coghill, "Love and 'Foul Delight': Some Contrasted Attitudes," *Patterns of Love and Courtesy*, ed. John Lawlor (London: Edward Arnold, 1966) 141–56. See also Colin Burrow, "C.S. Lewis"; Beach, "C.S. Lewis." For a more general study of the fortunes of the theory of courtly love, see Roger Boase, *The Origin and Meaning of Courtly Love: A Critical Study of European Scholarship* (Manchester: Manchester University Press, 1977), especially 35–6, 47–8, 51–2; see also Larry D. Benson, "Courtly Love and Chivalry in the Later Middle Ages," *Fifteenth-Century Studies: Recent Essays*, ed. Robert F. Yeager (Hamden: Archon, 1984) 237–57.

[12] Lewis dates the arrival in England of the courtly love ethos to the fourteenth century, ignoring—perhaps rightly—the possible influence earlier figures such as Eleanor of Aquitaine might have had; Lewis, *The Allegory of Love*, 158. He also ignores the influence

44 *Twentieth-Century Chaucer Criticism*

or less the same throughout this period, and would have been generally known by most medieval readers. As a result, Lewis argues, most medieval non-religious literature would have been interpreted via a courtly love framework.

At first glance, this theory of courtly love, which Lewis claims was pervasive in the literature of the Middle Ages, seems to contradict—especially in terms of its emphasis upon adultery—the equally pervasive Christianity which Lewis states existed in the Middle Ages. Lewis argues, however, that Christianity and the courtly love ethos are not as antithetical as they seem: courtly love is an ethic for this world, Christianity an ethic for the next. Most medieval writers and readers would advocate a turning-away from the courtly love ethos by the end—be it by the end of the poem, or the end of one's life. Lewis assumes that a medieval audience would have read love poetry primarily for entertainment, and would have eventually rejected the values of this poetry in favour of more pious sentiments. Christianity and other ethical systems, such as courtly love, do not conflict with each other in the medieval "Model of the Universe" so long as the proper order is understood: courtly love is for this world alone, Christian love is for all the spheres. In other words, the medieval reader could simultaneously hold two systems of belief in tension without having to choose one over the other until it became absolutely necessary—at the end of a book, or the end of one's life.

In *The Allegory of Love*, C.S. Lewis includes Chaucer within the arc of the courtly love tradition he describes. To Chaucer's contemporaries and early followers such as Deschamps, Gower, Usk, Lydgate and Hoccleve, Lewis notes, Chaucer was the poet of "dream and allegory, of love-romance and erotic debate, of high style and profitable doctrine," not the poet of comic realism and novelistic character depiction. Deschamps calls Chaucer the "English god of Love," Gower "the poet of Venus," Usk "Love's 'owne trewe servaunt'."[13] Instead of the *Canterbury Tales*, therefore, Lewis concentrates on *Troilus and Criseyde*, the poem about love and the poem most admired by Chaucer's fifteenth- and sixteenth-century successors. He rejects twentieth-century emphases on Chaucer's irony, satire, and humour, instead taking Chaucer "*au grand sérieux*"[14]—like he says Chaucer's contemporaries did. Lewis thus uses his belief in a medieval audience's understanding of the theory of courtly love to provide readings of Chaucer's work, but he checks and guides those readings with whatever actual responses survive from readers such as Deschamps, Gower, Usk, Lydgate, and Hoccleve. "Even if the first Chaucerians were dunces," he writes, we should not ignore their readings, because "the stupidest contemporary, we may depend upon it, knew certain things about Chaucer's poetry which modern

---

Anglo-Norman romances might have had on English culture, although the extent to which these adopted the courtly love ethos is debatable: see the discussion in Susan Crane, *Insular Romance: Politics, Faith, and Culture in Anglo-Norman and Middle English Literature* (Berkeley: University of California Press, 1986) 136.

[13] Lewis, *The Allegory of Love*, 162, 164.

[14] Ibid., 163.

scholarship will never know."[15] The "audience function" works here as both a creative and a limiting force: Lewis develops his interpretations by imagining the response of a medieval audience, and then refines and limits those readings on the basis of evidence from Chaucer's actual readers. Lewis is like Kittredge, then, in his method of assembling records of fourteenth- and fifteenth-century responses to support his initial reading of Chaucer. Ironically, as mentioned before, the two critics amass different evidence to prove completely different readings. Lewis uses some writers (Deschamps, Gower, Usk, Lydgate and Hoccleve) to prove that Chaucer was regarded as a courtly love poet and master rhetorician. Kittredge uses other writers (Chaucer himself in the "Envoy to Bukton" and the anonymous *Tale of Beryn*) to show that Chaucer was regarded as a great comedian and dramatizer of character. Lewis dismisses, by contrast, this evidence of Chaucer's "comic and realistic style," saying that the *Tale of Beryn* and Lydgate's Prologue to the *Book of Thebes* make "a small harvest beside the innumerable imitations of his amatory and allegorical poetry."[16]

Serious Chaucer

Based in part on this belief that the theory of courtly love would have been taken seriously, C.S. Lewis disagrees with modern critics who find irony and satire in works such as *Troilus and Criseyde*. He accuses modern critics of "read[ing] into Chaucer all manner of ironies, slynesses, and archnesses, which are not there."[17] In an article for the Cambridge student newspaper *Broadsheet*, Lewis lists as the third fault of undergraduate criticism the fact that most twentieth-century students lack the background in the Bible and the Classics which were taken for granted for centuries, thus "discovering 'irony' in passages which everyone hitherto has taken 'straight'."[18] Derek Brewer, recalling tutorials with C.S. Lewis, comments, "In general Lewis had a Johnsonian literalism. He always claimed to be baffled by the phrase, too often applied to Chaucer, 'with tongue in cheek,' and would put it to comic visual effect. Such literalism, both on this small scale, and more generally in his whole outlook, was a very important part of his criticism."[19] According

---

[15] Ibid., 163; cf. his comment that he "would give a great deal to hear any ancient Athenian, even a stupid one, talking about Greek tragedy. He would know in his bones so much that we seek in vain." C.S. Lewis, *Selected Literary Essays*, ed. Walter Hooper (Cambridge: Cambridge University Press) 13.

[16] Lewis, *The Allegory of Love*, 162. Neither scholar considers the manuscript evidence or print history to which later historicists turn for an image of Chaucer's actual fifteenth- and sixteenth-century audiences.

[17] Ibid., 164.

[18] Quoted in Green and Hooper, *C.S. Lewis*, 408 and Barbour, "Lewis and Cambridge," 474; cf. Lewis, *Experiment*, 85.

[19] Derek Brewer, "The Tutor: A Portrait" in Como, *At the Breakfast Table*, 47.

to Lewis, for example, the modern concept of a "mocking" Chaucer leads to misreadings of the ending of *Troilus and Criseyde*, by considering Troilus's final laughter ironic: irony in such a case can be used to explain away anything a critic does not like, or disagrees with ideologically. In this, Lewis is closer to Kittredge than to the ironists of mid-century Chaucerian criticism. While Kittredge speaks of Chaucer's "usual irony," the irony he sees in Chaucer tends to be the "irony of circumstance," a gentle laughter at the peculiarities of the world. At the level of the tale as a whole, however, as opposed to small jokes or ironic comments, Kittredge tends to take Chaucer "straight." Likewise, while Lewis will admit to the occasional moment of dramatic irony in Chaucer, this falls far short of the pervasive irony some critics see in Chaucer: "There is dramatic irony in the last sentence [of *Troilus and Criseyde*], but this must not be confused with the irony sometimes falsely attributed to Chaucer in this poem. It is destiny that laughs and Chaucer is far from laughter as he records it."[20] Neither in Kittredge nor in Lewis do we find the kind of irony required by later theories such as New Criticism or exegetical criticism, an irony that depends upon a major distance in perception and stance between characters in the text and the reader.

Lewis goes further than Kittredge in his rejection of ironic readings of Chaucer. For the most part, he believes that Chaucer's audience would have been quite "close" to the characters: most of the time, the reader shares the responses, feelings and values of the protagonists. Instead of reading Troilus's laughter ironically, Lewis argues, we should take it seriously, sharing Troilus's serious delight in the next world after he has left behind the pleasures and trials of this world. This fits perfectly with Lewis's theory of courtly love and its reconciliation with a Christian ethic: throughout most of the poem Chaucer follows the courtly love pattern of glorifying and praising worldly love, but turns to heavenly love in the final section. Likewise, the idea of an "ironic" Pandarus is rejected in *The Allegory of Love*. Pandarus is not a "vulgar scoffer" but "a convinced servant of the god of Love." His dictates and teachings about love should not be read as mocking or comic— the comedy comes because of Pandarus's pedantry and prolixity, not because the doctrines of love *themselves* are ridiculous. Indeed, we are meant to learn "the mystery of courtly love" from *Troilus and Criseyde*; the humour that there is in the poem does not detract from its overall seriousness.[21] Pandarus's sententiousness is not funny in itself, only in the response Troilus makes to it: "Chaucer's audience could listen with gravity and interest to edifying matter which would set a modern audience sleeping or sniggering," Lewis declares. "To assume that sententiousness became funny for Chaucer's readers as easily as it becomes funny for us, is to misunderstand the fourteenth century."[22] Lewis likewise reacts strongly against critics who read the courtly sentiment in the *Parlement of Foules* as ironic. Because Chaucer is a poet of love, and taken seriously as such by his contemporaries, we

---

[20]   Lewis, *The Allegory of Love*, 184.

[21]   Ibid., 191–2.

[22]   Lewis, *Experiment*, 23–4.

should consider the noble birds, who advocate noble refined love, and not the Duck or the Goose, who mock such sentiments, as his spokesmen. Critics who believe otherwise, Lewis says, "attribute to Chaucer a square-headed vulgarity of thought and feeling which would be regrettable in any age and all but impossible to a court poet of the age of Froissart" (although he concedes graciously that he "will not insist on [this] conviction").[23] Lewis's perception of the refined, courtly nature of both Chaucer and his audience leads him to reject readings which depend upon vulgar humour and base sentiment.

Lewis cannot dismiss the humour in Chaucer's writings entirely.[24] The humourous characters and passages, however, do not detract from the overall seriousness of Chaucer's writings, as they were received by his contemporaries and successors. Lewis argues that Chaucer, along with "every knight and dame among his listeners," allowed "the laughter of the vulgar" *inside* the poetry, so that it would not take on a more dangerous form from outside.[25] In other words, the Duck and the Goose in the *Parlement of Foules* give voice to the mocking cynicism of the commons so that the overall courtly ethos of the poem can triumph in the end, and protect itself pre-emptively against such cynicism and mocking common sense. Lewis thus uses the refined and educated nature of his vision of Chaucer's audience as a defence for his own reading, a reading that will allow gentle humour in Chaucer but nothing that might portray him as mocking or ironizing the courtly ethos in which Lewis situates Chaucer's writings. Chaucer's first readers, well versed in the "code" of courtly love, would have known how to interpret Chaucer's humour correctly.

Psychological Allegory

In parallel to the development of courtly love poetry, which Lewis describes from the eleventh century to the fourteenth century and beyond, Lewis outlines the development of the medieval tradition of allegory. The two traditions are linked: Lewis argues that allegory developed as a means of exploring the workings of courtly love in terms of the emotions of the lovers. Allegory grew out of a late Classical tradition, as the pantheon of Roman gods was allegorized to represent abstract ideas such as Nature, Love, or Fortune. Lewis traces the way allegory developed through writers such as Prudentius, Martianus Capella, and Bernardus Silvestris, until it reached its fully-medieval form in the *Anticlaudianus* of Alain de Lille. Courtly love writers such as Chrétien de Troyes, Lewis hypothesizes, drew on this tradition in attempting to describe the feelings at work in the inner minds of their characters. The courtly love tradition and the allegorical tradition meet most fully in the *Roman de la Rose*, a fully allegorized depiction of the

---

[23]   Lewis, *The Allegory of Love*, 172.

[24]   He believes the Miller's Tale, for example, was intended humourously. Lewis, *Experiment*, 12.

[25]   Lewis, *The Allegory of Love*, 173.

workings of courtly love which Chaucer himself translated. Medieval readers, Lewis concludes, used to the Christian allegorical tradition and books such as the *Roman de la Rose*, would have developed a competency in allegorical modes of reading and thought. They would have been familiar with the technique of allegory, and would have known how to read and decipher it without any of the alienation a modern audience, more accustomed to symbolism, would feel.[26] The extensive passages in *The Allegory of Love*, in which C.S. Lewis "translates" the allegory of the *Roman* for the modern reader, would have been unnecessary for a medieval reader. According to Lewis, a medieval audience would have enjoyed the dual nature of allegory, and would have had no problem in simultaneously retaining both the "literal" and the "allegorical" levels of narrative, neither reading the allegory simply for its own sake, nor dismissing the allegorical surface entirely in search of the inner message.

It is here, in his discussion of allegory, that Lewis makes another claim which has major critical implications for the interpretation of Chaucer. Lewis maintains that medieval allegory was fundamentally psychological. Allegory, he argues, is the way in which an "objective" culture (a culture whose mindset dwells primarily on externals, and little on the workings of the internal mind) describes "subjective" things—thoughts, feelings, emotions. Medieval psychological allegory developed from Chrétien de Troyes, who slips into allegory any time he wishes to describe the tensions in the minds of his characters, to the *Roman de la Rose*, which, Lewis argues, is almost entirely about the internal workings of the minds of the hero and heroine: "[The characters] may be conveniently divided into three groups, according as they are neutral qualities who may qualify now the hero's and now the heroine's mind; or qualities belonging to the hero; or, again, qualities belonging to the heroine."[27] Allegory, therefore, became a representation of the inner workings of the mind and soul—in other words, it became psychology. Lewis believes that a medieval audience would have shared this perception of allegory as being psychological. Allegory, then, to a medieval reader, is (rather paradoxically) psychological realism: "what we have in the *Roman de la Rose* is a story of real life. ... Young readers in the not ignoble ardours of calf-love, and elderly readers in the mood of reminiscence, whether wistful or ironic, could all find in it the reflection of their own experience." An allegorical love poem was a "natural mode of expression" for a medieval person.[28] Countering critics who claim that medieval literature is not "psychological" in the way in which a modern novel is psychological, Lewis contends that, because of allegories such as the *Roman de la Rose*, a medieval audience would have been entirely comfortable with psychologically-based characters and stories. Thus, while Lewis claims medieval poetry is not *visually* realistic, in terms of portrayal of perspective,

---

[26] For the distinction between symbolism and allegory, a key one in Lewis's thought, see Lewis, *The Allegory of Love*, 44–8.

[27] Ibid., 120.

[28] Ibid., 1, 116.

etc., he regularly suggests that it is *psychologically* realistic and true-to-life. The audience here functions for Lewis in such a way as to make certain readings permissible: since a medieval audience would have read stories psychologically, Lewis can counter criticisms that he is being anachronistic when he performs a psychological reading.

In this way, Lewis can fit Chaucer into what he sees as the allegorical tradition of courtly love stories such as the *Roman de la Rose*, despite the fact that *Troilus* is clearly not allegorical, and Chaucer's other poems are not radically allegorical in the way that the *Roman* is. Lewis sums up his thesis thus: "in his greatest work, we have the courtly conceptions of love, which Chaucer learned from the French allegory, put into action in poetry which is not allegorical at all. Chaucer achieves the literal presentation; but it is Guillaume's allegory which has rendered the achievement possible."[29] Chaucer's audience, Lewis suggests, would have read *Troilus and Criseyde* through the lens of the *Roman de la Rose*, and would have understood Troilus's and Criseyde's actions accordingly. In other words, they would have transferred the internal psychological motivations, allegorized in the *Roman de la Rose*, to the external actions Chaucer recounts in his tale. Thus, for example, Lewis describes Criseyde's first, tentative, admission of Troilus as being due to "Bialacoil" [*sic*], her "bettre chere" or "fair welcome."[30] In this way Lewis implies that Criseyde can be best understood through her parallels with the heroine of the *Roman de la Rose*, and suggests that contemporaries would have read her that way. Moreover, because of the medieval understanding of the courtly love ethic, a medieval audience would not have condemned her love for Troilus: "By Christian standards, forgivable: by the rules of courtly love, needing no forgiveness: this is all that need be said of Criseide's act in granting the Rose to Troilus."[31] The use in this passage of the allegorized term "Rose" for Criseyde's love shows the exent to which Lewis adopted the conventional language of the allegorical courtly love tradition and the *Roman de la Rose*. To a lesser extent, Lewis takes the same approach to the *Book of the Duchess*: he describes the Black Knight's falling in love as "looking into the well of Narcissus," and his approach to Blanche as "attempts to approach the rose." Again, the "psychology of love" developed in the *Roman*, Lewis argues, remains in the *Book of the Duchess*, but stripped of its covering allegory.[32] Chaucer, as a reader and translator of the *Roman*, deciphered the psychological discussion behind its allegorical code; his audience would likewise have recognized the *Roman* in the psychology of *Troilus and Criseyde* and the *Book of the Duchess*.

Having established that a medieval audience would have been able to understand—indeed, that it had a penchant for—psychological characters and stories, Lewis is free to provide a fully-blown psychological reading of *Troilus*

---

[29]   Ibid., 167.

[30]   Ibid., 181; cf. 136.

[31]   Ibid., 183.

[32]   Ibid., 167–9.

and Criseyde. In doing so, however, he tacitly moves beyond his understanding of Chaucer's medieval audience, and turns to Chaucer's universal audience. Great poetry, is, according to Lewis, defined as "great" in terms of audience reception: it speaks not only to its immediate audience, but to all audiences of all times. "In every age the achievements smack less of their own age than the struggles, and speak a more universal language," Lewis writes, "That is how we know they are achievements. Chaucer is most modern when he is most successfully medieval."[33] This universalizing tendency justifies particular psychological interpretations of *Troilus and Criseyde* which rest upon Lewis's implicit belief that human nature remains much the same over time, even if the manner in which it is expressed or portrayed in art and literature is radically different. Grounding his psychological reading in historical argument—a medieval audience's ability to understand the psychological aspect of allegory—Lewis broadens it out to show how universally appropriate, and understandable to audiences of all eras, such a reading is.

Much of this process is implicit. Lewis never clearly indicates when he is turning from a medieval appreciation of *Troilus and Criseyde* to a more "universal" reading (and one could not expect otherwise, since he explicitly believes that the most "medieval" reading will be the most universal). This movement from "medieval" to "universal" is clearly at work in Lewis's description of Criseyde. First, Lewis justifies Criseyde's actions in terms of the "medieval mindset" of courtly love: he judges her actions based on the eleventh-century Provençal ethos of Adultery and Courtesy, and pronounces her as "needing no forgiveness." If anything, within the terms of this ethic, Criseyde was too cautious. He then turns to a more universal psychology of human nature to explain her subsequent betrayal of Troilus. He attributes her betrayal to the emotion of "Fear." Although "Fear" is an allegorized character in the *Roman de la Rose*, Lewis explains the emotion in modern, not medieval terms. "Women of her kind have always some male relative to stand between them and the terrifying world of affairs," he writes; and again, "It may reasonably be asked whether there is not in such a woman ... a dash of what is now called masochism."[34] He imagines Criseyde's character in other circumstances, and describes her in terms equally suited to our society as to medieval society: "In happier circumstances she would have been a faithful mistress, or a faithful wife, an affectionate mother, a kindly neighbour—a happy woman and a cause of happiness to all about her—caressed and caressing in her youth, and honoured in her old age."[35] No longer is Lewis explaining Criseyde in terms of the medieval allegory of the Rose, or the ethic of courtly love. Instead, Lewis turns to a universal psychology understood by all ages. A medieval audience, in other words, would have reacted to Criseyde in the same way a modern one would, and attribute her betrayal to her "human" characteristics: her timidity and weakness.

---

[33] Ibid., 178.

[34] Ibid., 185–6.

[35] Ibid., 189.

The same universalizing tendency can be noted in Lewis's depiction of Pandarus. First described in terms Lydgate or Hoccleve would have used, drawn from the allegorical tradition, "Vekke in his scenes with Cryseide," "*Frend* in his scenes with Troilus,"[36] Pandarus is later described in obviously modern terms, as "the practical man, the man who 'gets things done' ... in the hands of such a man you can travel first class through the length and breadth of England on a third-class ticket; policemen and gamekeepers will fade away before you, placated yet unbribed ... a discreet, resourceful, indefatigable man." "Everyone has met the modern equivalent of Pandarus," Lewis writes, and says "the character is easily recognizable, for it is happily not uncommon in life."[37] Later, Lewis compares Pandarus to the "merry old Victorians"; in the end, he says, the character is a "richly concrete human being."[38] Troilus, too, is universalized, although with slightly less enthusiasm than Criseyde and Pandarus: his character traits must "be confessed to be true (intolerably true in places) to nature," and his experiences chime with universal human experience: "All men have waited with ever-decreasing hope, day after day, for some one or for something that does not come, and all would willingly forget the experience."[39] Lewis's double concept of audience—first, the immediate medieval audience, which must ground and limit all possible readings in terms of the "medieval mindset," and second, the universal audience, which appreciates the timeless aspects of Chaucer's depictions of "human nature"—supports and allows a reading which is at once psychological yet unironic. Criseyde, Pandarus and Troilus are psychologically true to the medieval courtly love mindset; they are also "true to life" in general.[40]

The Medieval Mindset

Lewis, therefore, takes an interesting stance with regards to historicism. On the one hand, he believes that certain aspects of human nature—the forms that love takes, the way in which people's actions are dictated by fear, etc.—are universal, and that a modern audience can understand medieval characters such as Criseyde by accessing and appealing to those universal emotions. At the same time, however, he believes that each age expresses that universal human nature in radically different artistic and cultural modes, modes so distinct that the underlying universal emotions become unrecognizable to people from different periods. He places a divide at the Romantic period, when artists turned from allegory to symbolism as tools through which to express psychology and abstract concepts.

---

[36]   Ibid., 180–81, *emphasis in original.*

[37]   Ibid., 190.

[38]   Ibid., 194.

[39]   Ibid., 195.

[40]   For criticism of Lewis's reading of the *Troilus*, see Sharrock, "Second Thoughts," 123–37.

The "medieval mind" is clearly differentiated from a modern one: "No one, as far as I know, has exaggerated the emotional and imaginative difference between such a universe and that which we now believe ourselves to inhabit," Lewis writes.[41] Lewis's contention is that if a medieval audience would have had certain perspectives, or assumptions, or cultural competencies, then modern people need to at least understand, if not share, those attitudes and competencies if we are to understand Chaucer. This is the main thesis of Lewis's inaugural address as the Chair of Medieval and Renaissance English at Cambridge University. He tells his audience, "It is my settled conviction, that in order to read Old Western literature aright you must suspend most of the responses and unlearn most of the habits you have acquired in reading modern literature."[42] This attitude is a major defining criterion for categorizing a critic. C.S. Lewis, then, is one of the first proponents of the belief that Chaucer should be read according to the values and attitudes of a medieval, rather than a modern, audience.

This belief—that medieval literature should be read by a modern audience in the way in which it would have been read by a medieval audience—is explicit in *The Allegory of Love*. It is developed most fully, and is the major impetus behind Lewis's other major work on medieval literature and culture, *The Discarded Image*. *The Discarded Image* is, in many ways, a handbook for the student of medieval literature: it systematically outlines the key aspects of the "mindset" which a medieval audience would have had, and which a modern audience no longer shares. Unlike the New Historicists of the end of the twentieth century, who study medieval *minds* and Chaucer's various *readers* or *audiences*, for Lewis, Chaucer's audience is singular, a roughly homogeneous entity which would react to Chaucer's writing in a more-or-less consistent way. Lewis is interested in the "characteristic medieval mood" and the "real temper of those ages."[43] He is not unsubtle in this: in *The Allegory of Love*, especially, he traces developments and changes to certain aspects of "the medieval mind" over time. He does not see "the medieval mind" as static and unchanging. He does, however, consider it more-or-less as homogeneous, continuous and coherent. He looks for, and is interested in, aspects of medieval culture and ways of thinking that were common to most people in medieval times, from which he can develop an approximate model of the medieval mindset. He is not interested in exceptions to or aberrations from that mindset, except as they clarify or provide insight into the mindset as a whole. This mindset in turn underlies Lewis's concept of Chaucer's audience: he is not interested in particular readers of Chaucer, or atypical responses, but in the way a typical person situated in the culture and mindset of the Middle Ages would have read Chaucer. Even if there are exceptions and discontinuities, Lewis believes that they had little impact upon literature or art. A good example of this attitude comes when Lewis is discussing medieval historians. He acknowledges that Matthew

---

[41] Lewis, *Studies*, 45–6.

[42] Lewis, *Literary Essays*, 13; cf. Green and Hooper, *C.S. Lewis*, 350; Sayer, *Jack*, 359.

[43] Lewis, *Studies*, 44.

C.S. Lewis (1894–1963): The Psychological Reader

Paris was a "scientific" and critical historian, by our standards, but dismisses this exception to the rule he is building. His justification for this procedure here is a good summary of his attitude throughout: "[Exceptions such as Paris] are not on that account especially important for our present purpose. We are concerned with the picture of the past, and the attitude to the past, as these existed in the mind of literary authors and their audience. The imagined past as part of the Model is the quarry we pursue."[44] It is indicative of Lewis's way of thinking that, in this passage, he uses the singular of "mind." He believes in, and is interested in studying, the "general mind of the period."[45] He believes there is such a thing as "the medieval mind,"[46] and the duty of a critic or scholar is to reconstruct this state of mind through "historical imagination."[47] Lewis calls this mindset of the audience a "backcloth," meaning both a set of assumptions and predispositions with which the audience comes to a piece of literature, and a set of knowledge and skills through which they can interpret the work. Our modern "backcloth" might include modernist poetry, Cartesian philosophy, and Mozart; the medieval "backcloth" included bestiaries, the Bible, and courtly love. The effects of this basic premise for Lewis's understanding of audience dynamic are twofold. First, he assumes that most of Chaucer's medieval audience would have read the works in roughly the same way, and that marginal or atypical responses—such as Matthew Paris's—are irrelevant. The audience in this formulation is unified and homogeneous, at least as far as the critic need be concerned. Second, Lewis works on the basis of the premise that knowledge and techniques of interpretation held by one group of medieval society (i.e., eleventh-century Provençal readers) can be relatively safely assumed for other groups of medieval society (i.e., fourteenth-century English readers) because they share the same general "mindset."

From his far-reaching reading of medieval texts, Lewis develops a thorough, clearly defined image of what he calls the "medieval mind," which he outlines in *The Discarded Image*. A medieval reader, according to this image, would have subscribed to an overarching "mental Model of the Universe."[48] This model of the cosmos would have been ordered, complex, and unified. Moreover, it was satisfying in its unity and certainty. Medieval texts are filled with re-workings and re-tellings of the model. Lewis concludes from this that medieval people must have enjoyed contemplating the model, dwelling on it and re-discovering or re-affirming its perfection again and again. He says, rather wryly, "One gets the impression that medieval people, like Professor Tolkien's Hobbits, enjoyed books which told them what they already knew."[49] From this contemplation and study, a medieval

---

[44]   C.S. Lewis, *The Discarded Image: An Introduction to Medieval and Renaissance Literature* (Cambridge: Cambridge University Press, 1964) 177.

[45]   Lewis, *The Allegory of Love*, 33.

[46]   Ibid., 17; Lewis, *Discarded Image*, 177.

[47]   Lewis, *The Allegory of Love*, 1.

[48]   Lewis, *Discarded Image*, 11, *capitals in original*. See also Lewis, *Studies*, 48–9.

[49]   Lewis, *Discarded Image*, 200.

reader would have had a competent knowledge of astronomy/astrology, alchemy, natural history (knowledge of bestiaries, etc.), theology, and philosophy, on which he could draw in his reading. This does not mean the knowledge was useful at a practical level—many medieval people would have had practical knowledge of animals, for example, which would have been at odds with the information given in bestiaries—but it was required for an understanding of literature.

The medieval reader was bookish.[50] The "medieval mindset" was founded upon certain key books, and even if an individual reader had not actually read a particular book, he would nonetheless have absorbed the key tenets of that book from other reading. Lewis believes the list of important books, from which medieval people assembled their "Model," included the Bible, Virgil, Ovid, Lucan, Statius, Claudian, Apuleius, Chalcidius, Macrobius, pseudo-Dionysius, and Boethius.[51] Not all people in the Middle Ages would have read all these books, but they would have had a general knowledge of what was in them—just as someone in our society would have significant knowledge of Marx or Freud even if he or she had never read their works. Unlike Kittredge, who, wherever possible, ascribed themes or subjects in literature to something the author had seen in real life (the whirling wicker House of Rumour to actual building techniques in Wales and Scotland, for example, or the Canterbury pilgrims to actual pilgrims Chaucer would have seen), Lewis was far more likely to ascribe them to something the author had read. His dependence on books does not allow entry to aspects of the medieval "mindset" that were not literary or clerkly. For example, he says, "Millions, no doubt, were illiterate; the masters, however, were literate, and not only literate but scholarly and even pedantic."[52] When he goes on in the next sentence to describe "medieval man," however, he has clearly dismissed the "millions" and is speaking solely of the "masters."

The Canterbury Omission

Problematically, the "medieval" concern for courtly refinement and psychology—a very specific kind of psychology descended from the allegory of the *Romance of the Rose*—seems clearly absent from what is commonly considered one of Chaucer's greatest works, the *Canterbury Tales*. So too is the "medieval" concern for order and harmonious unity, the "medieval" attitude of "profound and cheerful sobriety" as opposed to "renaissance frivolity," and the "age of Froissart's" courtly distaste for vulgar humour and base sentiment. Lewis's medieval universe had little room for a work as messy, chaotic, unfinished and, frankly, as "common" as the *Canterbury Tales*. "If medieval works often lack unity, they lack it not because

---

[50] Calin, *The Twentieth-Century Humanist Critics*, 90.

[51] Lewis, *Discarded Image*, chapters III and IV.

[52] Lewis, *Studies*, 43.

they are medieval, but because they are, so far, bad," he writes.[53] The *Canterbury Tales* seem to form a major lacuna in Lewis's criticism of Chaucer, and reveal the way in which a critic's concept of audience can shape his conclusions.[54] This, in turn, tells us important things about the *Canterbury Tales*, about what kinds of readings the implicit audience of the *Canterbury Tales* invites or precludes.

In part, Lewis glosses over the *Canterbury Tales* not only because they were not relevant to his study, but because he was reacting against an era of scholarship which considered "the great mass of Chaucer's work [as] simply a background to the *Canterbury Tales*, and the whole output of the fourteenth century [as] simply a background to Chaucer."[55] Yet this defence is also slightly disingenuous, for Lewis persistently shies away from dealing with the challenges the *Canterbury Tales* pose to his theory of medieval readership. He is so subtle in doing so that the reader of his works barely notices: in the *Allegory of Love*, for example, he justifies his omission of the *Canterbury Tales* on the grounds that Chaucer's heirs knew and revered his earlier work, not the *Tales*; he notes that the *Tales*, as opposed to Chaucer's earlier poems, begat few imitators in terms of style or content; and he then moves seamlessly into a discussion of the style of Chaucer's earliest writing. The *Canterbury Tales* never resurface. This method, of dealing with the *Tales* by not dealing with them, is typical. It is difficult to prove a negative, but the absence of the *Canterbury Tales* from Lewis's work is pronounced: there are three pages dealing with the *Canterbury Tales* in the *Allegory of Love*, as opposed to 26 dealing with *Troilus and Criseyde*, seven mentioning the *Book of the Duchess* and eight mentioning *Parlement of Foules*; in *Studies in Medieval and Renaissance Literature*, three of the six comments on the *Canterbury Tales* deal with an issue of style or etymology. Moreover, the defence that the *Canterbury Tales* had been over-studied does not hold at all for a work that Lewis *never* mentions, the *House of Fame*, yet the *House of Fame*, at first glance, contains many of the aspects Lewis ostensibly looks for in a medieval work: allegory, extreme bookishness (more than any other of Chaucer's works), and an ordered cosmos. However, the *House of Fame* is also chaotic, unfinished, and often irreverent or bawdy in its humour (the Eagle's joke about "ayr ybroken," for example). Since these are precisely the traits

---

[53]   Lewis, *The Allegory of Love*, 141.

[54]   Kerby-Fulton makes a similar use of Lewis's 'blind spots,' suggesting that Lewis's dislike of Langland and Donne provides important insight into Lewis's preference for complete, orderly works, which parallels his vision of the "finished and harmonious" medieval universe; I believe that this conception of Lewis's overall oeuvre (his preference for Spenser and Milton over Langland and Donne) is reflected in miniature in his criticism on Chaucer (his preference for *Troilus and Criseyde* and the dream visions over the *Canterbury Tales*). Kerby-Fulton, "Standing on Lewis's Shoulders."

[55]   Lewis, *The Allegory of Love*, 161. It is unsurprising that the *Canterbury Tales* were not included in a study of allegory, such as the *Allegory of Love*—but it must be remembered that *Troilus and Criseyde*, which is no more allegorical, was included.

that the *House of Fame* shares with the *Canterbury Tales*, they may point to the reasons Lewis omits discussion of the *Tales*.

The *Canterbury Tales* are messy, disorganized, and incomplete. They do not reflect a well-formed universe: the Miller disrupts the hierarchical structure of the three estates, the makeup of the pilgrims is heavily skewed towards the commoners, and some prologues are all out of proportion to their tales. The *Tales* do not present a bookish culture, but an oral one: some of the characters are almost surely illiterate, and others deliberately challenge the tenets of bookish authority. The pilgrims form a society that is far from genteel. The Miller's Tale is the epitome of base vulgarity, yet it is also exceedingly funny (and is clearly intended to be so); the humour in sections such as the Wife of Bath's Prologue or the Nun's Priest's Tale, far from reinforcing the hierarchies and the order of medieval society, wreaks havoc with traditional structures of morality and authority. The *Canterbury Tales* certainly contains as much so-called "renaissance frivolity" (the fabliaux, the Tale of Sir Thopas, the Nun's Priest's Tale) as "profound and cheerful medieval sobriety" (the Second Nun's Tale, the Man of Law's Tale). The *Tales* contain no allegory, and what psychology they include ranges from courtly love psychology to realistic characterizations of ordinary individuals. Few readers can take all the portraits in the General Prologue completely "straight," although they differ as to what extent the portraits should be considered ironic. Nobody (except the Host!) takes the Tale of Sir Thopas "straight." Finally, and perhaps most importantly, few readers would believe that all the extremely diverse pilgrims share one same, overarching "mindset" which governs their actions and their way of looking at the world.

Lewis's avoidance of the *Canterbury Tales*, his inability to fit the *Tales* into his model of medieval reading practices, suggests that the implicit audience encoded within the *Canterbury Tales* challenges his vision of a medieval audience. His difficulties seem to arise in several areas: in the vision of a "medieval mindset" that valued unity and order; in his sense that a medieval audience was overwhelmingly serious; in his image of the audience as upper-class, educated people who believed in and valued the courtly love ethos; and, perhaps most tellingly, in his insistence upon the singularity of "mind," his underlying assumption that all of Chaucer's readers would have read his works in predominantly the same way. These assumptions about medieval audiences seem to preclude several readings of Chaucer's works—readings of him as ironic, irreverent, or bawdy—and almost prevent entirely a reading of the *Canterbury Tales*. Lewis's "medieval mind," it seems, and the audience he imagines for Chaucer, for the most part overlooks commoners, non-courtiers, women, the overly pious, and the illiterate.[56]

---

[56] This depiction of a medieval audience as primarily upper-class, male and educated may contribute to Lewis's antipathy towards the anthropological approach: he dismisses the popular (lower-class) genres of ballad and romance, which anthropologists focus on, as "the reverse of typical." "Fragments" of "indigenous and spontaneous mythology" may survive in popular genres such as the ballad, he writes, but "we must insist that these things loom much larger in the popular [twentieth-century] picture of the Middle Ages than they did

These assumptions—especially that Chaucer's audience was male—are common to most scholars of the twentieth century. Only when we come to the feminist scholars of the last two decades of the twentieth century do we find a questioning of this assumption: an investigation into Chaucer's women readers and, more significantly, an interest in the way in which a woman might read differently than a man. These scholars address the problems that Lewis's vision of a medieval audience raises, especially its omission of women and non-courtiers, by eliminating the notion of a singular medieval mind, and envisioning "audiences," capable of multiple, diverse and conflicting responses. Later scholars also challenged other assumptions of Lewis's theory of audience. The exegetical critics attacked Lewis's ideas of psychological "tensions" in the medieval mind, especially between the courtly love and Christian frameworks, seeing the two as fundamentally incompatible. New Critics, by contrast, reacted against the overly serious, rigid, and conservative aspects of Lewis's criticism by envisioning an audience much more relaxed than Lewis's, one which did not take either the codes of courtly love or the strictures of the church too seriously. Both of these schools of thought, despite their differences, depended upon the concept of irony in their responses to Lewis's theories. E. Talbot Donaldson, a New Critic, envisions an audience for Chaucer capable of humour, alive to dramatic and structural irony, undisturbed by irreverence. D.W. Robertson and his exegetical followers move in the opposite direction, considering the medieval audience as even more serious, rigid and conservative than Lewis does. In response to the problems this poses—especially the problem of the *Canterbury Tales*, which Lewis avoids—they too answer with the tool of irony.

---

in the reality"—the "reality" of the aristocratic medieval man, as opposed to the common illiterate woman, one presumes. Lewis, *Studies*, 43.

Chapter 3

E. Talbot Donaldson (1910–1987): The Careful Reader

Two theoretical approaches began to dominate Chaucer studies by the middle of the twentieth century. The first, New Criticism, was prominent across English studies. New Criticism rejected the historicist claim that knowledge of the biography, historical circumstances, and context of a work would help the reader understand it. Instead, New Critics advocated taking a poem on its own terms, as "words on a page," without extensive reference to background or history. New Critics thus depended on a formal approach to literature, studying primarily the *form* of a text (its rhyme, rhythm, structure, etc.) and often focused on the overall unity and structural irony of the works. The other critical approach to affect Chaucer studies was exegetical criticism. This approach was less widespread, primarily restricted to Medieval Studies, and had little impact on English studies in general. Within the field of Medieval Studies, however, the exegetical approach was powerfully persuasive. Exegetics maintained that all medieval literature was written and read in accordance with St. Augustine's doctrine of *caritas*, and if a work did not seem on the surface to promote this doctrine, it should be read as allegorical or ironic. The next two chapters will consider two mid-century critics, E. Talbot Donaldson, the leading critic of Chaucerian New Criticism, and D.W. Robertson, the founder and primary advocate of exegetical criticism. These two scholars were engaged in controversy for much of their careers, and advocated radically different readings of Chaucer. However, as I shall argue, the two scholars are more similar than has been previously thought, since both Donaldson's and Robertson's readings of Chaucer depend upon an understanding of Chaucerian irony as pervasive, structural, and essential. Irony in Chaucer, by the middle of the twentieth century, came to be seen not just as a momentary humourous phrase or section, but as an underlying characteristic of his works; not simply a surface rhetorical technique, but embedded in the structures of the text. Understanding this irony became crucial to understanding Chaucer's works. This understanding of irony, in turn, was dependent upon a distinct vision of Chaucer's audience: the audience had to be situated at at conceptual distance from the text and its characters in order to perceive the irony.

Because Donaldson and Robertson were contemporaries, and responded to one another's ideas and theories in turn, they cannot be assessed in strict sequential order. Donaldson published several articles, most notably "Chaucer the Pilgrim," during the 1950s, and continued to publish throughout the 1960s. His edition of

60   *Twentieth-Century Chaucer Criticism*

Chaucer's works was published in 1958.[1] D.W. Robertson, meanwhile, published what in many ways could be called his "manifesto," the article "Historical Criticism," in 1950, along with several other articles in the 1950s, then produced his two major books in 1962 and 1963.[2] However, since Robertson was, in many ways, responding to the entire New Critical movement, of which Donaldson may be taken as representative, I will discuss him second. Donaldson belongs to what could be considered (by the 1950s) an older, more traditional theoretical approach going back to I.A.Richards and F.R. Leavis in the 1930s, and I will consider his work first.[3] Nevertheless, I will attempt to maintain a sense of the contemporaneity of Donaldson and Robertson, and address the ways in which their arguments were responses, rebuttals and critiques of the ideas of the other.

The New Criticism

E. Talbot Donaldson is primarily associated with Yale University, where he did his PhD in 1943 on the C-Text of Piers Plowman, and where he spent most of his career, although in later years he also taught at Columbia University, University of Michigan, and Indiana University.[4] Donaldson had a background in Classics

---

[1] "Chaucer the Pilgrim," in E. Talbot Donaldson, *Speaking of Chaucer* (London: Athlone Press, 1970) 1–12; E.T. Donaldson, *Chaucer's Poetry: An Anthology for the Modern Reader* (New York: The Ronald Press Company, 1958); E. Talbot Donaldson, "Chaucer's *Miller's Tale*, A3583–6," *Modern Language Notes* 69 (1954) 310–14; E. Talbot Donaldson, "Idiom of Popular Poetry in the *Miller's Tale*," *Explication as Criticism: Selected Papers from the English Institute 1941–1952*, ed. W.K. Wimsatt (New York: Columbia University Press, 1951) 27–51.

[2] D.W. Robertson, "Historical Criticism" in D.W. Robertson, Jr., *Essays in Medieval Culture* (Princeton: Princeton University Press, 1980); D.W. Robertson, Jr., *A Preface to Chaucer: Studies in Medieval Perspectives* (Princeton: Princeton University Press, 1962); Bernard F. Huppé and D.W. Robertson, Jr., *Fruyt and Chaf: Studies in Chaucer's Allegories* (Princeton: Princeton University Press, 1963). See also D.W. Robertson, Jr., "Why the Devil Wears Green," *Modern Language Notes* 69.7 (1954) 470–72; D.W. Robertson, Jr., "The Doctrine of Charity in Mediaeval Literary Gardens: A Topical Approach Through Symbolism and Allegory," *Speculum* 26.1 (January 1951) 24–49.

[3] For Donaldson as a representative of an "older" tradition, see Norman F. Cantor, *Inventing the Middle Ages* (New York: William Morrow, 1991) 200. Few Chaucerian scholars would argue with my choice of Donaldson as the archetypal "New Critic" for Chaucer studies: see Carolynn Van Dyke's comment, "Donaldson unquestionably represented those ... [new critical] critics." Carolynn Van Dyke, "Amorous Behavior: Sexism, Sin and the Donaldson Persona," *Chaucer Review* 41.3 (2007) 251. For the impact and enduring quality of Donaldson's scholarship, see the articles in the special issue of the *Chaucer Review*, vol. 41.3, 2007.

[4] For biography, see the introduction in the issue of the *Chaucer Review* devoted to Donaldson: vol. 41.3, 2007; Bonnie Wheeler, "The Legacy of New Criticism: Revisiting the

E. Talbot Donaldson (1910–1987): The Careful Reader   61

and had taught Latin and Greek before taking his doctorate; he also had extensive philological training, producing an edition of the B-Text of Piers Plowman with George Kane which won the Haskins Medal of the Medieval Academy. However, the New Critics who surrounded Donaldson at Yale were the primary milieu for Donaldson's scholarship. Alongside Donaldson, Cleanth Brooks, Maynard Mack, Louis Martz, W.K. Wimsatt, Jr. and other prominent New Critics worked at Yale in the 1950s and 1960s.[5] Wimsatt pioneered criticism attacking the "intentional fallacy," arguing that the text alone should be studied, and not the author's intentions as deduced from his biography, historical context, or other external evidence. Maynard Mack explored concepts of the "I-persona" of the speaker of a poem or work as distinct from its author. Both of these influences can be seen in Donaldson's work on the "Chaucer the Pilgrim" persona in the *Canterbury Tales.*[6] According to Ralph Hanna, Yale "didn't place a particularly high stock on learnedness"—meaning that despite Donaldson's undeniable breadth of learning, his criticism and the criticism produced by his colleagues tended to eschew the extensive reference and historical contextualizing depended upon by critics of the exegetical school of criticism.[7] As perhaps befits a scholar devoted to both philology and New Criticism, Donaldson, alone of the authors studied in this book, produced editions and articles but no monographs aside from his doctoral thesis and the post-retirement *The Swan at the Well: Shakespeare Reading Chaucer.*[8] However, his 1970 volume *Speaking of Chaucer*, a collection of his most important articles, was to have an impact on Chaucer studies comparable to that of Robertson's *A Preface to Chaucer* or Lewis's *The Allegory of Love.*

The New Critics of Donaldson's generation were, ultimately, heir to the critics C.S. Lewis so disliked, I.A. Richards and F.R. Leavis.[9] Donaldson and other

---

Work of E. Talbot Donaldson," *Chaucer Review* 41.3 (2007) 216–24; Rosalyn Rossignol, "Donaldson, E(thelbert) Talbot," *Chaucer: A Literary Reference to His Life and Work* (New York: Infobase Publishing, 2007) 412–13.

[5] Gretchen Mieszkowski, "'The Least Innocent of All Innocent-Sounding Lines': the Legacy of Donaldson's *Troilus* Criticism," *Chaucer Review* 41.3 (2007) 299; Ralph Hanna, "Donaldson and Robertson: An Obligatory Conjunction," *Chaucer Review* 41.3 (2007) 244–5.

[6] Geoffrey Gust, "Revaluating 'Chaucer the Pilgrim' and Donaldson's Enduring Persona," *Chaucer Review* 41.3 (2007) 315.

[7] Hanna, "Donaldson and Robertson," 245.

[8] E. Talbot Donaldson, *The Swan at the Well: Shakespeare Reading Chaucer* (New Haven: Yale University Press, 1985); E. Talbot Donaldson, *Piers Plowman: The C-Text and Its Poet* (New Haven: Yale University Press, 1949).

[9] For accounts of the development from Leavis and Richards to American New Criticism, see Raman Selden and Peter Widdowson, *A Reader's Guide to Contemporary Literary Theory, 3rd Ed.* (London: Harvester Wheatsheaf, 1993) 10–26; Terry Eagleton, *Literary Theory: An Introduction* (Oxford: Blackwell, 1983) 30–53. For the effect of New Criticism on Chaucer studies, see Corinne Saunders, ed., *Blackwell Guide to Criticism: Chaucer* (Oxford: Blackwell, 2001) 13–14; Lee Patterson, *Negotiating the Past: The*

New Critics downplayed Leavis's emphasis on the reading of English literature in terms of its moral or social value, and considered the study of literature as a pleasurable end in itself. This pleasure is crucial to a proper understanding of literature: in his introduction to his edition of Chaucer, Donaldson writes, "The assumption under which I have worked is that, in reading poetry, understanding is dependent on pleasure and will diminish proportionately as pleasure does."[10] New Critics turned away from the use of history or biography to explain literature, and focused on the text itself. So Donaldson comments that while Chaucer's "pretended inferiority complex" may have come from something real in his own life, "What interests me now however, is not the origin of the pose, but its literary value."[11] Authorial biography and its use in accessing the poet's mind is dismissed in favour of literary analysis. Much of Donaldson's criticism consists of close readings of texts, bringing his reader with him through a careful analysis of individual words, their connotations, and their implications for the text as a whole. Donaldson's New Criticical approach, unlike that of some of his colleagues, rested upon his philological and editorial training. E. Talbot Donaldson is the only one of the scholars studied in this book who produced his own edition of Chaucer's works. The format of this edition betrays New Critical values: historical and interpretative notes are kept to a minimum and put unobtrusively at the back of the volume, while the brief introduction emphasizes the need to experience the poetry directly, rather than through a screen of critical apparatus.[12] Donaldson believes that universal literature appeals to all time, and he emphatically denies the proposition, put forward by Robertson, that human nature or human minds have changed radically from medieval times to now.[13] This fundamentally New Critical approach determined Donaldson's latent, rarely-stated assumptions about Chaucer's audience. It also led him to the dominating controversy of his career, his opposition to the exegetical school of criticism championed by the followers of D.W. Robertson.

Historical Understanding of Medieval Literature (Madison: University of Wisconsin Press, 1987) 18–26.

[10] Donaldson, *Chaucer's Poetry*, iii. See Hanna, "Donaldson and Robertson," 244.

[11] Donaldson, *Speaking*, 84.

[12] Donaldson, *Chaucer's Poetry*, vi; see Lee Patterson's comments on this edition in Patterson, *Negotiating*, 19–20, and *Temporal Circumstances: Form and History in the Canterbury Tales* (New York: Palgrave MacMillan, 2006) 1.

[13] E. Talbot Donaldson, "Designing a Camel: Or, Generalizing the Middle Ages," *Tennessee Studies in Literature* 22 (1977) 2. For Robertson's beliefs about the change in human nature, see Robertson, "Some Observations on Method" in Robertson, *Essays*, 23, 29; Robertson, *Preface*, viii.

Opposing Exegetical Criticism

The main controversy of Donaldson's career came about through his rejection of the historicist stances taken both by contemporary scholars and by critics from the previous generation. Donaldson's wariness with regard to historicism seems to be based on more than the typical New Critical rejection of anything "outside the text": he was also reacting to the conflict among historicists themselves. Followers of C.S. Lewis, who emphasized the courtly love context of Chaucer's poetry as the "right" framework through which to read Chaucer's works, disagreed with other historicists, such as D.W. Robertson, who advocated a religious and biblical paradigm for reading Chaucer. Both approaches are "historicist," in that they argue that medieval poetry should be read as a medieval audience would have read it, but otherwise they contradicted one another, and the conflict undercut the certainty each approach claimed. Donaldson writes,

> I have eschewed the historical approach used by both the great Chaucerians of the earlier part of this century and by those scholars who have recently been reading Chaucer primarily as an exponent of medieval Christianity. The fact that the difference between what these two historical approaches have attained is absolute—if Chaucer means what the older Chaucerians thought he meant he cannot possibly mean what these newer Chaucerians think he means—has encouraged me to rely on the poems as the principal source of their meaning.[14]

The historical context is misleading, contradictory, and, ultimately, inaccessible as a means through which to read Chaucer's poetry. Donaldson instead claims that the poems themselves are the best guides to their own meaning. Donaldson wrote some criticism countering Lewis's interpretations, but he was much more concerned to oppose the new inroads exegetical criticism, as practised by Robertson and his followers, was making into Chaucerian and Medieval Studies: His conflict with Robertson was, in many ways, to set the tone in Chaucerian studies for the next 20 or 30 years.[15]

Donaldson's strong opposition to patristic exegetical criticism, as practised by the Robertsonian school, is based in large part upon his implicit assumptions about audiences. Donaldson states from the outset that he does not dismiss the influence

---

[14] Donaldson, *Chaucer's Poetry*, iv.

[15] For his opposition to Lewis's readings, especially of *Troilus and Criseyde*, see "The Myth of Courtly Love" in Donaldson, *Speaking*; cf. L.D. Benson, "A Reader's Guide to Writings on Chaucer," *Geoffrey Chaucer*, ed. Derek Brewer (London: G. Bell & Sons, 1974) 339. For Donaldson's most explicit critiques of patristic exegesis, see "Patristic Exegesis in the Criticism of Medieval Literature: The Opposition," Donaldson, *Speaking*, 134–53, and Donaldson, "Designing a Camel." For the impact of the controversy between Donaldson and Robertson on Chaucer studies, see the discussion in Patterson, *Negotiating*, 3–9, 32–9.

patristic exegesis may have had upon authors such as Chaucer or Langland. What he challenges is the claim that apparently non-allegorical poetry was actually read (and was intended to be read) as allegory, and that every work in the Middle Ages was read as promoting the doctrine of charity. Even if Chaucer might have *written* according to exegetical rules, in other words, Donaldson does not believe that medieval audiences would have *read*, or that modern audiences should have to read, medieval works in the manner Robertson advocates. Donaldson also objects to the inherent snobbery of Robertson's approach: he dislikes the requirement for complex, specialized knowledge on the part of the reader if he is to read the text correctly. Rather acerbically, Donaldson says, "Surely the burden of the proof is on the proponents of the critical method, who deny that I can understand what I read without possessing their special knowledge."[16] Donaldson's New Critical philosophy is evident here in his belief that "careful reading" is the main thing required to understand a text. Not only does Donaldson believe that he himself can understand what he reads without special knowledge, he thinks others can. He maintains that Chaucer's appeal extends well beyond the select group of critics with the expertise required to read Chaucer in what Robertson terms the "right" way. To read all of medieval literature through the techniques of exegetical criticism, or to read all of Chaucer through the lens of the Parson's Tale, as he claims Robertson's followers do, "is to miss the point of poetry. ... The best medieval literature does not necessarily have anything to do with sin, and it does just what Chaucer does—offers joy to the reader."[17] Donaldson's "reader" is not the specialist reader of the Robertson school, but any ordinary reader who reads for pleasure. As Lee Patterson writes, in many ways Donaldson's "mission" was to "rescue medieval literature from medievalists."[18]

Because Donaldson's image of Chaucer's audience is one of "ordinary" readers, Donaldson also objects to the method of reading which Robertson's approach implies. As opposed to Robertson's belief that reading a medieval text is an exercise analogous to solving a puzzle, requiring the intellect, Donaldson believes that reading involves an emotional, almost intuitive response to a work. Apparent contradictions, which to Robertson would indicate a challenge the reader must resolve, for Donaldson add to the emotional layers of a poem: "the fact is that we do not read poetry with the intellect alone, and that when poetry makes two contradictory statements they do not cancel each other out. Both remain as part of the essential poetic truth."[19] Readers do not consider Troilus as an abstract representation of all mankind, or Criseyde as a personification of the idea of worldly love—instead, they share in Troilus's suffering and fall in love with Criseyde. All the information a reader needs to understand a text is contained in the work itself; the application of outside information—be it of

---

[16]   Donaldson, "Patristic Exegesis," 135.

[17]   "Medieval Poetry and Medieval Sin" in Donaldson, *Speaking*, 173.

[18]   Patterson, *Temporal Circumstances*, 1.

[19]   Donaldson, *Chaucer's Poetry*, 970.

biblical symbolism, medieval hermeneutical practices, or complex patristic sign systems—is anathema to Donaldson's way of reading. In no way does Donaldson share Robertson's belief that medieval people knew the "right" way to read a text which we must recover to read it properly: "To give a reader a flat injunction to find one predetermined specific meaning in Middle English poetry is anything but the ideal way of preparing him to understand something old and difficult and complicated," he writes, "for in his eagerness to find what must be there he will very likely miss what is there; and in so doing he may miss a meaning arising from the poem that is better than anything that exegesis is able to impose upon it."[20] Donaldson does not concern himself with the possibility that the "better" meaning may be anachronistic or ahistorical. Moreover, as the preceding quotation shows, he is clearly sceptical of an approach which he believes imposes something on the text from the outside, as opposed to simply discovering "what is there" in the text itself. He also distrusts anything which might inhibit the reader's enjoyment, since a reader's enjoyment is crucial to his understanding of a text—and he clearly finds the extensive research and charting of iconographic symbolism, which Robertson's method requires, inhibiting to enjoyment.

Donaldson's vocabulary betrays assumptions about reading and audiences central to Donaldson's approach. The terms Donaldson uses are telling: meaning, to a New Critic like Donaldson, "arises" from a poem. The "summons" to interpretation must come from the poem itself: meaning is located within the poem or text, and a reader need only open himself up to that meaning.[21] Poems "yield up" their meaning to a reader—any reader who has a sufficient grasp of Middle English—without the need for complicated interpretative techniques or frameworks. Donaldson claims Robertsonian critics "substitute a special meaning for the one the poem yields without exegesis."[22] Instead, meaning comes from the poem itself, and if a reader needs special knowledge to understand certain passages, that knowledge should be embedded within the text. So, for example, when Langland uses symbols drawn from the patristic tradition, he explains them in such a way that a reader ignorant of the tradition will nonetheless understand the poem. No one who reads *Piers Plowman* could fail to realize that plowmen come to represent "spiritual plowmen" or priests, but this recognition comes from "having spent a good deal of time with the poem," not from any specialized, pre-existing knowledge in the reader.[23] The onus is upon the author to make the poem intelligible to his readers: Donaldson says emphatically that he "object[s] to a procedure which substitutes for the art of the poet the learning or good intentions of the reader."[24] No special techniques or specific knowledge

---

20   Donaldson, "Patristic Exegesis," 135.

21   Donaldson, "Myth of Courtly Love," 152.

22   Donaldson, "Patristic Exegesis," 138.

23   Ibid., 142.

24   Ibid., 152.

66 *Twentieth-Century Chaucer Criticism*

are required for understanding. If a reader pays close enough attention to a poem, the "text unfolds itself."[25]

Careful Reading

The underlying assumption behind the belief that meaning "arises" from the poem is, fundamentally, that all readers—or at least all reasonably intelligent readers who pay decent attention to the text (and this qualification is crucial to Donaldson's understanding of audience, as we will see)—will interpret a work in generally the same way. "Meaning" resides, in other words, within the poem itself, and surfaces through the reader's activity. In this, despite their radical differences, Donaldson's approach resembles Robertson's: both believe, essentially, that there is a "right" way to read a text. Robertson believes that the "right" interpretation will come about through the interpretation of the text using exegetical techniques, Donaldson through careful reading and close analysis, but both believe that readers who use the techniques advocated will produce similar interpretations of the poem. For example, if a reader believes that May, in the Merchant's Tale, only becomes bold and immodest after her marriage to January (rather than before), "he will be wrong," Donaldson states bluntly.[26] Because of his assumption that "careful" readers will individually come to the same "right" reading, Donaldson often describes the reactions of "the reader" to the text, without really considering that different readers, with different backgrounds, prejudices or assumptions, might react differently to a story, or that the same reader on a different reading might interpret a tale differently. So, for example, "the reader" will react with shock to the vulgarity in an otherwise innocuous passage of the Merchant's Tale; "the reader" shares the Merchant's horror at the deceitfulness of wives; "the reader" is deeply satisfied when the devil of the Friar's Tale carries the summoner off to hell; readers "delight" in the Nun's Priest's Tale, despite its rhetorical extravagance; "the reader" prizes Griselda's integrity and "trouthe" in the Clerk's Tale; "the reader" of *Troilus* momentarily wishes Troilus would keep Criseyde in the city by force; "the reader's" condemnation of Criseyde is increased by the narrator's defence of her; and "every reader" wants to identify himself with the hero of a story. "Every sensitive reader" feels that he "really knows" Criseyde, but "no sensible reader" will claim that he understands her.[27] Innumerable other examples could be quoted, for "the reader" is a continuous presence in Donaldson's criticism. This reader reacts in a predictable, sensible way, and underlies many of the claims Donaldson makes about the texts he analyzes.

---

[25] Donaldson, *Speaking*, viii.

[26] "The Masculine Narrator and Four Women of Style," in Donaldson, *Speaking,* 52.

[27] "The Effect of the Merchant's Tale" in Donaldson, *Speaking*, 34, 42; Donaldson, *Chaucer's Poetry*, 917; Donaldson, "Patristic Exegesis," 146; Donaldson, *Chaucer's Poetry*, 919, 974, 978, 935; "Criseide and Her Narrator" in Donaldson, *Speaking*, 83, respectively.

E. Talbot Donaldson (1910–1987): The Careful Reader   67

In this formulation of the reading dynamic, both text and reader are stable, uniform, predictable entities. The reader's response is conditioned by the text, and every reader will react to the text in approximately the same way. So, for example, the shifts in perspective in the Merchant's Tale first make the reader sympathetic to May, as he sees the wedding night from her point of view, but then, as the narrative point of view shifts and we no longer see things from May's perspective, the reader begins to feel disgusted with her as well as with January. Likewise, Chaucer carefully controls the reader's responses to Criseyde, by having the narrator of *Troilus and Criseyde* raise possibilities which the reader would not have originally considered, but which he gradually comes to believe by the very force of the narrator's denial. This "makes" the reader into "an involuntary critic of the action instead of a mere spectator."[28] In the Knight's Tale, readers dislike Emily because Chaucer has worked "very hard" to ensure she "has no character."[29] The reader's dislike, in other words, is an effect the text evokes, rather than a result of the reader's personality or individual taste. In the same way, the reader is shocked at May's vulgarity in the Merchant's Tale not because May is inherently shocking (although she may be) or because the reader is a prude (although he might be) but because of the *way* in which Chaucer introduces the vulgarity, injecting it into an otherwise innocuous passage. In other words, had the vulgarity been introduced into the story in another manner, the reader would not have been equally shocked.

Because the reader's response is evoked by the text, and because the text is perceived as a stable entity, individual readers should have more-or-less the same responses to the same text (hence Donaldson's ability to talk about a generalized entity, "the reader" rather than specific, differing, "readers"). This creates serious problems for Donaldson when he encounters intelligent readers or critics who disagree with what he believes to be the "right" reading of a text. Donaldson's ideal image of the reader glosses over the fact that actual readers come to a text with particular and individual histories, biases, moods, and attitudes, and thus he is uncomfortable with the possibility of different, but equally valid, readings.[30] Such a quandary forms the impetus behind Donaldson's article "The Effect of the Merchant's Tale." In it, he attempts to come to terms with the fact that critics such as B.H. Bronson consider the Merchant's Tale to be a lighthearted romp, while he himself finds it almost unbearably dark and bitter. He concludes that the difference in opinion arises because both he and Bronson write descriptive criticism, which

---

[28]   Donaldson, *Chaucer's Poetry*, 970; cf. 978.

[29]   Donaldson, "Masculine Narrator," 48.

[30]   Donaldson's attitude to diverging readings seems to have softened over the course of his career: in an article printed almost 20 years after some of the articles in *Speaking of Chaucer* were written, he admits, "no two readers will make precisely the same inference. Much will depend upon one's moral and intellectual predispositions. ... there can be no right answer." E. Talbot Donaldson, "Chaucer and the Elusion of Clarity," *Essays and Studies* 25 (1972) 27.

means that "while we both pretend to be describing the tale objectively, we are in fact describing our reactions to it." He proposes, therefore, to perform a close reading of the poem in order to justify his claim that the Merchant's Tale is "in truth a grim thing."[31] So, for example, he demonstrates that the juxtaposition of January's statement that he wants "old fissh and yong flessh" with the later description that January's bristles, when kissing May, were "lik to the skin of houndfissh," creates feelings of aversion and disgust in the reader.[32] Such close readings of individual words are often bolstered by analyses of other contexts for similar terms in Chaucer's poetry, or of the common usage for the words in Middle English. In this way Donaldson grounds his interpretation in the philology of Middle English, and shows that his "close reading" is not merely a subjective reaction. At times, however, Donaldson's evocation of the response "the reader" has to particular words or images experiences the same problems as it does for his more generalized descriptions of "the reader's" response: it does not take into account differences between different readers, or the sliding, slippery nature of signification itself. The problem with close reading is the same as the problem for more generalized "descriptive criticism": when the critic thinks he is being objective about individual words, he may in fact just be describing his own reaction to them. For example, when Donaldson describes the effect of the juxtaposition of the word "softly" with the word "privee," he writes, "*softly* also has, and cannot help having, another range of meanings that associate it with warm weather, warm May, tender, gentle, alluring womanhood, femininity at its most romantically attractive."[33] The reader here is implicitly coded as masculine, and the connotations of the word depend upon this coding. Likewise, Donaldson performs a close reading of the term "bely-naked," he launches into an account of the way boys in his own youth used the word when skinny-dipping, and would never have used it in front of their own mothers. From this Donaldson constructs a reading of the passage which depends upon the word "bely-naked" having a certain amount of vulgarity.[34] Donaldson goes on to convincingly support his reading with a philological discussion of the term "belly" in Anglo-Saxon and Middle English, and Chaucer's other clearly vulgar uses of the term in the Summoner's Tale and the Pardoner's Tale, but it is evident nonetheless that Donaldson himself has highly personal connotations and associations with the term, and noticed it in part because of these connotations. For a New Critic, the difference between an expert and an "ordinary reader" is not in their response, which is shared, but in their ability to explain and analyze that response. Donaldson responds emotionally to the term "belly," but then justifies and supports that response with philological evidence; however, another less scholarly reader, unable to provide the philological expertise, should nonetheless experience the same emotional reaction. On the basis of usually convincing, but often equally

---

[31] Donaldson, "Effect," 31.

[32] Ibid., 35–6.

[33] Ibid., 37.

[34] Ibid., 39.

E. Talbot Donaldson (1910–1987): The Careful Reader   69

personal, close readings such as the ones discussed above, Donaldson concludes that "it is a literary *fact* that [the Merchant's Tale] is an intensely bitter story."[35] Bronson's reading, in other words, is wrong.

How, therefore, does one account for such wrong readings? Donaldson answers, albeit implicitly, with a term which appears throughout his criticism: the "careful reader." This "careful reader" fills an audience function which disqualifies some readings of the text and justifies others. Since the text itself evokes responses in the reader, the "careful" reader will react with the right response. If a critic such as Bronson disagrees with Donaldson, the implicit suggestion is that he was not reading carefully enough. "Careful readers" are "those with attentive ears," those who perceive the delicately shaded connotations of the specific words the author has chosen and respond with the right emotion.[36] The "careful reader" is contrasted with "the reader reading quickly"—such a reader "will be wrong."[37] Readers who "read [a problematic] line fast enough" will perceive only "a very slight blur," but a slower, more careful reader will perceive all the subtleties and complexities of the poetry.[38] This "careful reader" is the same "sensitive" and "sensible" reader who knows but does not understand Criseyde. This same reader, according to Donaldson, feels an off-putting, "cool hardness" about May.

Donaldson himself is, of course, the "careful reader" *par excellence*, and frequently uses the first-person plural pronoun to describe this universalized reader's reactions.[39] So, for example, throughout the article "The Effect of the Merchant's Tale," he writes about the poem "affronting *our* aesthetic sense, bringing *our* emotions into play in such a way as to confuse *our* moral judgment," the fish passage is "made rank enough seriously to effect [*sic*] the quality, if not the quantity, of *our* laughter," "*we* have to surrender to laughter, but not without some of that sense of sadness *we* feel when what *we* have been emotionally involved with moves beyond the point where *we* can any longer care," and "*our* natural sympathy for May, evoked by her physical loveliness, and *our* natural disgust with January. ..."[40] In this use of the first person plural, he betrays a basic assumption

---

[35]   Ibid., 34, *emphasis mine*. Cf. Donaldson's statement in *The Swan at the Well*, 3, that Shakespeare, unlike many modern critics, understood *Troilus and Criseyde* "for what it is"—"what it is" being, of course, Donaldson's interpretation of *Troilus and Criseyde* as "a marvellous celebration of romantic love containing a sad recognition of its fragility, a work full of ironic contradictions and yet ringing true."

[36]   See David Lawton, "Donaldson and Irony," *Chaucer Review* 41.3 (2007) 233.

[37]   Donaldson, "Masculine Narrator," 52.

[38]   Donaldson, "Idiom," 25.

[39]   Carolynn Van Dyke writes that she has found "no pseudo-universal references to readers or critics in Donaldson's work"; however, I believe that Donaldson's ubiquitous use of the first-person plural pronoun, as well as his term "the reader" perform a universalizing gesture. Van Dyke, "Amorous Behavior," 256.

[40]   Donaldson, "Effect," 34–5, 36, and 42 respectively, *emphasis mine*. I am uncertain whether the word "effect" in the second passage is a typo: one would expect "affect," but

of his criticism: that his own response to a text can be generalized to include most readers. This assumption is likewise evident in the way Donaldson generalizes from his own individual responses to specific words or images, as I discussed above. To consider Donaldson's image of Chaucer's audience, therefore, and, more importantly, to assess the effect this image has on Donaldson's criticism, we face a problem we do not face with critics such as C.S. Lewis or D.W. Robertson: because Donaldson does not posit a medieval (or modern) audience clearly differentiated from himself, it is difficult to distinguish Donaldson's own response from the one he expects Chaucer's audience to have. Since Donaldson assumes any "careful reader" of Chaucer will come to a similar interpretation of the texts, and since Donaldson is himself a careful reader, it is unsurprising that Donaldson's "reader" seems remarkably like Donaldson himself.[41] In order to explore Donaldson's assumptions about audiences, therefore, we must tease out the representation of this "careful reader" implicit in his criticism.

So what are the characteristics Donaldson assumes for this typical reader of Chaucer? The first, evident in Donaldson's use of the techniques of close reading, is that the reader will be a "good" reader, alive to the shadings of meaning, connotation and implication that individual words can have. This necessitates, it would seem, a *reader*, rather than a listener, or at the very least a listener who listens like a reader—one who pays close attention to individual words, rather than absorbing sentences or phrases as single units of meaning. Donaldson knows that Chaucer's original audience may have listened to Chaucer reading aloud, rather than reading his words themselves; however, this knowledge does not affect his criticism. He does not posit one response from medieval listeners and a different response from modern readers. Instead, he collapses Chaucer's audience into the single unit of "the reader," and bases his criticism upon this composite being. For example, when discussing the description of the Friar as "a virtuous man," Donaldson writes, "our instinct—and that of Chaucer's first readers—is to take the phrase in its broadest sense."[42] For the most part, it seems, it can be assumed that medieval readers had more or less the same instincts as modern readers. When Donaldson does note the differences between modern and medieval audiences, he is concerned to maintain the validity of the modern response, refusing to sacrifice it to a more "authentic" medieval appreciation. For example, when deciding upon the spelling conventions of his edition of Chaucer, Donaldson explicitly chooses to retain medieval spellings, rather than modernizing the spellings completely, because "Historically we have become readers of rather than listeners to poetry,

---

Donaldson's emphasis on the way in which the text evokes the reader's response makes "effect" highly suggestive. For more examples of a pervasive first person plural, see Donaldson, "Elusion of Clarity," 41.

[41] Carolynn Van Dyke argues that this reader is in fact a persona of Donaldson's, not Donaldson himself; nevertheless she agrees that this persona "model[s] the reader's experience." Van Dyke, "Amorous Behavior," 255.

[42] Donaldson, "Elusion of Clarity," 27.

E. Talbot Donaldson (1910–1987): The Careful Reader   71

and the visual image has become part of our poetic experience."[43] The modern poetic experience of Chaucer includes an awareness of visual archaism which a medieval audience would not have had, yet Donaldson does not privilege the listening experience or the non-archaic experience of Chaucer as more authentic.

Reading in Time

Donaldson's reader partakes of a reading process that happens in time. Crucially, this time-situated image of the reader only pertains when the reading process is actually taking place—otherwise, the reader is universal and timeless, and does not change according to his historical situation, his age, or even his mood on any given day. Medieval and modern readers read Chaucer in more-or-less the same way and an individual reader's response to the poem does not change on a second or third reading because of intervening experiences or the fact of the poem having been read before. Nevertheless, despite this overarching ahistoricity in the representation of the reader, in the actual process of reading the reader is represented as being located in time.[44] In this, Donaldson differs from many New Critics, who approach a poem as a static object to be considered as a whole entity—their interpretation of the poem, in other words, takes place after the poem has been completely read. In Stanley Fish's words, "in formalist readings meaning is identified with what a reader understands at the *end* of a unit of sense (a line, a sentence, a paragraph, a poem) and that therefore any understandings preliminary to that one are to be disregarded as an unfortunate consequence of the fact that reading proceeds in time."[45] By contrast, Donaldson emphasizes the way in which the responses the poem evokes in the reader follow in succession, and the experience of the poem depends upon this succession of responses. So, for example, when Donaldson explains the effect of the Merchant's Tale, it is the changing effect of May which interests him: he writes, "Initially she seems a

---

[43] Donaldson, *Chaucer's Poetry*, iv. Donaldson standardized the spelling in his edition by choosing among the possibilities offered by the manuscripts the spelling which would be easiest for a modern reader to recognize.

[44] This formulation of the reading process as being a phenomenon dictated by time was clearly developed in the work of Stanley Fish, in Stanley Eugene Fish, *Surprised by Sin: The Reader in Paradise Lost* (Berkeley: University of California Press, 1967); see, for example, the statement on page 23: "the reading experience takes place in time, that is, we necessarily read one word after another." Fish was Donaldson's student: I will not speculate here whether Fish influenced Donaldson's thinking or *vice versa*. Nevertheless, a theory upon which Donaldson depends but never makes explicit (the time-oriented nature of the reading process) is fully elaborated and consciously theorized in Fish's work. See also Fish's more theoretical discussion of his approach in the article "Literature in the Reader: Affective Stylistics" in Stanley Fish, *Is There a Text in This Class? The Authority of Interpretive Communities* (Cambridge, Mass: Harvard University Press, 1980) 21–67.

[45] Fish, *Is There a Text?* 3.

sort of Galatea created in response to the fantasies of January. ..." then takes his analysis through the poem in progression, concluding, "But later, when May's female resourcefulness begins to work, some of the disgust we felt for January begins to spill over into our feeling for May ... [and] some of the sympathy we felt for May is displaced and spills over into our feeling for him."[46] In other words, the reader's response to May is not a unified effect or interpretation, but one which changes over the course of reading the poem. Likewise, in his analysis of Criseyde, Donaldson is particularly concerned with the effect on the reader of the fact that the reading takes place in time, both at the level of the overall structure of *Troilus and Criseyde*, and at the level of individual passages. The reader follows the narrator through the poem, from a position of enamoured liking for Criseyde to a slight "sense of distrust" to, finally, a full acknowledgement of her betrayal.[47] On a more detailed level, the order in which a reader encounters the components of a particular passage is important as well in creating its ultimate meaning and effect, as meanings first created are undercut, reversed or questioned as the passage moves on.[48] This image of the reader—as a being who encounters the unfolding of a text or narrative *in time*—has a major effect on Donaldson's criticism. Without it, he would have been unable to develop the crucial aspects of his analysis of *Troilus and Criseyde*: the narrator's changing relationship to Criseyde is paralleled in the reader's changing relationship to the narrator, as the reader becomes increasingly unable to accept the narrator's statements about Criseyde's character without distrust or scepticism. A crucial characteristic of Donaldson's image of the reader, therefore, is his temporal nature.

The Masculine Reader

Donaldson's reader betrays other characteristics. He seems indubitably masculine: the reader is put in a position of desire with relation to the feminine and the female characters in the text. He falls in love with Criseyde, he is sexually repulsed by May, and he finds the Prioress's femininity appealing. In his article "The Masculine Narrator and Four Women of Style," Donaldson comments that women are the hardest thing for a male author to deal with, and that "male narrators in literature so often fall in love with their heroines—to encourage the reader also to make an emotional investment from which he will expect, though not necessarily get,

---

[46]   Donaldson, "Effect," 36, 43.

[47]   Donaldson, "Criseide," 71; cf. "The Ending of *Troilus*" in Donaldson, *Speaking*.

[48]   See, to cite only a few examples, the reversed effect of the euphemism in the narrator's summary of his tale (Donaldson "Criseide," 69–70); the anticlimax of Criseyde getting off her horse (Donaldson, "Criseide," 75); and the anticlimax of Criseyde's age in her description (Donaldson, "Criseide," 77).

a return."[49] The "he" in this sentence is clearly not just a grammatically neutral generic pronoun: the reader is gendered masculine in order to fall in love with the female heroine.[50] This gendering of the reader is made explicit when Donaldson discusses Criseyde: "Criseide is as beautiful as an angel, and we romantic-minded men may expect that she will show a heroine's integrity."[51] Likewise, he describes the Prioress as "surely capable, like other attractive women, of making even bigger fools of us male critics"—this despite the fact that he just quoted a female critic in the previous paragraph.[52] In a later passage, Donaldson seems to admit there might be readers who are not masculine, by saying that "on most masculine readers ... the effect of this lovely meek woman whose look can be a challenge will be devastating," but he does not follow this through with a consideration of the effect of Criseyde on non-masculine readers, instead subsuming all readers under the ubiquitous first-person plural pronoun: "So charmed are *we* that *we* readily forget that *we* still know nothing about her."[53] The reader shares "*our* natural sympathy for May" because of her "physical loveliness," but then transfers to her the disgust he feels for January, because of her subsequent crudeness.[54] Donaldson describes the careful reader's reading of May almost in the vocabulary of a courtship: "the narrator's elaborate clumsiness must make a careful reader feel that there is something impenetrable about May's loveliness, a cool hardness that puts one off. ... The suspicion that May has a shrewd mind of her own, though it is confirmed only late in the poem, is intermittently aroused in the reader during the intervening action."[55]

---

[49] Donaldson, "Criseide," 47. For discussion of this passage and the implications for the gender of the reader, see Carolyn Dinshaw, *Chaucer's Sexual Poetics* (Madison: University of Wisconsin Press, 1989) 37. As Dinshaw also notes, in his professional life Donaldson does not seem to have demonstrated this male bias, but in fact championed the careers of many women and increased the percentage of woman graduate students in Yale's English Department from 10 percent to 50 percent during his time as Director of Graduate Studies. See Mary J. Carruthers, "Speaking of Donaldson," *Acts of Interpretation: The Text in Its Context: Essays in Honor of E. Talbot Donaldson,* ed. Mary J. Carruthers (Norman: Pilgrim Books, 1982) 368–9. Several of Donaldson's students have joined in the defence of Donaldson against the charge of anti-feminism: see Judith H. Anderson, "Commenting on Donaldson's Commentaries," *Chaucer Review* 41.3 (2007) 271; Elizabeth D. Kirk, "Donaldson Teaching and Learning," *Chaucer Review* 41.3 (2007) 286. Geoffrey Gust sees Donaldson as a "kind of feminist-sympathizer": Geoffrey Gust, *Constructing Chaucer: Author and Autofiction in the Critical Tradition* (New York: Palgrave Macmillan, 2009), 136.

[50] Likewise, I have consciously used male pronouns throughout this chapter to refer to Donaldson's reader, since he seems so clearly masculine.

[51] Donaldson, "Masculine Narrator," 54.

[52] Ibid., 63–4.

[53] Ibid., 57, *emphasis mine.*

[54] Ibid., 42, *emphasis mine.*

[55] Ibid., 52.

74 *Twentieth-Century Chaucer Criticism*

Donaldson's implicit image of Chaucer's audience—this clearly masculine reader who desires or is put off by the female characters of the poems—would be seriously challenged by later critics, who object that such a universalized reader subsumes individualized responses under one norm, a norm that does not include women, homosexuals, or various other readers. While other critics, such as C.S. Lewis, make assumptions similar to Donaldson's about the gender of the reader, these assumptions do not always have a significant impact upon their criticism. Donaldson's entire interpretation of *Troilus and Criseyde,* however, depends upon the reader falling in love with Criseyde alongside the narrator, and resisting the inevitable disillusionment over the course of the poem. Likewise, his feeling that the Merchant's Tale is a sordid story arises, at least in part, from his assumption that the reader will be attracted to May's youth and beauty, but will then be disgusted and shocked by her actions. Donaldson's universal reader, therefore, upon which his interpretation depends, is less universal than he may at first seem.

The Use of History

Despite the fact that Donaldson bases most of his criticism on the probable response that an ahistorical, universalized reader would have to Chaucer's works, he is not unaware of the differences between medieval times and now. He notes, for example, that a medieval reader might find the association of May with a "fairye" more disquieting than a modern reader would, and that a modern reader, more concerned about antiseptic cleanliness than a medieval person, would wince more at the joke about the Cook's suppurating sore. For the most part, however, he downplays or ignores the historical distance between medieval times and modern, preferring to put the focus of his attention and emphasis on the "text itself," and only using historical information to shore up, elaborate on, or explain interpretations which have arisen from the text. He likewise encourages that approach in his students. In his edition of Chaucer's poetry, he deliberately places all the critical apparatus except a brief introduction at the back of the book, so that the student encounters the poetry first, before he receives any interpretation or explanation of it.[56] The critical and historical apparatus is given solely as an "aid to experiencing, rather than a justification for reading, the poetry." Donaldson's aim is to "make history serve Chaucer's poetry rather than be served by it."[57]

As this phrase suggests, Donaldson is not averse to historical explanation when it aids the reader's comprehension of the poem; he simply does not believe that such explanations should take precedence over Chaucer's actual text. When Donaldson does turn to historical explanations it seems to happen when he finds a passage or fact inexplicable in other terms. At these times Donaldson invokes Chaucer's medieval audience, rather than the universal "reader," to clarify sections

---

[56] See Patterson's discussion of this edition in Patterson, *Negotiating*, 19–20.

[57] Donaldson, *Chaucer's Poetry*, iii–vi.

E. Talbot Donaldson (1910–1987): The Careful Reader 75

a modern reader would not understand or would dislike. So, for example, the Prioress's anti-semitism, to which a post-Holocaust reader would react extremely negatively, Donaldson explains with reference to common medieval attitudes to Jews. Likewise, Donaldson accounts for the seemingly inexplicable fact that what he considers to be a thoroughly boring story, the Melibee, was copied in multiple manuscripts by saying that in the Middle Ages "readers did not entirely distinguish between pleasure in literature and pleasure in being edified."[58] At times, Donaldson's turn to a historical explanation has the air of a person throwing up his hands: the apparent popularity of the tragedies the Monk tells (tragedies which Donaldson finds tedious), is blamed rather helplessly on the "pessimistic Middle Ages."[59] Unlike Lewis or Robertson, Donaldson rarely invokes the concept of "the medieval mind" to explain differences between modern readings and medieval readings of Chaucer. Only when elucidating the implications of a detail with which a modern person would be completely unfamiliar, such as the Pardoner's eunuchry, does Donaldson turn to that kind of explanation: "To the medieval mind, which liked to find in the visible world the patterns of the invisible, this lack of manliness would suggest the barrenness of the Pardoner's spirit."[60] Similarly, the allegorical and theological overtones that a pilgrimage would have in the Middle Ages are explained for the modern reader. Such explanations, however, are secondary to the text of the poem itself, given only when the story would be incomprehensible without them.

Donaldson's hesitation in using historical data as the primary means through which to interpret Chaucer's stories, however, does not extend to Middle English vocabulary. Because of the emphasis he and other New Critics place on the text itself, and because of his reliance upon the connotation, implication and subtle suggestion latent within individual words, he believes it is important to recover the original meanings of Middle English words. This is where English critics and scholars are important: they can provide such knowledge for the ordinary reader. In his criticism Donaldson relies heavily on reference works such as the Middle English Dictionary and Chaucer concordances. His own "careful reading" of Chaucer includes discovering what the connotations of individual words would have been for a medieval reader or listener through an analysis of other contexts in which the words were used. So, for example, Donaldson argues in his article "Idiom of Popular Poetry in the Miller's Tale" that interpretation of the Miller's Tale depends upon the reader knowing the diction of medieval romance. Donaldson claims in this article that the diction imported from romance would have had a comic effect in the Miller's Tale, as the audience would perceive the irony of romance diction being used in a farcical *fabliau* context. This irony depends upon the reader knowing the conventions of one literary genre or social milieu, and perceiving the gap in tone when those terms and conventions are

---

[58] Ibid., 937.

[59] Ibid., 939.

[60] Ibid., 928.

applied in another genre or milieu. In other words, Donaldson's reading requires a distance between the character and the reader: the reader has a superior knowledge which the character does not have. In this case, for example, the reader knows the usual context—courtly love romance—of certain words, and is aware that the present context—*fabliau*—is unsuitable for such romantic terms. The characters, on the other hand (who probably think they are in a romance) are unaware of the disjunction of words and context. What is perfectly serious for a character such as Absolon, who thinks he is the epitome of a courtly lover and who acts accordingly, is ridiculous for the reader, who knows Absolon is a *fabliau* dupe.

New Critical Irony

The existence of this ironic distance between reader and characters is a key aspect of Donaldson's criticism. Unlike the scholars of the first part of the twentieth century, who acknowledge occasional dramatic or situational ironies but for the most part think Chaucer should be taken "straight," Donaldson posits a much more pervasive irony in Chaucer's works.[61] This requires a particular concept of an audience for Chaucer's works. It implies an audience which constantly anticipates double meanings and veiled innuendo, and which does not identify closely with the characters but is situated at some distance from them. Such a distance would seem to contradict Donaldson's emphasis, discussed earlier, on the emotional impact stories have on the reader: on the identification of the reader with the sufferings of Troilus, for example. This apparent contradiction is resolved by the fact that not every character, or every situation, is ironic. In *Troilus and Criseyde*, the ironic distance exists between the narrator and the reader, not the characters within the drama. The reader, in other words, is aware of subtleties, complications and contradictions of which the narrator is unaware.

This idea of the distance between narrator and reader is perhaps Donaldson's most important contribution to Chaucer criticism.[62] In the article "Criseide and Her

---

[61] Lawton, "Donaldson and Irony," 235; Harold Bloom, ed., "Introduction," *Bloom's Modern Critical Views: Geoffrey Chaucer* (New York: Infobase Publishing, 2007) 11.

[62] Ethan Knapp, "Chaucer Criticism and its Legacies," *The Yale Companion to Chaucer*, Seth Lerer, ed., (New Haven: Yale University Press, 2006) 343; Thomas J. Farrell, "The Persistence of Donaldson's Memory," *Chaucer Review* 41.3 (2007) 293. For criticism of this theory, see Derek Brewer, "The Reconstruction of Chaucer," *Studies in the Age of Chaucer: Proceedings 1* (1985) 3–19; Geoffrey Gust, "Revaluating 'Chaucer the Pilgrim' and Donaldson's Enduring Persona," *Chaucer Review* 41.3 (2007) 311–23; Gust, *Constructing Chaucer*, 30–31. See also Derek Brewer, "The History of a Shady Character: The Narrator of *Troilus and Criseyde*," *Modes of Narrative: Approaches to American, Canadian and British Fiction*, eds. Reingard M. Nischik and Barbara Korte (Würzburg: Königshausen and Neumann, 1990) 166–78.

Narrator," Donaldson argues that Criseyde is presented to the reader entirely from the point of view of the narrator, and his reactions condition our responses. The distance between the narrator and Chaucer himself is clear: the narrator, Donaldson argues, is in love with his heroine, but Chaucer is not. Over the course of *Troilus and Criseyde*, the distance between the narrator and the audience, by contrast, gradually grows. Chaucer allows cracks to slip into the narrator's presentation of Criseyde, and we as readers gradually move from sharing the narrator's opinion of Criseyde to coming to doubt it. In other words, over the course of the poem the audience changes position, from one very close to the narrator to one distant from the narrator. Donaldson writes,

> Chaucer interferes with the work of his narrator. ... At some of the moments when his narrator is striving most laboriously to palliate Criseide's behaviour, Chaucer, standing behind him, jogs his elbow, causing him to fall into verbal imprecision, or into anticlimax, or making his rhetoric deficient, or making it redundant—generally doing these things in such a way that the reader will be encouraged almost insensibly to see Criseide in a light quite different from the one that the narrator is so earnestly trying to place her in.[63]

The distance between reader and narrator in *Troilus and Criseyde* can be called ironic: statements the narrator makes about Criseyde come to suggest their opposite to the reader. Thus the more the narrator tries to convince us that Criseyde loved, and still loves, Troilus, the more we suspect she is acting primarily in the interests of practical necessity. Donaldson examines this process in some detail. He quotes the lines, "And thus to him she said as ye mowe here. / As she that hadde hir herte on Troilus / So faste that ther may it noon arace; / And straungely she spak, and saide thus," and then remarks,

> Regardless of what the narrator intended, his imprecision here is fatal. The simile which is not a simile finally realizes the full potential it has, I think, always had of suggesting the opposite of what it purports to be saying—of turning its own sense inside out. Criseide spoke *like* a woman who loved Troilus, but she was most imperfectly like a woman who loved him, as her speech shows.[64]

Because of the growing distance between the narrator and the reader, even a seemingly straightforward remark of the narrator's "starts to contain a complex of possible meanings, endlessly dynamic and interactive, amplifying, qualifying, even denying the simple statement."[65] By the end of *Troilus and Criseyde*, Chaucer's

---

[63] Donaldson, "Criseide," 68.

[64] Ibid., 78, *emphasis in original*.

[65] Donaldson, "Ending of *Troilus*," 86.

78   *Twentieth-Century Chaucer Criticism*

manipulation of "a narrator capable of only a simple view of reality" has created for the reader a much more complex view both of reality and of Criseyde.[66]

Donaldson's concept of audience, which situates Chaucer's reader at some distance from Chaucer's narrator, enabling irony to pervade the reading experience, is similar for the rest of Chaucer's writing. However, nowhere is it so important as for the *Canterbury Tales*. Donaldson's article "Chaucer the Pilgrim" was groundbreaking in this sense: other critics had suggested a distance between Chaucer and the narrator of the *Canterbury Tales*, but no one had fully explored the ironic implications of that distance. In this article, Donaldson argues that the pilgrim Chaucer is an entirely distinct entity from the author Chaucer who created him, and that readers of Chaucer need to remain aware of this distance because it creates the irony so important to the poem. Readers of the *Canterbury Tales*, in other words, share an ethical and moral position with Chaucer the Author rather than Chaucer the Pilgrim, and both the humour of the poem and its ethical force arise out of the distance between the two positions. In the General Prologue, for example, the narrator's "undiscriminating attitude" on a literal level seems to show appreciation for his fellow pilgrims, but ironically condemns them all, as the reader perceives the gap between the way they are and the way they should be.[67] So, whereas Kittredge takes the General Prologue narrator's admiration for the Prioress as straightforward, assuming the narrator's opinions to be similar to Chaucer's, Donaldson considers the portrait of the Prioress highly ironic. The narrator finds the Prioress charming, but his over-the-top superlatives highlight for the reader the discrepancy between the actual characteristics of the Prioress (fine manners, liking for small creatures, physical beauty) and the ideal traits of a nun (devotion to God, charity for all humanity, contempt for the things of this world). The reader is superior to the narrator, both in terms of acuteness of perception and in terms of moral values, and this results in a double satire: on nuns who act like the Prioress, but also on the foolish narrator himself, and therefore on people who admire the same kinds of things he does.

The same mechanism is at work in most of the other portraits of the General Prologue. These portraits, Donaldson claims, can be read "upside down."[68] The narrator is quite overawed by the Monk's virility, without perceiving the contradiction—which the reader perceives—between such virility and a monk's religious calling. The same gap is present in the description of the Friar: the narrator evinces a wholehearted approval for the values and lifestyle of the Friar, while the reader remains aware of the difference between such values and the ideal promoted by St. Francis. Donaldson, in all these cases, attributes the irony to Chaucer, and takes the narrator's words at face value: he does not consider that it might be the narrator, rather than Chaucer, who is being sarcastic, satirical, or

---

[66]   Ibid., 99.

[67]   Donaldson, *Chaucer's Poetry*, 880.

[68]   Ibid., 880.

E. Talbot Donaldson (1910–1987): The Careful Reader   79

ironic.[69] Chaucer is always the one with his tongue in his cheek, in other words; the narrator never is. So Donaldson believes the narrator is sincere when the latter expresses admiration for the Summoner's "moderation in extortion, his fellow-feeling for his victims"; the Shipman, too, is described by the narrator as a "good fellow," and Donaldson sees no reason to doubt that the narrator actually considers him as such.[70] Unlike Kittredge and Lewis, who would consider such descriptions to be momentary "tongue-in-cheek" humour, and would not worry about whether such irony should be ascribed to Chaucer or to the narrator, Donaldson envisions an irony much more pervasive, dependent upon the extreme naiveté of the narrator as a literary pose Chaucer adopts. The narrator is almost invariably presented as "intellectually simple," and, unlike the reader, he is usually "acutely unaware of the significance of what he sees, no matter how sharply he sees it."[71] This obliviousness, paradoxically, makes the ironic significance of particular details even more apparent to the reader.

In the rest of the *Canterbury Tales*, a similar distance exists between Chaucer and the various narrators of the tales. Chaucer's irony "becomes operative in the no man's land that exists between the poet Chaucer ... and the assigned teller of the tale."[72] Although Donaldson does not explicitly say so, an identical "no man's land" must exist between the narrator and the reader, or the reader would no more be able to perceive Chaucer's irony than the narrator can. If the reader shared the same moral, ethical or perceptive position as the narrator, he would not perceive the works as ironic: since the narrator is sincere, the reader, sharing the narrator's values and perceptions, would interpret the narrative as equally sincere. Only when the reader occupies a different "position" from the narrator—when there is a gap between the reader and the narrator in terms of knowledge, perception or moral stance—is it possible for irony to exist. For example, Donaldson's reader would not consider the Knight's Tale ironic, because he is assumed to accept some of the Knight's values of chivalry, love, honour and so on. The reader emphatically does not share what Donaldson calls the Merchant's bitterness or thorough-going misogyny, however, and therefore the Merchant's Tale is structurally ironic. The reader, according to Donaldson, takes from the Merchant's Tale a message about the "kind of world that can come into being if a man's approach to love and marriage is wholly mercantile and selfish"—a message that the mercantile and selfish Merchant himself does not perceive.[73] Likewise, Donaldson attributes the expansive, dilatory use of rhetoric in the Nun's Priest's Tale to the Nun's Priest, who attempts to make sense of the world through (usually inappropriate)

---

[69] For this argument, that it is the narrator who is the "subject" and therefore he is the only one responsible for the irony, see H. Marshall Leicester, *The Disenchanted Self* (Berkeley: University of California Press, 1990) 387–90.

[70] Donaldson, "Chaucer the Pilgrim," 6; cf. Donaldson, *Chaucer's Poetry*, 879, 898.

[71] Donaldson, "Chaucer the Pilgrim," 8, 3.

[72] Donaldson, "Idiom," 28–9.

[73] Donaldson, "Effect," 45.

rhetoric. It is Chaucer, not the Nun's Priest, who is in control—the Nun's Priest is not making fun of rhetoric through his own use of it, but is seriously, naïvely, and in good faith trying to make a proper use of rhetoric, and it is Chaucer who is mocking the excessive use of rhetoric through his failure to do so. Again, we can see that the irony depends on the distance between the narrator of the tale and the audience. This is not "tongue-in-cheek" irony, where the Nun's Priest deliberately says something he doesn't mean, but a thorough-going irony where the reader must be constantly alive to the fact that Chaucer might be making fun of his own characters. This kind of irony—a pervasive, structural irony which can make a tale mean the opposite of what it says on a literal level—will be developed even more fully in D.W. Robertson's criticism. Such a structure of irony is important to this discussion because it is Donaldson's and Robertson's positioning of the audience which allows their critical insight into and interpretation of the *Canterbury Tales*: without the gap between narrator and reader, ironic readings such as Donaldson's or Robertson's would not be possible.

Donaldson, then, shares with Robertson—and against Kittredge and Lewis—an understanding of the *Canterbury Tales* as pervasively ironic, as having a distance between narrator and author, and between narrator and reader, which allows for a thorough-going irony in which every word a narrator says is potentially suspect. Like Robertson as well, Donaldson believes this irony is not just used for humourous purposes but is profoundly moral, although he would disagree with Robertson about the nature of Chaucer's morality. In the *Canterbury Tales*, the vision of the social world, which the narrator sees, is imposed on the vision of the moral world, which the reader and the author perceive. In other words, the narrator perceives the world solely how it is; the reader, knowing how the world *should* be, perceives the gap between how the world is (described by the narrator) and how it should be. This gap is ironic. Such gaps, according to Donaldson, creates a kind of "moral realism," in which traditional stock satirical characters, drawn from traditional moralistic texts, are placed in a genre of literary realism, and described, "with all their traditional faults upon them, by another pilgrim who records faithfully each fault without, for the most part, recognizing that it is a fault and frequently felicitating its possessor for possessing it."[74] The reader then sees the characters with a "double vision," which is Chaucer's "ironical essence," knowing how they *should* be but perceiving them realistically through a narrator who goes on "affirming affectionately" how they *are*.[75] In this way the reader receives the moral, satirical message of the General Prologue portraits without compromising his affection for the flawed humanity of Chaucer's characters. Interestingly, and perhaps because of this over-arching moral view, Donaldson, having emphasized the pervasive irony throughout the *Canterbury Tales*, drops this reading at the Parson's Tale. Like Robertson, he takes the Parson's Tale and Chaucer's Retraction "straight." The Retraction is read as auto-biographical: "The

---

[74]   Donaldson, "Chaucer the Pilgrim," 9.

[75]   Ibid., 11.

retraction must be taken as heartfelt. The poet was about to die and he feared for his soul."[76] The elaborate narratological structure he had proposed, with a clear gulf between Chaucer and his narrator, and between the reader and the narrator, disappears, and Donaldson assumes that by the end of the *Canterbury Tales* the narrator and the poet are one, and that the reader will treat them as such.

The Listening Audience

Donaldson, in his discussion of response to Chaucer, collapses the distance between the medieval listener of Chaucer and the modern reader, conflating them, more-or-less, into one entity called "the reader." This requires the assumption that a medieval listening audience would have been able to perceive the subtleties and connotations of individual words and phrases which a modern reader can apprehend through close reading. However, Donaldson does not always ignore the fact that a medieval audience would often have listened to Chaucer's poetry rather than reading it. Donaldson uses the historical facts about the situation of Chaucer's actual audience to support his argument about the ironic distance between the author Chaucer and the pilgrim Chaucer, and infers that a medieval audience would have come to the same conclusions that a modern audience, used to the trope of the "fallible narrator," would come to.

In his discussion of Chaucer's irony, Donaldson focuses on the aural nature of Chaucer's original audience. Chaucer, as a medieval poet, would not have only been the composer, but also the performer, of his poetry. Donaldson concludes that the medieval audience would have had a heightened awareness of Chaucer as an individual, as a person, which we as readers do not have. Donaldson argues that because of this, medieval audiences would have been *more*, not less aware of the distance between the poet Chaucer and the narrator Chaucer. This seems a bit counter-intuitive: since the poet and the narrator occupy the same body and share the same name, and since the poet speaks in the first person, one might conclude that a medieval audience would be *more* likely to confuse the two. But Donaldson argues that the discrepancy between the astute, perceptive poet, whom the audience knew personally, and the naive, bumbling narrator, would have been acute enough that the audience would have had no problem perceiving it. It is clear, for example, that the poet Chaucer can write very good poetry—he has written the whole of the *Canterbury Tales*—yet he gives his own character the worst narrative of the story collection, the Tale of Sir Thopas. The audience, fully aware of Chaucer's skill and talent, would have had no trouble perceiving Sir Thopas as parody, and to an audience with the real poet in front of them, Sir Thopas "seems a joke on a far larger scale."[77] For an audience who knows the real Chaucer, both the irony and the humour are heightened: Donaldson writes, "one can imagine the delight

---

[76] Donaldson, *Chaucer's Poetry*, 949.

[77] Ibid., 936.

of the audience which heard the [General] Prologue read in this way, and which was aware of the similarities and dissimilarities between Chaucer, the man before them, and Chaucer the pilgrim, both of whom they could see with simultaneous vision."[78] Chaucer obviously exploits his physical presence—his plumpness, his odd appearance—in order to increase the humourous qualities of his narrator, but there is a deeper humour as well, as Chaucer attributes to "himself" traits—such as naiveté or superlative exuberance—the audience would know were false. For Chaucer's original audience, "the constant interplay of these two Chaucers must have produced an exquisite and most ingratiating humour."[79] Chaucer's medieval audience, then, has advantages which are different from a modern audience's advantages: where the modern one must depend on close reading to perceive the ironic distance between Chaucer the Pilgrim and Chaucer the Narrator, the medieval audience would have readily noted the disparity between the two, and would have had cues of facial expression, vocal tone, and mannerisms to aid in their grasp of the irony. The end result, however, is the same: both sets of audiences are situated at an ironic distance from the narrator, and thus Donaldson feels no compunction about conflating the responses of the two. In each case, the positioning of the audience functions as a structural element which enables an interpretation of Chaucer heavily dependent upon irony.

Donaldson's image of Chaucer's audience, then, is of a man much like himself, a "careful reader," who would be more-or-less the same whether he were medieval or modern. This concept of audience acts as an "audience function" which allows for the key elements in Donaldson's interpretations of Chaucer's works. Based on his image of Chaucer's audience, Donaldson concludes that Chaucer's poetry does not require extensive learning or a thoroughgoing understanding of patristic symbolism to be read; that Chaucer's works are pervasively, profoundly, ironic; that this irony is used to moral purpose; that Chaucer's narrator is clearly distinct from the poet. The exegetical critics, Donaldson's contemporaries, come to some of the same conclusions about Chaucer's poetry: that it is profoundly ironic, for example, and that the irony is highly moral in its purpose. For both Donaldson and D.W. Robertson, the "audience function" works in a similar way. Both posit an audience situated at some distance from the narrator or the characters in a story: the audience knows things or holds attitudes which the characters do not, and this gap between the audience's knowledge and the characters' creates irony and humour. The audience can perceive double meanings—meanings which often are the exact opposite of the text's literal meanings—that the characters within the story miss. In this dynamic, the audience is envisioned as slightly suspicious and wary. It never takes a statement at face value, but always remains alive and watchful for double meanings or semantic inversion. For both New Critics and exegetical critics, the audience has a sense of humour: it perceives the disparity between the surface meaning of the text, and the underlying meaning that Chaucer is conveying through

---

[78] Donaldson, "Chaucer the Pilgrim," 10.

[79] Ibid., 11.

irony, and it finds this disparity funny. Robertson comes to these conclusions from assumptions radically different from those of Donaldson: instead of conflating the historical distance between Chaucer's medieval and modern readers, and positing an "ideal" reader who is conditioned to read in certain ways by the text, Robertson emphasizes the distance between medieval and modern audiences, and insists that to read Chaucer properly, modern audiences need to learn to read like medieval audiences. This historicizing of Chaucer's audience, and this insistence upon the extreme gap between the present and the past, has an effect on Robertson's criticism as profound as the New Critical "ideal reader" uniformity of audience has upon Donaldson's.

Chapter 4
D.W. Robertson (1914–1992):
The Allegorical Reader

D.W. Robertson was one of the most important and most controversial Chaucer scholars of the twentieth century. He is the only medievalist to have had a "school" of criticism named after him: "Robertsonianism" has become synonymous with the theory of patristic exegetical criticism which he introduced to the mainstream of Medieval Studies, and insisted be applied rigorously to all medieval literature.[1]

---

[1] See David Lyle Jeffrey, ed., *Chaucer and Scriptural Tradition* (Ottawa: University of Ottawa Press, 1984) xv; Pamela Gradon, "Review of *Essays in Medieval Culture*," *The Review of English Studies* 34.133 (February 1983) 52. Many scholars have adopted or used Robertson's method; see, to name only a few, numerous articles by R.E. Kaske, including R.E. Kaske, "Patristic Exegesis: The Defense," *Critical Approaches to Medieval Literature*, ed. Dorothy Bethurum (New York: Columbia University Press, 1960) 27–60; numerous articles by John Fleming, as well as books such as *Reason and the Lover* (Princeton: Princeton University Press, 1984); articles and books by Judson Boyce Allen, including Judson Boyce Allen and Theresa Anne Moritz, *A Distinction of Stories: The Medieval Unity of Chaucer's Fair Chain of Narratives for Canterbury* (Columbus: Ohio State University Press, 1981) and Judson Boyce Allen, *The Ethical Poetic of the Middle Ages* (Toronto: University of Toronto Press, 1982); see also B. Koonce, *Chaucer and the Tradition of Fame: Symbolism in the* House of Fame (Princeton: Princeton University Press, 1966); Leigh DeNeef, "Robertson and the Critics," *Chaucer Review* 2 (1968) 205–34. Critique of "Robertsonianism" and exegetical criticism is extensive, but see D.S. Brewer, "Review of *Fruyt and Chaf*," *The Review of English Studies* 16.63 (August 1965) 305; "Patristic Exegesis in the Criticism of Medieval Literature: The Opposition" and "Medieval Poetry and Medieval Sin" in E. Talbot Donaldson, *Speaking of Chaucer* (London: Athlone Press, 1970); E. Talbot Donaldson, "Designing a Camel: Or, Generalizing the Middle Ages," *Tennessee Studies in Literature* 22 (1977) 1–16; Rodney Delasanta, "Chaucer and the Exegetes," *Studies in the Literary Imagination* 4.2 (1971) 1–10; Francis Lee Utley, "Chaucer and Patristic Exegesis," *Chaucer's Mind and Art*, ed. A.C. Cawley (Edinburgh: Oliver and Boyd, 1969) 69–85; Glending Olson, *Literature as Recreation in the Later Middle Ages* (Ithaca: Cornell University Press, 1982); William Rogers, "The Raven and the Writing Desk: The Theoretical Limits of Patristic Criticism," *Chaucer Review* 14.3 (Winter 1980) 260–77; William Calin, "Defense and Illustration of Fin'amor: Some Polemical Comments on the Robertsonian Approach," *The Expansion and Transformations of Courtly Literature*, ed. Nathaniel B. Smith and Joseph T. Snow (Athens: University of Georgia Press, 1980) 32–48. See also Halverson's parody of exegetical criticism, as applied to Tom Sawyer: John Halverson, "Patristic Exegesis: A Medieval Tom Sawyer," *College English* 27.1 (October 1965) 50–55.

86   *Twentieth-Century Chaucer Criticism*

Robertson's approach moved Medieval Studies away from the folkloric approach that still bore traces of the romanticized Victorian view of the Middle Ages, and it offered a historicist alternative to New Critical ahistoricity.[2] As opposed to both the folkloric approach of anthropology and the dangerously subjective "close reading" approach of the New Critics, exegetical criticism opened up a methodology that aimed to achieve in literary criticism the standards of proof used in the sciences: externally verifiable evidence, objective analysis, and clear criteria for determining "right" and "wrong" answers. More than any school of criticism, Robertson and his followers rigorously applied the "audience function" in determining which interpretations of Chaucer's works were permissible. Robertson's image of Chaucer's audience was explicit and detailed. In fact, works such as *A Preface to Chaucer* are primarily devoted to outlining and exploring the composition and assumptions of that audience. Robertson had very definite ideas about how a medieval audience would have read literature in general and Chaucer in particular, and those ideas uncompromisingly demarcated the readings which he deemed acceptable for Chaucer's works.

Robertson's career spanned over forty years, and hence his writings are extensive.[3] Essays such as "Historical Criticism" and "Some Observations on Method in Literary Studies," as well as the introduction to *Fruyt and Chaf* (co-written with Bernard Huppé), lay out the theoretical grounds of his approach. This theory was then fully developed in his major work, *A Preface to Chaucer: Studies in Medieval Perspectives*.[4] Other articles either put his theory of exegetical criticism into practice ("The Doctrine of Charity in Mediaeval Literary Gardens" and "The Physician's Comic Tale") or establish the historical facts of medieval culture and society upon which his theory depends ("Frequency of Preaching in Thirteenth-Century England," "'And For My Land Thus Hastow Mordred Me?' Land Tenure, the Cloth Industry, and the Wife of Bath," and the full-length work *Chaucer's London*).[5] Rather surprisingly for someone who had such a long career,

---

[2]   Ethan Knapp, "Chaucer Criticism and Its Legacies," *Yale Companion to Literature*, Seth Lerer, ed. (New Haven: Yale University Press, 2006) 344–5.

[3]   For a brief critical biography, which bizarrely does not mention exegetical criticism, see Rosalyn Rossignol, "Robertson, D(urant) W(aite), Jr.," *Chaucer: A Literary Reference to His Life and Work* (New York: Infobase Publishing, 2007) 552.

[4]   "Historical Criticism" in D.W. Robertson, Jr., *Essays in Medieval Culture* (Princeton: Princeton University Press, 1980) 3–20; D.W. Robertson, Jr., "Some Observations on Method in Literary Studies," *New Literary History* 1.1 (October 1969) 21–33; Bernard F. Huppé and D.W. Robertson, Jr., *Fruyt and Chaf: Studies in Chaucer's Allegories* (Princeton: Princeton University Press, 1963) 3–31; D.W. Robertson, Jr., *A Preface to Chaucer: Studies in Medieval Perspectives* (Princeton: Princeton University Press, 1962). The preface to *Fruyt and Chaf* states explicitly that both authors "endorse heartily" everything in the book, therefore I will not attempt to distinguish, in this chapter, between Huppé's views and Robertson's: Huppé and Robertson, *Fruyt*, vii.

[5]   D.W. Robertson, Jr., "The Doctrine of Charity in Mediaeval Literary Gardens: A Topical Approach Through Symbolism and Allegory," *Speculum* 26.1 (January 1951) 24–49;

especially one so riddled with controversy, Robertson seems to have changed his views remarkably little over the course of time. Later articles such as "And for My Land," "Chaucer and the Commune Profit—the Manor" and "Who Were the People?" seem slightly more subdued than his earlier writings, aimed more at establishing legal and social history rather than advancing specifically exegetical criticism. Other late articles, however, such as "The Probable Date and Purpose of Chaucer's Troilus" and "The Physician's Comic Tale," depend upon a critical approach little changed from the one Robertson championed in the 1950s and 1960s.[6] Robertson's writings, then, form a complete "oeuvre," with each individual piece working to advance and support the overarching project.

D.W. Robertson studied at the University of North Carolina under H.K. Russell and George Coffman, first doing a master's thesis on the Aristotelian definition of "catharsis" and tragedy, then, under George Coffman alone, a doctoral thesis on Robert Mannyng's *Handlyng Synne*. Robertson writes that his master's thesis established for him the importance of historical context when studying literature, since Aristotle's theories were interpreted very differently in different times and cultures.[7] Likewise, one can surmise that a doctoral thesis on a collection of sermon exempla was foundational in his development of an argument which maintains that all medieval literature, in essence, should be read as exemplary and moral. His two graduate theses, therefore, may have formed the basis for a theory of literature which emphasized the need to read works as they were read by their original audience, and which maintained that, for the medieval period, this method of reading was exemplary and didactic. Hired by Princeton in 1946, where he was to spend the rest of his career, and where most of his books were to be published, Robertson shared an office with Bernard F. Huppé, and the two scholars worked out the basics of the theory of exegetical criticism together, which they published in *Piers Plowman and Scriptural Tradition* and the later *Fruyt and Chaf*. Robertson was heavily influenced by the art historian Erwin Panofsky, who was also at Princeton.[8] Panofsky believed that art should be studied according to the framework through which it would have originally been perceived. He developed a series of iconographical interpretations of art, outlining the symbols and figures in medieval art which signaled various theological concepts, and

---

D.W. Robertson, Jr., "The Physician's Comic Tale," *Chaucer Review* 23.2 (1988) 129–39; D.W. Robertson, Jr., "Frequency of Preaching in Thirteenth-Century England," *Speculum* 24.3 (July 1949) 376–88; D.W. Robertson, Jr., "'And For My Land Thus Hastow Mordred Me?' Land Tenure, the Cloth Industry, and the Wife of Bath," *Chaucer Review* 14 (1980) 403–20; D.W. Robertson, Jr., *Chaucer's London* (New York: John Wiley and Sons, 1968).

[6]   Robertson, "'And For My Land Thus'"; "Chaucer and the Commune Profit—the Manor" in Robertson, *Essays*; "Who Were The People" in Robertson, *Essays*; D.W. Robertson, Jr., "The Probable Date and Purpose of Chaucer's *Troilus*," *Medievalia et Humanistica* 13 (1985) 143–71; Robertson, "Physician."

[7]   Robertson, *Essays*, xiii.

[8]   Norman Cantor, *Inventing the Middle Ages* (New York: William Morris, 1991) 201–2.

which an educated medieval person would have been able to "read" at a glance. Because of Panofsky, Robertson became interested in art history and the role of iconography; he adopted many of Panofsky's theories of iconography into his own theory of allegory and imagery in medieval literature.[9] Both scholars believed that the artistic output of a whole period should be studied in order to understand individual works or genres: thus literature can inform art history, and art and sculpture can inform literary study. However, Robertson did not adopt Panofsky's distinction between iconography (defined as the symbols and motifs of particular images) and iconology (defined as the underlying, psychological, wide-ranging principles which lie beneath a particular work of art and particular instances of iconography, and which reveal the basic attitude or mindset of a culture or time period), thus simplifying and perhaps distorting Panofsky's theory. Bernard Huppé, Robertson's early partner in developing Panofsky's theories for literature, later left Princeton, and thus Robertson became the sole champion of the theory of exegetical literary criticism, and bestowed his name upon the theoretical school which grew out of their approach.[10]

Robertson writes that early in his career, he discovered he was unable to publish on Old English literature—according to him, the field was so dominated by "folklorists" and scholars interested in Germanic pagan influences, that any suggestion of Christian influence upon Old English literature was resisted strenuously.[11] He fought for several years against the "pagan influence" theory of medieval literature, claiming that the symbols, images and motifs which earlier scholars ascribed to "paganism" could be explained by the framework of Christian iconography.[12] At the same time, Robertson was challenging the previous generation of scholars, such as C.S. Lewis, over the theory of courtly love. Like so-called pagan symbolism, Robertson believed that the concept of "courtly love" depended upon attitudes and beliefs which would have been fundamentally anathema to the Christian Middle Ages. In the final section of *Preface*, as well as the article "The Concept of Courtly Love as an Impediment to the Understanding of Medieval

---

[9] "The Allegorist and the Aesthetician" in Robertson, *Essays*, 85; cf. Robertson, "Some Observations," 32. Robertson cites Panofsky several times in *Preface*—in a work notoriously short on footnotes, these citations carry greater weight than one might assume at first glance. Panofsky's most influential works for Robertson seem to have been *Early Netherlandish Painting* (Cambridge, Mass.: Harvard University Press, 1953) and *Gothic Architecture and Scholasticism* (New York: Meridian, 1957), although the work *Studies in Iconology*, published in 1939, established the basics of Panofsky's approach: Erwin Panofsky, *Studies in Iconology* (Oxford: Oxford University Press, 1939).

[10] For biographical details, see Chauncey Wood, "In Memoriam: D.W. Robertson Jr., 1914–1992," *Chaucer Review* 28.1 (1993) 1–4.

[11] Robertson, *Essays*, xiii.

[12] See, for example, the discussion of *Beowulf* in Robertson, "Doctrine of Charity," as well as articles such as D.W. Robertson, Jr., "Why the Devil Wears Green," *Modern Language Notes* 69.7 (1954) 470–72.

Texts," Robertson outlines his argument most fully: courtly love, as defined by modern scholars, would not have been acceptable in a society as fully Christian as medieval Europe, since it required the idolizing of someone (the beloved) other than God. Writers who seem to be portraying earthly love are actually giving a warning against cupidity. Indeed, he argues, the term "courtly love" was not even used in the Middle Ages—Chaucer never would have heard of either the term or the concept.[13]

These controversies with anthropologists and courtly love enthusiasts were eclipsed by a far greater one: the conflict between the Robertsonian school of exegetical criticism, and the New Critical school which at the time held sway in most university English departments. Robertson calls New Critics "Croceans," after Benedetto Croce, whose theory of aesthetics Robertson claims most New Critics follow, in which art is valued for its ability to express intense emotion and its rejection of any use-value or practical purpose. In the quasi-allegorical article "The Allegorist and the Aesthetician," Robertson outlines his opposition to the Aesthetic/Crocean theorists: calling in a figure dubbed the "Stylistic Historian," he concludes that styles (or values) of literature and art have changed over time, and that so-called "Aestheticians" should limit themselves to post-eighteenth-century writings, while the "Allegorists" (such as Robertson himself) should study Classical, Medieval and Renaissance art and literature.[14] The intensity of the controversy between Robertson and the New Critics is evident in the passage Robertson writes giving the reasons for the need of an article defending his theory: he says, "At the outset, I had no intention of offending anyone ... However, the reactions of both the Aesthetician and the Conventional Scholar to what I have said have been so violent, and at times ... wrathful ... that I feel that some answer to their attacks is appropriate."[15]

Robertson's main opponent in this debate was, of course, E. Talbot Donaldson, although, unlike Donaldson himself, Robertson (to my knowledge) never mentions his opponent by name. As discussed in the previous chapter, one of the main areas of disagreement between Robertson and Donaldson was over the difference between a modern audience and a medieval one. Donaldson believes that any careful modern reader of Chaucer's works will come to more-or-less the same interpretation as a medieval reader. Robertson, by contrast, maintains that there is a major distance between medieval and modern audiences in outlook, beliefs and values, and that a scholar must carefully recreate the medieval worldview in order to read Chaucer's works "properly." Robertson disagrees with Donaldson's theory about the ironic gap between narrator and author. With reference to the *Canterbury Tales*, for example, he argues that in the link between the Tale of Sir Thopas and the Tale of Melibee, Chaucer "is speaking in his own

---

[13]   Robertson, *Preface*, 110, 391–503; "The Concept of Courtly Love as an Impediment to the Understanding of Medieval Texts" in Robertson, *Essays*, 257–72.

[14]   Robertson, "Allegorist and the Aesthetician," 87, 101.

[15]   Robertson, "Allegorist and the Aesthetician," 86.

person as well as in the person of Chaucer the pilgrim to Canterbury," at least as far as the *sentence* of the tales is concerned (in contrast to the surface meaning), and he considers all the characters in the *Book of the Duchess* (the dreamer, the Black Knight, etc.) to be allegorical aspects of the poet.[16] Interestingly, however, Robertson posits a different structural irony in Chaucer's works and indeed all medieval literature—and it is this similar dependence upon irony as a fundamental structuring device and tool of interpretation which links Donaldson and Robertson, and betrays them as members of the same generation, despite their irreconcilable differences.[17]

The Language of the Past

D.W. Robertson's most important premise, when it comes to studying literature, is that works should be read in the way that their original audience would have read them. In this he shares a stance with C.S. Lewis, and ranges himself against critics such as Kittredge and Donaldson, who focus less on the gap between medieval and modern audiences and more on the universal nature of great literature. Robertson sets out this approach most explicitly in his articles "Historical Criticism" and "Some Observations on Method in Literary Studies," and this attitude underlies most of his other writings. In an echo of C.S. Lewis, he characterizes the past as a foreign country "inhabited by strangers," whose customs, tastes and attitudes can broaden our own perspectives if we understand them properly. By contrast, if we visit these foreign countries with modern attitudes and prejudices about art and literature, we will achieve only the "stultification" of "concealed self-study."[18] Over and over again Robertson insists that aesthetic values we regard as "universal truths" are in fact historically contingent and transitory, and if we apply those "truths" to eras and cultures which held different "truths" we will misread their literature. Instead, Robertson argues, the proper task of the scholar is to evaluate art and literature according to the criteria the original audiences would have used. We should place ourselves "by an act of historical imagination" into Chaucer's original audience, thinking and feeling as they thought and felt.[19] Robertson admits that it is impossible to fully recreate the perspectives and attitudes of a medieval audience, but denies that this fact justifies the application of modern ways of reading to medieval texts. He uses the metaphor of language: the signs and symbols medieval authors used form a kind of "language" which

---

[16] Robertson, *Preface*, 367, 465, Huppé and Robertson, *Fruyt*, 35, 52, 91.

[17] David Lawton distinguishes between the two, calling Donaldson's irony "unstable" or "minor," and Robertson's "major irony." David Lawton, "Donaldson and Irony," *Chaucer Review* 41.3 (2007) 237.

[18] Robertson, "Some Observations," 31; cf. 29.

[19] Ibid., 32; Robertson, "Historical Setting of the *Book of the Duchess*" in Robertson, *Essays*, 254; cf. Robertson, *Essays*, xi; Robertson, *Chaucer's London*, 170.

the original audience would have understood, and which we need to be able to "decode" in order to even approximate an understanding that would have come naturally to a medieval audience. At all costs, however, we should refrain from applying modern concepts of romantic love, or modern ideas of "psychology," or emotions of modern "sentimentality" to medieval literature.[20] The literature of the past, Robertson suggests, is interesting not because it is "modern" or foreshadows modernity, but because it is so different.

Robertson, therefore, despite the fact that he spent much of his career arguing against the school of criticism inspired by C.S. Lewis and the theories of courtly love, nonetheless shares Lewis's belief that medieval society was fundamentally different from modern society.[21] Just as Lewis was reacting against the universal, humanistic approaches of Kittredge and others, so Robertson reacts against the "universalizing" theory of his day: New Criticism. Robertson rejects the New Critical claim that "good art" transcends time and place. Instead, he suggests, the "universals" we find in medieval art are likely to be projections of ourselves or our own values onto something otherwise completely alien. In his statements about the interpretative gap between medieval and modern times, however, Robertson goes farther than C.S. Lewis. Lewis, as discussed in Chapter 2, admits that while society changed drastically since medieval times certain elements of human nature remain constant. Robertson, by contrast, argues that "human nature" is inescapably structured by the environment in which it is bred, and thus the "human nature" of one time and place is fundamentally different from the "human nature" found in another place or era.[22] Changes in the structure of society and the nature of language, Robertson writes, "frequently imply changes in very basic attitudes toward reality, toward the location of reality, and toward its relation to space and time."[23] Not only human society, but human nature itself, therefore, has undergone significant change since the Middle Ages:

---

[20]   Robertson, *Preface*, 463; Robertson, *Chaucer's London*, 170.

[21]   Robertson also shares with Lewis a rejection of the traditional view that the change in society took place in the Renaissance; like Lewis, he posits the eighteenth century and the Romantic movement as the moment of the change: D.W. Robertson, Jr., *The Literature of Medieval England* (New York: McGraw-Hill, 1970) 2, cf. 491; Robertson, *Preface*, 9–10, 31; Robertson, "Some Observations," 30–31; C.S. Lewis, *The Allegory of Love* (New York: Oxford University Press, 1958) 46.

[22]   Robertson, "Some Observations," 23; cf. Robertson, *Preface*, viii. Robertson does admit grudgingly that there may be certain aspects of human nature which do not change, but insists that human behaviour and the interpretations of that behaviour vary so much with changes in social structure that whatever "constants" there may be in human nature become irrelevant: Robertson, *Preface*, 462. See also L.D. Benson, "A Reader's Guide to Writings on Chaucer," *Geoffrey Chaucer*, ed. Derek Brewer (London: G. Bell & Sons, 1974) 348.

[23]   Robertson, "Some Observations," 29.

Writers about the past frequently seek to reassure their readers that people have always been like themselves, that human nature is universal, and that the special periods with which they are concerned are in many respects like the period in which they live. I have sought to point out on the contrary that people in the late Middle Ages were different, that their world was very much unlike ours, and that in general human nature has changed considerably.[24]

Medieval people were not, Robertson insists, "humans like ourselves," and to treat them as though they were is to over-sentimentalize and fundamentally misunderstand them.

The Medieval Mind

Because human nature was so different five hundred years ago, Robertson can make generalizations about "the medieval mind," and contrast this mindset to the worldview or outlook we have today. The stated purpose of *A Preface to Chaucer* is to detail aspects of the medieval mind and world for modern scholars. One of the fundamental assumptions upon which Robertson's argument rests is that the "medieval mind" influenced all aspects of medieval culture, that there is a basic "continuity of medieval culture," so Robertson can use visual art, for example, to illuminate and explain literature. Not only human nature, Robertson declares, but aesthetic values differ between medieval times and modern, and in *A Preface to Chaucer* Robertson seeks to describe "an aesthetic attitude which became typically medieval."[25] He argues that fourteenth-century stylistic conventions did not value characteristics such as "psychological profundity, dramatic intensity, well-rounded characters, realism, and well-structured plot development," and so to look for such things in medieval literature is essentially taking the wrong approach. Instead, medieval artists tended to think in terms of "symmetrical patterns" and "abstract hierarchies," and the modern tendency to look for patterns of opposites and dynamic conflicts leads to misreadings of medieval literature.[26]

D.W. Robertson's vision of Chaucer's medieval audience is largely dependent upon his image of medieval society as a whole. Robertson's most famous description of medieval society comes at the end of the introduction to *A Preface to Chaucer*, where he contrasts the "medieval world" with the ills of modernity:

The medieval world was innocent of our profound concern for tension. We have come to view ourselves as bundles of polarities and tensions in which, to use one formulation, the ego is caught between the omnivorous demands of the id

---

[24]   Robertson, *Chaucer's London*, vii.

[25]   Robertson, *Preface*, 139, 52–3; cf. Robertson, "Some Observations," 22.

[26]   Robertson, *Preface*, 276, 6, 31. One can see here the influence of medieval art on Robertson's theories of literature.

on the one hand, and the more or less irrational restraints of the super-ego on the other. ... We project dynamic polarities on history as class struggles, balances of power, or as conflicts between economic realities and traditional ideals. ... But the medieval world with its quiet hierarchies knew nothing of these things.[27]

Robertson believed that medieval men and women were almost all orthodox, conservative, and content in their places in the "quiet hierarchies" which made up medieval society. This vision of medieval society is elaborated most fully in the book *Chaucer's London*, but pervades Robertson's writings. According to Robertson, medieval society was structured by personal obligations and familial ties, and these small hierarchies built into the great hierarchies of the kingdom as a whole. Because every individual knew his "degree" or place, and those degrees were narrowly defined with reference to the surrounding degrees, there were no large "classes" and hence no class struggle. "No one had any special desire to be dynamically progressive," Robertson writes, for since medieval men knew their place and trusted in God, they "lacked that essential uneasiness and lack of confidence in the past and future that characterizes much of modern life."[28]

This social hierarchy was stable and "quiet" because it reflected the hierarchy of the universe, and medieval society, Robertson believes, was profoundly Christian. Robertson writes of the "rigorous Augustinian Christianity of the Middle Ages" and argues that medieval Christianity was not a "system" but "essentially a way of life."[29] Christianity pervaded every aspect of medieval society: the division commonly made between "secular" and "religious" attitudes did not apply in medieval times, for religion then was a social and political institution and phenomenon, not simply a spiritual one. Clergymen and laymen shared the same basic Christian ideals and attitudes, and those ideas "shaped the thinking of men in all walks of life."[30] Because of this, social and political problems in the Middle Ages were fundamentally moral issues, for moral rot in one group or level of society could infect or destabilize the whole hierarchy. Political stability was the fruit of moral stability, and social instability could only be a symptom of a more deeply-rooted threat to the order of society. Morality was not a personal matter, but worked to maintain and improve the order of society: people and characters, be they fictional or real, were judged "on

---

[27] Ibid., 51. In the language he uses in this passage Robertson is explicitly rejecting both Freudian ("ego," "id," "superego") and Marxist ("dynamic polarities," "class struggles") claims to universalism and trans-historicity.

[28] Robertson, *Chaucer's London*, 4, 109.

[29] Robertson, "Historical Criticism," 4; D.W. Robertson, Jr., "Chaucer and Christian Tradition," *Chaucer and Scriptural Tradition*, ed. David Lyle Jeffrey (Ottawa: University of Ottawa Press, 1984) 3–32, 4; cf. Robertson, *Essays*, xv.

[30] Robertson, *Chaucer's London*, 10–11; cf. 8, 68. Robertson admits the existence of heresy, but tends to deny that any person of worth or social standing could have held heretical beliefs and maintained their position in society: see, for example, Huppé and Robertson, *Fruyt*, 30; cf. "Chaucer's Franklin and His Tale" in Robertson, *Essays*, 280.

94   *Twentieth-Century Chaucer Criticism*

the basis of their moral qualities and on their abilities to contribute to the coherence of community life with self-restraint and industry."[31]

On the basis of the pervasiveness of this Christian and hierarchical mentality in the Middle Ages, Robertson believes that certain attitudes which we take for granted today would have been literally unthinkable in medieval times. For example, we cannot attribute modern ideas about marriage to Chaucer (by arguing that in the Franklin's Tale Chaucer promotes the idea of marital equality, for example), because such ideas would have been "absurd" in Chaucer's society. According to exegetical criticism, the Franklin's Tale simply cannot legitimately be read to suggest that love and mastery are incompatible, since that principle "would have undermined the entire structure of Chaucer's society, not to mention the Christian religion as it was then understood."[32] Likewise, the theory of "courtly love" as developed by modern scholars such as C.S. Lewis would have been considered heretical to a medieval person, since it advocates the idolizing of a creature (the beloved) who is not God.[33] In the same way, doubting the Boethian philosophy of the mutability of the world and the fickleness of Fortune would have been "strange indeed" in fourteenth-century English court circles, Robertson writes, and this means, for example, that Chaucer could not have had a modern conception of tragedy, since modern tragedy depends upon an uncaring universe and a lack of understanding of the workings of Providential order.[34] This ultimate trust in the workings of Providence which Robertson ascribes to medieval people leads him to some occasionally startling conclusions: "Society did not then systematically protect itself from contact with disease, death and bloodshed," he writes, "hence these things caused relatively little anguish and provoked little sentimentality."[35] Tragic situations would not have been sentimentalized, and tragic works would not have provoked sympathetic emotions in the way in which they do today. We can see in these statements the way in which the "audience function" becomes a key aspect of Robertson's criticism: Robertson's image of Chaucer's audience works as a severely limiting factor on the interpretations a critic produces. Some interpretations are simply inadmissable because the medieval audience, according to Robertson, would not have been able to think or react in such a way. The audience here is functioning as a structural device which enables the claims Robertson makes in his criticism.

---

[31]   Robertson, "Christian Tradition," 3.

[32]   Robertson, "Chaucer's Franklin," 281.

[33]   See Benson, "A Reader's Guide," 339.

[34]   Robertson, *Preface*, 473–4. See also, as the converse of this, Robertson's description of Chaucer's sense of comedy: Huppé and Robertson, *Fruyt*, 147.

[35]   Robertson, *Chaucer's London*, 9; cf. 11.

Christian Reading

Because of what he perceives as the thorough-going Christianity of the Middle Ages, D.W. Robertson believes that medieval people would have read literature in accordance with both Christian "methods" of reading and in accordance with Christian values and doctrine. Christian methods of reading are essentially the techniques used or advocated by the exegetes of scripture. Robertson postulates that medieval individuals would have known and understood the techniques of patristic scriptural exegesis used in studying the Bible, and that they would have applied those techniques to non-Biblical writings. Robertson argues that the model of the four senses or levels of Scripture, in which the Bible is interpreted literally, tropologically, anagogically and allegorically, became a "habit of mind," so that other writings came to be read in the same way.[36] In this method of reading, seeming contradictions or problems in the literal level are resolved by interpreting them as allegory, referring either to the Church, the morality of the individual, or the afterlife. Limiting these allegorical readings, which could be quite imaginative, was the guiding principle of charity or *caritas*. Charity is anything which brings one closer to God; cupidity is anything which takes one away from God and closer to the self. Since the Bible's ultimate message, its *sentence*, was *caritas*, any reading which did not reinforce the message of *caritas* was, according to Augustine, invalid. Augustine writes, "Scripture teaches nothing but charity, nor condemns anything except cupidity … in the consideration of figurative expressions a rule such as this will serve, that what is read should be subjected to diligent scrutiny until an interpretation contributing to the reign of charity is produced."[37]

Robertson extends this guiding principle to all Christian literature, in which he includes all literature written in the Middle Ages. Robertson cannot envision a Christian author writing in defiance of Augustine's system, and since all serious writers in the Middle Ages, according to Robertson, were Christian, all medieval writing conforms to the test of charity: "Medieval Christian poetry, and by Christian poetry I mean all serious poetry written by Christian authors, even that usually called 'secular,' is always allegorical when the message of charity or some corollary of it is not evident on the surface."[38] Charity is "the message of the Bible, of the *Consolation of Philosophy*, of Andreas Capellanus, of Chrétien de Troyes, and of a great many other medieval writers. The idea, indeed, was a part of the normal expectation of the medieval reader, and to say that an author

---

[36] Robertson, *Preface*, 355; cf. Robertson, *Preface*, 347; Robertson, *Literature of Medieval England*, 26. For definitions of the four levels of interpretation, see Robertson, *Preface*, 292.

[37] Augustine, *On Christian Doctrine*, trans. D.W. Robertson, Jr. (Upper Saddle River: Prentice Hall, 1958) 88, 93.

[38] Robertson, "Historical Criticism," 10.

intends it is simply to say that he is a Christian."[39] Since the grounding element or control on interpretations of scripture was Augustine's theory of charity—that everything in the Bible points to a meta-narrative about charity, and thus seemingly contradictory sections must be read as allegories about charity—Robertson adopts the same ground or control for interpretations of all medieval literature. Thus he asserts that medieval readers would have interpreted literature using the principle of *caritas*, and any story which does not seem to promote the message of charity would have been read allegorically, either as a negative exemplum depicting a cupidity the reader is warned to avoid, or as a symbolic narrative in which the characters symbolize abstractions which teach charity.[40] So, for example, in his article "The Doctrine of Charity in Mediaeval Literary Gardens," Robertson demonstrates how gardens in literature could symbolize either charity or cupidity: charity through their associations with the Garden of Eden, the Tree of Life, God's creation, etc.; cupidity through associations with worldliness, the Fall, luxuriant bestial Nature, and so on.[41] Which way a garden should be read would depend upon the context and the ultimate message of the particular work.

The goal of reading for modern scholars, therefore, as it was for medieval people, should be to discover the ultimate *sentence* of charity beneath a medieval poem, and to do this medieval literature should be read allegorically. The "audience function" is harnessed again as a limitation upon criticism: since, according to Robertson, medieval audiences read allegorically, modern critics should likewise limit their interpretations to allegorical readings. Robertson defines allegory with reference to the exegetes and the grammarians: "allegoria" is the practice of "saying one thing to mean another."[42] Like C.S. Lewis, he distinguishes between symbolism and allegory, assigning the first to post-eighteenth-century writing, and the second to Classical, Medieval and Renaissance works.[43] Likewise, he maintains that allegory is different from an extended metaphor, or any kind of metaphor: metaphor replaces one object with another, but allegory says one thing to mean

---

[39]   Robertson, *Preface*, 501. Again, this quotation shows Robertson's extensive use of the audience function in his criticism. See also Robertson, "Doctrine of Charity," 46. For criticism of this application of Augustinian principles to all medieval literature, see Kaske, "Patristic Exegesis: The Defense," 29; R.E. Kaske, "Chaucer and Medieval Allegory," *English Literary History* 30.2 (June 1963) 176.

[40]   Robertson, "Doctrine of Charity," 25; Robertson, *Preface*, 343. For discussion, see Kaske, "Chaucer and Allegory," 175; Gradon, "Review," 51.

[41]   Robertson, "Doctrine of Charity"; see especially page 36: "An ironic presentation of the evil garden for purposes of satire has the same ultimate effect as a straightforward presentation to illustrate Christian herosim [*sic*] on the part of one conquering evil."

[42]   Robertson, *Preface*, 57, 291, 300; Robertson, *Literature of Medieval England*, 26, 29; Robertson, "Historical Criticism," 10; Robertson, "Allegorist and Aesthetician," 95.

[43]   Robertson, *Preface*, 286. See also Lewis, *Allegory of Love*, 46. Robertson occasionally confuses the issue by speaking of medieval "symbolism"; what he means by this, however, is the system of symbols and signs through which medieval allegory is read.

another, often its exact opposite. In this definition of allegory, Robertson comes fairly close to both modern and medieval definitions of irony as "The expression of meaning using language that normally expresses the opposite."[44]

In Robertson's understanding of allegory and irony, the role of the audience is crucial. The allegory cannot function without the audience's understanding of the double meaning: "poets ... compose enigmatic fables which *are understood* to mean something other than what they say."[45] For allegory to work, therefore, it is entirely dependent upon the audience. As in the Christian allegorizations of classical texts, the allegorical meaning may, in fact, not be "in" the text at all, but is produced by the reader. The surface of a medieval work, according to Robertson, is often deliberately obscure—the inner didactic meaning is concealed so that the reader might have the pleasure of unveiling it. Robertson harnesses medieval exegetical vocabulary for his purposes here: the chaff must be discarded for the fruit, the shell for the inner kernel, etc.—indeed, the title of *Fruyt and Chaf* indicates the tradition on which he depends. The proper communication of the message, in Robertson's theory, depends on the reader realizing that the poem is allegorical and that he has to look for another meaning. It depends upon his knowing the conventions of the symbolism and allegory, and being able to interpret the "beautiful surface" in a way that reveals the Christian message beneath. The modern reader who values the surface level of the text, therefore, misreads the poem: the aesthetic "quality" of the surface—its realism, poetic effects, consistency, etc.—is hardly relevant to the true worth of the work. Robertson, in a sense, sees every story told in the Middle Ages as a sort of exemplum, a tale told with a moral lesson: "It is but a step from an elaborate *exemplum* to a Canterbury Tale, except that the Tale conceals its *sentence* under what Petrarch called a 'veil' of fiction, instead of employing an elaborate moralization at the close."[46] The nature of the "veil" itself matters little, except as a means of enticing the reader.

Chaucer's Educated Audience

In order to sustain his interpretation of Chaucer's works, Robertson needs to support his claim that a medieval audience would have had reading practices shaped in accordance with the principles of allegorical interpretation, and would have had at least some understanding of the complex network of symbols and signs that would enable them to interpret a text correctly. Robertson makes this

---

[44] Oxford English Dictionary, s.v. "irony." See discussion in Beryl Rowland's introduction to Earle Birney, *Essays on Chaucerian Irony* (Toronto: University of Toronto Press, 1985) xvi.

[45] Robertson, *Preface*, 59, *emphasis mine.*

[46] Robertson, "Christian Tradition," 20. See also Robertson's comment that the link to the *Melibee* suggests that poetic fables are to be read, like the Bible, for their underlying meaning not their surface content: Robertson, *Preface*, 369; cf. 502.

argument in several ways. First, in articles such as "The Frequency of Preaching in Thirteenth-Century England," he establishes that most individuals in the Middle Ages would have had regular exposure to preaching and scripture, and hence to Biblical symbols and images, to the techniques of scriptural exegesis, to the wealth of attendant symbolism which developed parallel to the symbolism in the Bible, and to the symbols and images of the commentary tradition. Second, he argues that because of the art, stained glass windows, sculpture and other decoration in the churches of the Middle Ages, the common people would have developed a mental store-house of images and signs, an understanding of the uniform "iconographic language" upon which allegory depends.

A commoner in medieval times, therefore, would have had a reasonable cultural competency which he could access when listening to or reading a medieval text. However, Robertson posits an increased likelihood of the audience being able to understand a wide breadth of references by arguing for a select audience for Chaucer. Chaucer's audience, he claims, would have been primarily men and women of the court and educated clerics—in other words, an educated, chivalric, orthodox, literary elite, "the thinking public, that is, the courtly audience."[47] Chaucer's audience was "royalty, lords lay and spiritual, great ladies and minor members of the court such as squires, pages, ladies-in-waiting, and clerks, as well as more substantial men of the City."[48] These men and women would have been able to understand a far wider range of reference than commoners. According to Robertson, the courtiers and the élite of English society would have had their ideas about literary interpretation shaped by the theories of authorities such as Peter Lombard, Boethius, Augustine, Jerome, Gregory, Bede, Hugh of St. Victor, and others, as well as the classical tradition of Ovid and Virgil. As a result, figurative readings or allegorical interpretations of common images and phrases would have been well-known, and literate people, when encountering them in Chaucer's works, would have thought of them almost automatically. Chaucer's audience would have caught the humour when sources with which they were familiar were deliberately distorted for purposes of satire, irony or inversion. They would have known the symbolic implications of details such as the Miller's bagpipe or his wrestling, for example, and would have understood the clothing imagery of the Clerk's Tale. They would have remembered St. Paul's comments on proper marriage when the Wife of Bath describes her own marriages, and they would have recognized the Boethian elements of *Troilus and Criseyde* and understood their implications with reference to Troilus's love for Criseyde. They would have known the metaphor of Christian life as a pilgrimage, and would have silently

---

[47] Robertson, *Preface*, 396; cf. Robertson, *Preface*, 80, 272, 280; D.W. Robertson, Jr., "Some Disputed Chaucerian Terminology," *Speculum* 52.3 (July 1977) 572; Robertson, "Chaucer's Franklin," 280; Robertson, "The Historical Setting," 237–8, 252; Robertson, *Literature of Medieval England*, 491.

[48] Robertson, *Chaucer's London*, 216–17; cf. Robertson, "Probable Date," 143; Robertson, *Literature of Medieval England*, 28.

contrasted the ideals of that metaphor with the actions of Chaucer's pilgrims on their way to Canterbury. Almost innumerable other examples could be given. Robertson regularly uses phrases such as "the implications would have been clear at once to most persons in Chaucer's audience" or "this fact could hardly have escaped Chaucer's audience" or "this probably suggested to the audience ..." or "we can rest assured ... that this commonplace analogy did occur to them" or "needless to say, no one in Chaucer's audience would have needed to be reminded of the Augustinian principle that. ..."[49] Throughout his books and articles, D.W. Robertson thus continually refers to the audience's extensive knowledge in order to underpin his readings of Chaucer's works.

This claim that Chaucer's courtly, educated audience would have read his works as allegories either promoting charity or condemning cupidity has, as one might expect, far-reaching consequences for Robertson's reading of Chaucer. *Troilus and Criseyde*, for example, he reads as a warning poem directed at the English chivalric elite: Troilus (like the Squire in the *Canterbury Tales*) symbolizes a new, dandified, frivolous chivalry, and through his devotion to a woman rather than to his country, he brings about the destruction of Troy. Troy itself symbolizes London or England (in the fourteenth century, London was sometimes called "New Troy"). Pandarus's symbolic role is as an "inverted Lady Philosophy," a bad adviser. The poem, therefore, is an admonition to the English knighthood not to fall into the same lifestyle as Troilus—it is neither a tale of "true love" nor of "courteous love," but a depiction of the evils of worldly love.[50]

The *Canterbury Tales* are likewise interpreted as moral exempla. The overall framework of the *Tales* points to the pilgrimage of the life of every Christian, and the pilgrims themselves offer various examples of "right" and "wrong" ways of making this pilgrimage. All the *Tales*, therefore, agree in *sentence*, if not in surface meaning. The Franklin's Tale and the Knight's Tale, like *Troilus and Criseyde*, are, according to Robertson, negative exempla about worldly love, and Robertson reads them as warnings about the dangers of *cupiditas*. The moral of the Physician's Tale is that one should beware of "wolf-like" doctors who take advantage of their "sheep and lambs," their patients. The characters of January and Arcite, despite their differences, both symbolize the abuse of the beauty of the world; the Wife of Bath represents the inversion of the proper order of things (especially between the sexes). Innumerable other examples could be quoted, since *A Preface to Chaucer* is essentially an exploration of the possible exegetical interpretations of Chaucer.

The corollary of D.W. Robertson's assumption that a medieval audience would have read a story for its moral value and charitable message, is that the audience *wouldn't* have valued literature for its psychological insights, realistic characters, or gripping drama. Robertson argues that the "vicarious participation in the fictional experience of at least one of the characters in a dramatic context," which

---

[49] Robertson, "Chaucer's Franklin," 282; Robertson, "Historical Setting," 241; Robertson, *Preface*, 260; Robertson, "Probable Date," 161; Robertson, *Preface*, 486.

[50] Robertson, "Probable Date," 143; Robertson, *Preface*, 472.

most modern readers would experience when reading a story or watching a play, was a phenomena that was, for the most part, absent from the medieval experience of literature.[51] Only the lower classes in medieval times, the audiences of popular ballads and Robin Hood stories—classes which Robertson does not consider to have been a materially important part of Chaucer's audience—would have read stories "for the story," becoming caught up in the action and involved with the characters, and Robertson maintains that such a method of reading literature only entered the mainstream during the Romantic period.

Robertson bases this claim in part upon his assumption that medieval audiences would have read stories for the moral message, and not for the plot or the drama. He also, however, claims that our modern concepts of "personality," "psychology," and "character" only developed with the rise of individualism in the eighteenth century.[52] Thus his argument that medieval people would not have looked for psychological development in their characters rests upon the assumption not that medieval audiences would have *chosen* not to read stories for the characters, but that fundamentally they would have been unable to do so. "No one in antiquity or the Middle Ages, or even the Baroque period," Robertson writes, "either had a personality in this sense or accused anyone else of having one; and we should not look for personalities either in the artists of these periods or in the characters they portray in their works."[53] Instead of being "personalities" or "psychologies," medieval characters are personifications of abstract, moral, ideas. (In other words, they are not depictions of the inner worlds of distinct, unique individuals, but moral aspects of character which we all share.) Social problems or inner conflicts would have been perceived not in terms of psychological crises but in terms of moral philosophy.

Thus Robertson dismisses the critical debate about whether the Canterbury pilgrims are "individuals" or "types" by stating that a medieval audience would have perceived them as neither: the Canterbury pilgrims would have been envisioned as exemplary figures, personifications of various virtues or vices, neither "typical" nor "individualized." So the Plowman, for example, is neither a representation of a typical plowman nor an individualized character, but a "statement of ideals"; other characters, such as the Reeve, are depictions of the "failure of ideals." The

---

[51]   Robertson, *Preface*, 37; cf. Robertson, *Literature of Medieval England*, 28.

[52]   Robertson, "Some Observations," 28; Robertson, *Literature of Medieval England*, 5; Robertson, *Chaucer's London*, 6; cf. Robertson, *Preface*, 276. Robertson occasionally goes further, and claims that not only did medieval people not share our modern *concepts* of personality or psychology, but that people in the Middle Ages actually had neither personalities nor psychologies: see Robertson, *Chaucer's London*, 5, 117. In this assumption, of course, he disagrees strongly with C.S. Lewis's argument that medieval allegory was "psychological" and depicted the inner struggles of the characters: instead, allegories such as the *Romance of the Rose* are "description[s] of human actions in terms of abstractions belonging to an objective scheme of moral values": Robertson, *Preface*, 35.

[53]   Robertson, "Allegorist and Aesthetician," 97.

Physician is an "exemplar of medical fraud"; the Friar is a "vivid exemplar of mendicant weaknesses"; the Wife of Bath is "an elaborate iconographic figure" representing misled, aggressive, femininity; the Parson provides a contrast with the common vices of London clergymen; the Sergeant of Law exemplifies the "grasping qualities and worldly wisdom" of lawyers; the Miller signifies gluttony, vainglory and avarice.[54] The characteristics which most critics perceive as "individualizing," such as the Miller's bagpipes, the Knight's list of battles, or the Wife's clothing, are "keys to ideas," which point to the characters' exemplary qualities, rather than "features of personalities."[55] The links between the tales are to be read morally, rather than dramatically: since there can be no "psychological rapport" or "connection between characters," all the speeches become "soliloquies," "the function of which is to present ideas to the audience rather than any of the other characters."[56] Similarly, the characters within the various tales are representations of ideas, rather than characters or personalities: Custance represents constancy, Griselda patience, Prudence prudence. Despite the radical "personality" differences which a modern audience would perceive between the characters of January and Arcite, as far as a medieval audience would have been concerned, the two would have represented a similar moral message: the dangers of an over-emphasis upon worldly beauty. In all of these cases, Robertson distinguishes between "realism" and "verisimilitude": Chaucer's characters may display strong verisimilitude, but they are not realistic.[57] Robertson reads Chaucer's other works in a similar way. *Troilus and Criseyde* is not a "study in the vagaries of sexual love" but a "monitory story." Characters such as Pandarus have no "psychological motivation," but act in accordance with the "moral structure of his person," or their exemplary role. Troilus himself is "hypersensitive, sentimental, romantic," but these are "the results of a moral process, not the operations of a psychology."[58] The *Book of the Duchess* is likewise a moral poem: the Black Knight and the dreamer are "not 'characters' at all in modern sense, and what happens to them is not a 'story.'"[59] Modern critics have misunderstood the poem because they were inclined to see the grief of the Black Knight as psychological, rather than moral or philosophical.

---

[54] Robertson, "Physician," 137; Robertson, *Chaucer's London*, 195, cf. Robertson, "Chaucer's Franklin," 99; Robertson, *Preface*, 330; Robertson, *Chaucer's London*, 81, 110, 204; Robertson, *Preface*, 243.

[55] Robertson, *Chaucer's London*, 218; cf. Robertson, *Preface*, 247.

[56] Robertson, *Preface*, 270–71.

[57] Ibid., 247, 257. For the distinction between "realism" and "verisimilitude" see "The Reality Effect" in Roland Barthes, *Rustle of Language* (Oxford: Basil Blackwell, 1986) 141–8.

[58] Robertson, *Chaucer's London*, 221; Robertson, *Preface*, 480, 497. In statements such as these, the distinction between "moral process" and "psychology" is usually undefined; the key difference seems to be that an audience would "learn" from "moral processes" but "identify" with a "psychological" character.

[59] Robertson, "Historical Setting," 253.

102   *Twentieth-Century Chaucer Criticism*

When Troilus "dies for love," therefore, the reader would not have felt a "strong sympathetic response," but would have responded intellectually and rationally.[60] The intellectual response to a poem is the proper one: emotion ought to be controlled and guided by the reason. Romantic art, according to Robertson, moves the audience to feel—to identify with the characters, to experience the author's emotions, to feel the stirring power of the symbolism. Medieval art, by contrast, encourages the audience to think.[61] The Middle Ages was a time of ideas, of reason, and not of "sentiment."[62] A medieval poem or story is an intellectual puzzle for the audience to solve, a moral message to decode, not a dramatic situation to experience.[63] The artistic and fictional "surface qualities" of a poem or story are "allurements only to the senses," which must be discarded if the intellect is to gain access to the doctrinal truth which is the true *sentence* of the poem.[64] The appeal of a medieval poem is not "sentimental," in Robertson's terms, but logical and intellectual. Emotion, where it exists, works only to reinforce the essential ideas of the poem.[65] Readers who "like" the Wife of Bath, cheer on John and Aleyn, identify with Dorigen, fall in love with Criseyde, pity Arcite, or are amused by the Miller are, according to Robertson, fundamentally responding "wrongly" to Chaucer's works. A medieval audience would have felt none of those emotions.

Allegory and Irony

Robertson's theory and his precise, strict image of a medieval audience have broader implications for interpretations of Chaucer. As I mentioned above, Robertson's definition of allegory is almost indistinguishable from the modern definition of irony, and is a sub-category of the medieval definition of irony.[66] Both involve a

---

[60]   Robertson, *Preface*, 46.

[61]   Ibid., 33, 37; cf. Robertson, "Allegorist and Aesthetician," 95. Again, the only audiences for which this was not true are the "unsophisticated" audiences of popular ballads and romance tales; such emotionalism, according to Robertson, was not a "respectable method of appealing to the thinking public, that is, the courtly audience": Robertson, *Preface*, 38, 396.

[62]   Robertson, "Historical Criticism," 5; Robertson, "Allegorist and Aesthetician," 94.

[63]   Robertson, *Preface*, 15, 32, 272.

[64]   Huppé and Robertson, *Fruyt*, 7, 10, 13; Robertson, *Preface*, 60, 63, 67, 83, 137, 216.

[65]   Robertson, *Preface*, 396, 230. For criticism of Robertson's use of the term "sentimental," see Kaske, "Chaucer and Allegory," 182, 186.

[66]   It should be stressed that this is *Robertson's* definition of allegory; for a discussion of other definitions, see Suzanne Conklin Akbari, *Seeing through the Veil: Optical Theory and Medieval Allegory* (Toronto: University of Toronto Press, 2004) 7–22. Robertson's allegory, however, would fall into Akbari's category of "vertical" allegory: it "points toward a hidden meaning that the reader must construct within his own mind, a transcendent truth that cannot be conveyed through literal language"; 14.

D.W. Robertson (1914–1992): The Allegorical Reader 103

text "meaning something other than what it says": the literal or surface meaning of a text is different, in many cases the exact opposite, of its "real"—ironic or allegorical—meaning. Since the two definitions are so close, and Robertson insists that all medieval literature is allegorical, his reading of medieval literature thus depends heavily on what many modern critics would call irony. Robertson, too, often uses the term irony to describe the allegorical aspect of medieval literature. He thus posits a distance between the audience and the text—a distance covered by irony—whereby the audience, secure in its knowledge of charity and Christian doctrine, sees irony and humour working against the literal meaning of the text. To put it another way, the allegorical distance between the inner meaning of a text (its kernel or grain) and the literal meaning (the chaff or shell) can be equivalent to the distance between the reader (who perceives the spiritual meaning) and the characters within the work (who do not).

Robertson's reading of Chaucer depends on his assumption that Chaucer's audience would find inversions and reversals of Christian doctrine funny—that they would perceive such inversions as satire, and find the gap between "the way things are" in the text, and "the way things should be" amusing. The ironic distance between how things are and how things should be, according to Robertson, formed the key means by which medieval authors criticized society. Thus if a story or poem seems to be depicting *cupiditas*, it is to be read ironically, as a mockery of people who act in such a way, as opposed to acting through *caritas*. Through this ironic reading it becomes an allegory of cupiditas, rather than a mere story. Therefore, writers such as Chrétien de Troyes, who write stories about love and chivalry, actually intend "to show the foolishness of idolatrous cupidity in an entertaining way that his audience could understand."[67] Andreas Capellanus likewise presents a "double lesson" of his work about love through irony, "the art of condemning something while seeming to praise it."[68] Capellanus seems to advocate worldly romantic love, but is actually mocking or satirizing it. According to Robertson, an ironic presentation of cupidity for the purposes of satire has the "same ultimate effect" as a straightforward presentation of charity or Christian heroism. The basis of Robertson's understanding of medieval humour is outlined most clearly in the work *Fruyt and Chaf*:

> Aberration from patterns clear, ordered, and omnipresent in men's lives offered the basis for medieval humor. When the contrast between illicit love and love in accord with God's order is absolutely clear, the solemn nonsense of the protestations of the irrational lover, the absurdity of his sufferings, and the foolishness of his hot desires are equally clear, and are a perennial subject for

---

[67] Robertson, "Doctrine of Charity," 40; cf. with reference to *Troilus and Criseyde*, Robertson, *Preface*, 487.

[68] Robertson, *Preface*, 400; Robertson, "Doctrine of Charity," 37–8; Robertson, *Preface*, 391, 405, 447. Robertson does not consider the possibility that Capellanus's third book, rather than the first two, might be ironic.

medieval laughter, especially when there is something in every one of us which warns that the lover's foolishness may be our own.[69]

The distance, then, between the way things should be—the "clear, ordered patterns" of medieval life—and aberrations from this order, creates irony. This irony is essential both to the humour of the text and to the moral lesson encoded within it.

Two-fold Irony

Although Robertson treats his allegorical/ironic method of reading as undifferentiated, his concept of irony is actually two-fold. The first kind of irony upon which Robertson's theory depends is textual irony: an aspect of allegory, texts in Robertson's readings are ironic because they say one thing and mean another. The audience reads medieval works as, at times, the exact opposite of what the text literally says, in order to make the text conform to the dictates of the imperative of *caritas*. As mentioned above, the literal story becomes an allegory of *caritas* or *cupiditas*. Worldly love really means heavenly love, disorder and disobedience really teach order and obedience, inversion and reversal actually depict or suggest the proper order of things, and cupidity really transmits the message of charity. This sense of irony is applied to most of Chaucer's works: every work apart from, perhaps, the Prioress's Tale, the Clerk's Tale, the Parson's Tale, the Man of Law's Tale, and the Second Nun's Tale (all of which portray the values of *caritas* directly) is interpreted ironically. Chaucer's more "worldly" writings, from *Troilus and Criseyde* to the *Canterbury Tales'* General Prologue, should be read as meaning the opposite from what they seem to say literally. By means of this pervasive, structural textual irony, Robertson can argue that all medieval texts essentially contain the same message, and that a medieval audience would have read such texts in according to a consistent, exegetical, Christian method of reading. In this way, through positing ubiquitous ironic readings of medieval works, Robertson can reconcile his image of Chaucer's audience as Christian, orthodox, educated and socially conservative with the reality of texts which seem bawdy, worldly, disorderly, or unchristian.

A second irony, however, underpins this theory at an even more basic, more fundamental level. Robertson's understanding of the way in which medieval audiences read medieval works rests upon an even more thorough-going concept of medieval irony: that medieval people would have read the *whole world*, essentially, as ironic. This definition of irony is, obviously, different from the definition meaning a text which "says one thing and means another"; instead, it is closer to the Oxford English Dictionary's third definition of irony, a "discrepancy between the expected and the actual state of affairs; a contradictory or ill-timed outcome of

---

[69]   Robertson, "Doctrine of Charity," 36; Huppé and Robertson, *Fruyt*, 146.

events as if in mockery of the fitness of things."[70] The whole world, essentially, is ironic: the discrepancy between the way things "seem to be" (disordered, chaotic, unhappy, unjust), and the way things "actually are" (ordered by God, ultimately just, ultimately reasonable), reminds the onlooker of God's divine wisdom and providence. Dorigen, looking at the cruel rocks, should have remembered the Boethian philosophy of the ultimate fitness of all things, rather than lamenting their existence. A medieval person, according to Robertson, would have found Dorigen funny because she does not properly understand the irony of the world—that is, the injustice of the world does not point her to the ultimate justice of God. Aberration from the proper patterns and order of the universe "offered the basis for medieval humor." The *Parlement of Foules* is "high comedy," because the birds cannot perceive their proper roles in the order of Nature and God's universe.[71] This worldly irony can also be turned inward: as Robertson's comment that "the lover's foolishness may be our own" suggests, the distance between the way the world is and the way it should be is paralleled by an equivalent distance between the way *we* really are and the way *we* should be. A good medieval reader, reading a courtly lover ironically, would turn the moral lesson back on himself and recognize the duality within his own soul. A bad reader, by contrast, despite knowing the "proper" way to read, would choose to ignore the story's lesson, avoid applying the story's moral to himself, and would read the work solely at a carnal level—that is, for entertainment or aesthetic pleasure. This reader would miss the key element of Chaucer's humour: ultimately, Robertson writes, "[Chaucer's] humor, which is based on the confident acceptance of a Providential order underlying the apparent irrationality of the world and its inhabitants, is sometimes more profound and more persuasive than any 'highly serious' discourse couched in the grand style can possibly be."[72] This irony is the irony in the laughter of Troilus at the end of *Troilus and Criseyde*, as he looks back upon those who are sentimentally caught up in the sorrows of the world and who don't perceive the ultimate ordering of God's universe.

Quite obviously, this concept of irony is a world apart from the more limited irony Donaldson posits in his distinction between Chaucer the author and his narrator. Nonetheless, both critics' readings of Chaucer depend upon a method of reading which does not take the text at face value, but posits a radical structural irony which indicates what the text "really means." Both critics use the "audience function" in justifying their turn to irony: they both depend upon a concept of the audience as distrustful of the surface of the text, and an audience situated at some distance from the characters within the text (be it from the general narrator, or

---

[70] Beryl Rowland describes "philosophic irony" or "cosmic irony," saying that this kind of irony "is compatible with medieval thought in that Christianity sought to reconcile the futility of man's endeavours with a belief in the justice of an omniscient Deity": Birney, *Essays*, xxii.

[71] Huppé and Robertson, *Fruyt*, 146–7.

[72] Robertson, *Preface*, 281.

106   *Twentieth-Century Chaucer Criticism*

individuals such as Troilus or Dorigen). This distance is necessary for the audience to catch the ironic message. Donaldson's concept of irony is restricted to the narrator and the text: the audience perceives the ironic gap between the narrator and the author, and so understands the satire of sections such as the General Prologue portraits. Robertson's concept of irony seems more far-reaching: not only does the audience perceive a textual irony, a disparity between what the text says and what it "actually means," but a philosophical irony, a sense of the whole world being, in some way, ironic. The individuals of a medieval audience, in these terms, are not just readers of *Chaucer*'s text, they are readers of *God*'s text, the book of the world. Using a metaphor drawn from Hugh of St. Victor, Robertson explains that the voice of God could be heard "in the things mentioned in Scripture or in the created world itself, which came to be called the 'Book of God's work.'"[73] The world, of course, did not have to be ironic: things of beauty or order could point the way to God straightforwardly as easily as things of ugliness or disorder could point the way ironically or through opposition—but what is interesting here is that Robertson extends the concept of reading, or of audience, to the whole world.

Characters as Readers

In this sense of the term "audience," Robertson's concept of audience broadens to include not just Chaucer's actual audience, but to include the characters *within* Chaucer's works, as well. Kittredge, Lewis, and Donaldson, when they envisioned Chaucer's audience, all envisioned the *real* audience: Chaucer's actual readers, be they medieval or modern. In Robertson's formulation, however, the readers *within* Chaucer's text form a key part of the image of the audience, the representation of the way in which audiences function. Just as Chaucer's actual medieval audience read not only Chaucer's works but the world around them (nature, society, each other) according to the dictates of the rule of *caritas*, so too do Chaucer's characters. Robertson writes about Chaucer's characters as *readers*: readers of the world, readers of each other, readers of the stories they themselves tell. These in-the-text readers then become exemplary readers for the out-of-text readers of Chaucer's actual audience. Good readers, those who read according to the dictates of charity, become examples of good hermeneutical practice for Chaucer's real readers, while bad readers, those who read according to worldly desires and cupidity, become examples of how not to read. So, for example, what Robertson calls Harry Bailey's consistent blindness to the *sentence* of the other pilgrims' tales—Harry does not "read" the tales in accordance with patristic exegetical methods—serves as a "jocular warning" to Chaucer's audience to avoid similar blind readings. Harry's glaring misinterpretations of the tales (interpreting the Merchant's Tale as illustrating the wiles of women, for example) encourages the audience to think about what the tale *really* means, its message in terms of

---

[73]   For this concept, see Robertson, *Preface*, 76.

Christian values. The other Canterbury pilgrims are likewise interpreters—or misinterpreters: the Wife of Bath's misinterpretation of scriptural authorities leads the real audience to wonder what else she has misinterpreted. The Franklin's interpretation of his own story as a question of freedom or gentility—neither of which, according to Robertson, is present in the tale—leads the audience "to consider the problem of just what the Franklin has actually said." The Clerk outlines for the other pilgrims the charitable *sentence* of his tale.[74] In each case, the actual reader is asked to evaluate the "in-text" reader's judgment, and decide whether it meets the criteria for a "proper" charitable interpretation. If it does not, that reading is to be rejected, and taken as an example of how not to read. Many of the pilgrims, by missing the Christian or charitable implications of their own tales, subtly comment on their own moral state, and thus the tales become commentaries on their own narrators. The *Canterbury Tales* contain readers not only at the level of the frame-tale but within the inner tales, and these, too, Robertson claims, serve as examples of good or bad reading practices. So, the summoner in the Friar's Tale "misreads," failing to see the "fruit" beneath the "chaff"; the friar in the Summoner's Tale misinterprets his own exempla, thus alerting the audience to the deeper implications of the story. Robertson divides these various readers or "exegetes" within the *Canterbury Tales* into categories: the Wife of Bath is "hopelessly carnal and literal" in her reading, the friar in the Summoner's Tale is an "arrant hypocrite," the Pardoner is "aware of the spirit" or *caritas* of the tale but defies it, and the Parson is a reader "altogether admirable."[75] All of them are perceived as exemplary of good or bad methods of reading.

Robertson's concept of audience, therefore, is not limited to the actual medieval audience he details in such particularity in *A Preface to Chaucer* and other works. It expands to include characters located *within* the works, as he considers those characters themselves as readers—readers of their own tales, of other tales, of the world around them and of each other. This shift in the concept of audience had major repercussions on the course of Chaucerian studies for the rest of the century. The concept of "reader" was no longer limited to Chaucer's *actual* readers, but extended to his fictional readers as well, and later critics take these readers, and these readings, into account in developing their criticism. This development cannot in any way be traced only to Robertson, of course: many scholars in the last third of the twentieth century began considering texts as themselves allegories for the reading process. Self-reflexivity entered English studies with a vengeance, and many works were beginning to be read as commentaries upon their own creation and poetic status. In Robertson's turn to Chaucer's own characters as exemplars of the reading process, he was consonant with other theorists who were beginning to explore self-referentiality in literature.[76] Later Chaucerian critics who consider the

---

[74] Ibid., 275, 366–7.

[75] Ibid., 317.

[76] Innumerable examples of the turn to self-reflexivity could be cited, but for two of the most important, see Paul de Man, *Allegories of Reading: Figural Language in*

relationships between Chaucer's various characters as allegories or metaphors for the relationships between texts and readers, may be able to trace their ideas back to Robertson as much as to deconstructionism and post-structuralism.

Despite this inclusion of Chaucer's own characters in his image of the audience, Robertson's "audience" is still, for the most part, singular, at least as far as it affects his criticism—"the medieval audience" is a singular entity, sharing the same values, worldview and method of reading. Not all of Chaucer's characters share these medieval Christian values, but according to Robertson's interpretation those who do not are examples of "bad readers," and thus do not affect Robertson's overall interpretation. Likewise, Robertson raises the possibility that a reader might ignore the tropological turn, and refuse to apply the morals of the story to himself—again, these interpretations are "wrong" and hence do not come into consideration in Robertson's own readings of the texts except as examples not to follow. To put it another way, these readers do not enter into the "audience function" except in a negative way: by being dismissed from Robertson's image of the audience proper, they limit the proliferation and diversity of readings by indicating readings which are *not* permissible. So while the actual audience in medieval times may have been multiple, and while the audiences depicted in Chaucer's works certainly were—in that they contain both good and bad readers—as far as it works as a function in Robertson's criticism, the audience is singular and unified.

Later scholars, noting the diversity of the figures Robertson himself details within his description of Chaucer's readers, and likewise becoming aware of the diversity of Chaucer's real audience, posited theories of audience which describe multiple, non-unified audiences for Chaucer. In the last third of the twentieth century, Chaucer's audience becomes plural: critics begin to consider Chaucer's *audiences*, both his medieval audiences and his different audiences through time. The extreme ironies both the New Critics and the Exegetes depend upon were toned down, and many of their main claims were rejected or modified. However, Donaldson's "careful reading" and Robertson's historical grounding became important for all breeds of critics. Robertson's expansion of the audience to include Chaucer's own characters as readers, moreover, was to become fundamental, as critics were to develop interpretations of Chaucer not just based upon the way real people read Chaucer, but the ways in which Chaucer's characters read themselves.

Rousseau, Nietzsche, Rilke and Proust (New Haven: Yale University Press, 1979); Jacques Derrida, *Of Grammatology*, trans. Gayatri Chakravorty Spivak (Baltimore: Johns Hopkins University Press, 1976).

Chapter 5
Carolyn Dinshaw (1957–):
The Gendered Reader

In the mid-century, a new idea about audiences appeared in literary criticism, but was never fully developed. D.W. Robertson, in envisioning Chaucer's characters as readers themselves, raised the suggestion of the possibility of *misreading*. What this means is that Chaucer's audience was beginning to be envisioned as multiple: different readers can read a text in different, even contradictory ways, and those differences arise out of differences in their own personalities, situations, or—especially for Robertson—relative piety or sinfulness. Robertson almost immediately closed down this suggestion of multiplicity in Chaucer's audience with the division of that audience into "good readers" and "bad readers." Multiple readings might be possible, but only a reading that accords with *caritas* is the "proper" or "correct" reading, the way the text is "meant to be read." Scholars of the last two decades of the twentieth century developed both these ideas about audiences—the image of the audience as multiple, and the idea that Chaucer's characters are themselves readers—without adopting Robertson's moral framework. These later critics would almost certainly consider themselves to be the philosophical heirs of such post-structuralist thinkers as Paul de Man, Jacques Derrida, Luce Irigaray or Michel Foucault, rather than of D.W. Robertson. Certainly the idea of a text being about itself—a self-referential commentary on the concepts of writing and reading—neither began nor ended with Robertson. Nevertheless, the turn to a vision of the audience as multiple and heterogeneous in late-twentieth-century Chaucerian criticism was in many ways presaged, if then rejected, by Robertson.

The movement towards the concept of multiple and diverse audiences arose out of several philosophical and political trends in the late 1970s and early 1980s. With the development in literary studies of approaches such as feminism, Marxism, and black studies, academics became more interested in diversity, whether of characters, writers, or readers. At the same time, New Historicism exerted more and more of an influence on Medieval and Renaissance studies, and brought with it a focus on power, discourse, and the creation of identity in historical texts and documents. In Medieval Studies, there also developed increasingly honed applications of the old techniques of paleography, codicology, and manuscript work, which resulted in very specific and detailed studies of particular individuals, books, or documents. In other words, at the very time that some scholars were developing theories that emphasized the multiplicity of audiences—the way a female reader, or a black reader, is different from the white male reader traditionally envisioned—other

110   *Twentieth-Century Chaucer Criticism*

scholars were performing detailed studies of individual readers of medieval texts, whether through studies of the history of a particular manuscript, or analyses of the practices of a certain scribe, or examinations of the inheritors of particular books in wills or legal documents. They studied Chaucer's medieval audience not in terms of an over-arching "medieval mind," but in terms of particular, individual readers of specific texts and manuscripts. I have argued that although the readings of Donaldson and Robertson were diametrically different, they nonetheless shared a similar ground in their dependence upon irony. Likewise, in the next two chapters I will suggest that despite the differences between identity criticism and New Historicism, they nonetheless share a similar ground that would characterize Chaucer studies for the last quarter of the twentieth century: an awareness of the multiplicity of Chaucer's audience, and an insistence on readings and interpretations that reflect that diversity, as opposed to readings based on the homogeneous unity of audience assumed by earlier critics.

Whether because we as yet lack historical distance and perspective on the late twentieth century, or because the number of Chaucerians and leading Chaucer scholars has multiplied, it is more difficult to select a clear representative scholar of the two most recent movements in Chaucerian studies than it is for earlier periods.[1] A wealth of feminist studies of Chaucer were published during the 1980s and 1990s; Marxist readings were perhaps less numerous, but still influential; masculinism, queer theory and post-colonialism/orientalism were fields only beginning to be explored. Yet Carolyn Dinshaw can be taken as representative in many ways, since she touches on many of these different fields. Dinshaw's work *Chaucer's Sexual Poetics* was the first full-length feminist study of Chaucer, and set a tone for Chaucer studies in the way that *Chaucer and His Poetry, The Allegory of Love, Speaking of Chaucer*, and *A Preface to Chaucer* all did. Dinshaw's article, and later chapter, on the Pardoner's Tale marked a turning point in studies of the Pardoner's Tale, and no study written after Dinshaw can fail to take Dinshaw's reading into account, be it by building on it or by countering it.[2] Dinshaw also

---

[1]   Nevertheless, a kind of consensus seems to be forming: several scholars note the importance of the same critics I have chosen to focus on, Carolyn Dinshaw and Lee Patterson. See, among others, David Matthews, "Foreword: The Spirit of Chaucer," *The Canterbury Tales Revisited—21st Century Interpretations*, ed. Kathleen A. Bishop (Cambridge: Cambridge Scholars Publishing, 2008) xii. Lee Patterson himself singles out Carolyn Dinshaw, as well as Donaldson and Robertson, in his brief survey of Chaucer criticism in the introduction to his latest book: *Temporal Circumstances: Form and History in the Canterbury Tales* (New York: Palgrave MacMillan, 2006) 14. Ethan Knapp lists Dinshaw among others for both feminist criticism and queer theory; he does not discuss post-colonial theory. Ethan Knapp, "Chaucer Criticism and Its Legacies," *Yale Companion to Chaucer*, Seth Lerer ed. (New Haven: Yale University Press, 2006) 350–51.

[2]   Carolyn Dinshaw, "Eunuch Hermeneutics," *English Literary History* 55.1 (Spring 1988) 27–51; Carolyn Dinshaw, *Chaucer's Sexual Poetics* (Madison: University of Wisconsin Press, 1989) chapter 6. Several earlier readings did carry out considerations of the Pardoner's possible homosexuality; however, Dinshaw's combination of the Pardoner's

Carolyn Dinshaw (1957–): The Gendered Reader 111

straddles several fields which made a major impact on Chaucer studies in the final two decades of the twentieth century: *Chaucer's Sexual Poetics* takes a feminist approach for the most part, while its final chapter and her later book, *Getting Medieval*, use a queer studies approach.[3] In her more recent work, Dinshaw has become increasingly interested in post-colonial theories as well. Thus she is in many a convenient choice, since she allows a discussion of all of these disparate approaches. Moreover, in her explicit concern with the ramifications of the act of reading, Dinshaw develops, counteracts, or responds to many of the themes and problems that emerged over the course of the century.

Reading Like a Woman

Carolyn Dinshaw's scholarly training incorporated both the New Criticism of the likes of Robert Burlin (who taught her as an undergraduate at Bryn Mawr College), and exegetical historicism still prevalent at Princeton, where Dinshaw did her doctorate.[4] In later years, Dinshaw moved away from this Princetonian influence,

---

sexuality with his hermeneutic practices and the symbolic valence of his relics was very influential. This chapter is often excerpted in important collections of criticism on Chaucer: see Derek Pearsall, ed., *Chaucer to Spenser: A Critical Reader* (Oxford: Blackwell, 1999) 65–106; Corinne Saunders, ed., *Blackwell Guide to Criticism: Chaucer* (Oxford: Blackwell, 2001) 314–24.

[3] Carolyn Dinshaw, *Getting Medieval: Sexualities and Communities, Pre- and Postmodern* (Durham: Duke University Press, 1999). It should be noted that throughout her works Dinshaw defines "queer" very broadly: while the category includes gays and lesbians, it goes beyond these to designate anyone who has some sort of deviant or abnormal sexuality, or who goes against the sexual or community norms of the culture; queerness by its very nature is "fundamentally indeterminate" and sex is "heterogeneous and multiple." Thus the Pardoner is "queer" although we do not know whether he is homosexual or a eunuch; Margery Kempe is "queer" because of her refusal to fulfill traditional gender and sexual roles. See Dinshaw, *Getting Medieval*, 12, 13, 117; Dinshaw, *Sexual Poetics*, 157. To complicate matters further, Dinshaw uses the term "queer" to designate the kind of historical act she is performing, a history which "creates a relation across time that has an affective or an erotic component": Dinshaw, *Getting Medieval*, 50. Dinshaw acknowledges that her use of the term is anachronistic, that the word "queer" did not exist in Middle English: Carolyn Dinshaw, "New Approaches to Chaucer," *The Cambridge Companion to Chaucer*, 2nd ed., ed. Piero Boitani and Jill Mann (Cambridge: Cambridge University Press, 2003) 280.

[4] Carolyn Dinshaw, email, July 16, 2005. I am grateful to Professor Dinshaw for communicating with me and for graciously providing me with this personal and biographical information. Dinshaw's earliest work may reflect the influence of D.W. Robertson's continued presence at Princeton, although she does not see herself in any way as a Robertsonian: her first article, published while she was still a doctoral student, studies the role of games in the text "Le Jeu de Saint Nicolas," arguing that although they seem to imply doubt in the existence of God (because they depend on chance), ultimately they symbolize both providential

although its traces are still left in the thoroughness of her use of historical evidence, her interest in medieval allegory, and in her use of exegetical sources to prove her arguments. Indeed, one reviewer called *Sexual Poetics* a "feminist revision of a Robertsonian reading," indicating both Dinshaw's traces of Robertsonianism, and her critique of and movement away from it.[5] But "Foucault was in the air" in the late 1970s, Dinshaw says, and like many post-structuralists at the time she was attempting to find a historicism that was not exegetical. In 1982 Dinshaw was hired by the University of California at Berkeley, and in the "overtly politicized" atmosphere there she was drawn into, and became a leading practitioner of, the surge in feminist criticism of the 1980s. There she also encountered the beginnings of gay criticism. *Sexual Poetics* is heavily dependent upon feminist theory, but in her later career Dinshaw has turned to queer theory, as a theory which can incorporate elements of feminism but addresses other elements of sexuality, not just female heterosexuality.

This grafting of a strong political commitment to marginalized figures such as women or queers onto a New Critical training and a Robertsonian heritage makes Dinshaw's concept of audience—along with that of most of her generation—starkly different from that of previous generations. Dinshaw's image of Chaucer's audience is multiple, diverse, and differentiated. It includes historical and modern audiences, mainstream individuals and marginalized characters. Dinshaw explicitly calls her vision of Chaucer's audience "diversely imagined."[6] Dinshaw also picks up on Robertson's analysis of the characters *within* Chaucer's stories as readers, and pushes this concept one step further. Not only are Chaucer's characters themselves readers, but in Dinshaw's analysis they become metaphors and symbols for the reading process itself. Dinshaw's vision of audience in Chaucer is thus three-fold: first, there is Chaucer's actual audience, be they medieval or modern readers and listeners; second, there are the characters themselves, who are readers of other texts and of each other; and third, there is a representation of reading or interpretation developed through the characters' roles as metaphors for the hermeneutic process.

Dinshaw's early interest in feminist criticism provided the starting point for her first, and perhaps most important, re-envisioning of Chaucer's audience. Like many other feminists of her generation, she realized that the supposedly neutral universal "reader" of New Critics such as Donaldson actually had all the characteristics—and characteristic blindnesses—of a white, Western, heterosexual man. Literary critics,

---

control and God's cosmic game with the devil. Carolyn L. Dinshaw, "Dice Games and Other Games in Le Jeu de Saint Nicolas," *PMLA* 95.5 (October 1980) 802–11. For a brief critical biography, see Rosalyn Rossignol, "Dinshaw, Carolyn," *Chaucer: A Literary Reference to His Life and Work* (New York: Infobase Publishing, 2007) 410–11.

[5]   Monica E. McAlpine, "Catching the Wave to Canterbury," *College English* 54.5 (September 1992) 601; see also Carolynn Van Dyke, "Amorous Behavior: Sexism, Sin and the Donaldson Persona," *Chaucer Review* 41.3 (2007) 252, 254.

[6]   Dinshaw, *Getting Medieval*, 104.

Carolyn Dinshaw (1957–): The Gendered Reader 113

for the most part, had always considered the "normal" reader to be male, and they did not think about the ways in which a female reader might react differently to a text. An awareness of difference in reader-response between the genders, then, is the first step in envisioning a multiple audience. Dinshaw, in her book *Sexual Poetics*, takes earlier Chaucerians and literary critics to task for their assumption of a universal, homogeneous audience for Chaucer—because, as she points out, that audience is always implicitly white, male and heterosexual. In Chapter 1 of *Sexual Poetics*, she argues that E. Talbot Donaldson and D.W. Robertson are remarkably similar in their approaches to Chaucer, despite their well-known controversies.[7] While I have argued that the similarities between Donaldson's and Robertson's readings are centred in their mutual dependence upon irony, Dinshaw suggests that the two are alike in their gendered methods of reading. Both Donaldson and Robertson (and Kittredge and Lewis, I might add) assume Chaucer's readers were male. In response to these assumptions, Dinshaw imagines a more diverse audience. When Donaldson comments that almost every male reader falls in love with Criseyde, she writes, "This leads to intriguing questions: What about the female reader of this text? Will she love Criseyde, too? Or, as Criseyde herself fears, will women hate Criseyde most of all? What about that male reader who *doesn't* fall for her? Is he not sufficiently 'masculine,' or is he just a churl?"[8] Likewise, Dinshaw explores the way in which Criseyde reads texts, and how the actual women of Chaucer's courtly audience read *Troilus and Criseyde*. She maintains an image of the Wife of Bath as a reader of misogynist, anti-feminist texts throughout Chapter Four of *Sexual Poetics*, and she notes the way in which Petrarch's translation of Boccaccio's story of Griselda out of the vernacular and into Latin excludes women (for whom, according to Boccaccio's conclusion, the *Decameron* was originally intended) from the audience of the tale.

Dinshaw quickly moves from imagining a woman's response to Chaucer's texts into a consideration of the way in which "men" and "women"—or better, "masculine" and "feminine" readers—might read differently, and this becomes the focus for and key interest of her book.[9] More interesting to Dinshaw than the fact that Chaucer's audience is diverse and multiple, and thus contains previously ignored individuals such as women and queers, are the theoretical implications of that multiplicity. Times have changed since Robertson and Donaldson wrote, and Dinshaw takes it relatively for granted that the "norm" for Chaucer's reader is not necessarily a heterosexual man. What she is most interested in are the ramifications of the fact that men *and* women make up Chaucer's audience, and her project in *Sexual Poetics* is to explore the way in which masculine and feminine readers might read differently. She grounds her analysis on the proposition that "reading

---

[7]   See Carolynn Van Dyke for a critique of Dinshaw's reading of Donaldson: "Amorous Behavior," 250–60.

[8]   Dinshaw, *Sexual Poetics*, 37, *emphasis hers*.

[9]   For Dinshaw's discussion of the difference between male/female and masculine/feminine, see Dinshaw, *Sexual Poetics*, 12.

114   *Twentieth-Century Chaucer Criticism*

like a man," or performing a masculine reading on text, has historically been depicted as fundamentally different from "reading like a woman." Traditionally, female readers have been characterized as subjective, irrational and illogical, while male readers are intellectual, rational and objective. Dinshaw retains the poles of this binary opposition, but inverts the hierarchy of values: according to the traditional dichotomy, female readers could be seen as open, tolerant, flexible and sensitive, while male readers are restrictive, controlling, intolerant and insensitive. In other words, Dinshaw accepts the characterizations of "masculine reading" and "feminine reading" which patriarchy establishes, but inverts the patriarchal evaluation of the merits of each way of reading.

According to this newly-valued opposition, Robertson and Donaldson, despite their "diametrically opposed theoretical principles," are alike because they both "read like men."[10] Not only do they assume Chaucer's reader is male, but their *methods* are masculine. That is, in their readings of *Troilus and Criseyde*, they try to impose a "firm control" on the dangerously "slyding" Criseyde, and this is paralleled by their attempts to impose a similar control on the dangerously sliding text.[11] Donaldson, according to Dinshaw, "eagerly participates in the emotional vicissitudes of the narrative," while Robertson "urgently resists such subjectivity as he tries to escape solipsism." Nevertheless, a "pervasive literary structure subtend[s] and inform[s] their contrasting projects," and this is the inherited patriarchal structure of literary activity. Each performs "masculine" readings of *Troilus and Criseyde*, but in the end each presents those readings as neuter and normative.[12] Other readers of *Troilus and Criseyde* have performed similar moves: Dinshaw argues that Henrysson's sequel to Chaucer's poem, *The Testament of Cressid*, was motivated by the need to "finish off the narrative by finishing off Criseyde"—again the desire to close down and limit the "slyding" of the text is linked with the need to constrain and limit the feminine.[13] It is the presentation of a "masculine" reading as normative which is dangerous, and Dinshaw states that a "denaturalization" of the masculine response—the recognition that there might be other perspectives, other responses or ways of reading, than the dominant one—is the first step of a feminist analysis. Only once it is recognized that the "masculine" response is neither natural nor universal can the question of what it might be to "read like a woman" arise.

"Reading like a man" and "reading like a woman," in Dinshaw's theory, are not different-but-neutral ways of approaching a text, but take on ideological significance. "Reading like a man" is totalizing, controlling, and, ultimately, negative, while "reading like a woman" is inclusive, disruptive of totalitarianism,

---

[10]   Ibid., 28.

[11]   Ibid., 28.

[12]   Ibid., 28ff. My analysis of the "masculine" nature of Donaldson's "careful reader" in chapter 3 parallels Dinshaw's understanding of Donaldson in many ways.

[13]   Ibid., 67.

Carolyn Dinshaw (1957–): The Gendered Reader 115

and, therefore, ultimately positive. This hierarchy of reading—an inversion from the traditional patriarchal hierarchy—is clear in Dinshaw's definitions:

> To "read like a man" in this poem is to impose a structure that resolves or occludes contradictions and disorder, fulfills the need for wholeness. It is to constrain, control, or eliminate outright the feminine—carnal love, the letter of the text—in order to provide a single, solid, univalent meaning firmly fixed in a hierarchical moral structure. Donaldson, Robertson, the narrator, Pandarus, Troilus all read like men: they invoke structures of authority in order to order the disorder, to stop the restless desire represented in and enacted by their texts, to find rest.[14]

"Reading like a man" is "constituted by opposition, by exclusion, by oppressive mastery and consequent constriction"—indeed, the "hierarchical moral structure" of Dinshaw's own politics is self-evident in the terms she uses.[15] In retaining the binary opposition she has inherited from patriarchy—despite the fact that she inverts its ideological valence—Dinshaw's work runs the risk of preserving the same essentialism that she objects to in patriarchal structures.[16] Although she tries to avoid such essentialism by claiming that "reading like a man" and "reading like a woman" are categories for practices of reading, and that men can read like women and vice versa, nonetheless she perpetuates the patriarchal definitions of masculine and feminine and the absolute nature of the distinction between them. Nevertheless, this perception of multiple audiences, and Dinshaw's development of the categories of "masculine" and "feminine" reading, allow her to shape a unique understanding of Chaucer. She argues throughout *Sexual Poetics* that not only is *she* exploring the *Canterbury Tales* and Chaucer's other works in terms of the gendered nature of reading, but that *Chaucer* is performing precisely the same experiment. In his works, Dinshaw suggests, Chaucer explores the gendered nature of reading he has inherited from the patriarchal structures he inhabits, and considers the real, lived effects of that gendering. The entire project of the *Canterbury Tales*, *Troilus and Criseyde* and *The Legend of Good Women* is, according to Dinshaw, an experiment in the theory of audience reception and response. It is an investigation which Chaucer himself is performing into the nature of reading and interpretation.

---

[14] Ibid., 51.

[15] Ibid., 63.

[16] For criticism of this aspect of Dinshaw's theory, see Pearsall's review of *Sexual Poetics:* Derek Pearsall, "Review of *Chaucer's Sexual Poetics*," *Speculum* 67.1 (January 1992) 134–8; and the discussion in Stephanie Trigg, *Congenial Souls: Reading Chaucer from Medieval to Postmodern* (Minneapolis: University of Minnesota Press, 2002) 216–20.

Reading Readers

Chaucer's investigation takes two forms: first, Chaucer considers and depicts his own characters as *readers*, and therefore performs an analysis of the nature, function and workings of audience through them; second, Chaucer uses his characters as metaphors for texts, textuality, and the reading process. So, in her consideration of *Troilus and Criseyde*, Dinshaw argues that Troilus, Pandarus, and the narrator are *readers* just as Donaldson and Robertson are, and that Chaucer depicts them as such. The narrator is a reader of the story of Troilus and Criseyde which he is retelling for us, Pandarus "reads [Troilus and Criseyde] as if *they* constituted 'an old romaunce,'"[17] and Troilus both literally reads Criseyde's letters and figuratively "reads" Criseyde herself. All of these readers, Dinshaw argues, read in the same way that Donaldson and Robertson read: they read, that is, "like men." Dinshaw goes on to ask,

> But if that's "reading like a man," what might it be to "read like a woman"? Is there any alternative to this masculine reading response suggested in the poem? Is there such a thing in this work as a feminine response? To begin to answer these questions, we must turn now to Criseyde, for she is not only a text read but is herself a reader.[18]

As we can see, not only does Dinshaw explore the multiplicity of Chaucer's audience, but she believes Chaucer himself does the same. Criseyde's methods of reading are fundamentally different from Troilus's and Pandarus's: she "tak[es] in every word" without closing down the text, so her response "keeps the whole in view," instead of excluding possible responses or options, and thus she enacts the way "reading like a woman" is different from "reading like a man."[19] Alceste and Cupid, in the *Legend of Good Women*, are also readers: they read *Troilus and Criseyde* and react negatively, demanding from Chaucer a tale of good women. According to Dinshaw, these characters for the most part "read like men." They want "entirely totalizing literary activity" which leaves little room for ambiguity or variety of interpretation.[20] Again, Dinshaw uses the categorization she has inherited from patriarchy to classify styles of reading, which do not necessarily accord with the actual sex of the reader. Chaucer, in the *Legend of Good Women*, is re-enacting in fiction the response of actual readers to his stories, and exploring the intricacies of their culturally-determined and gendered responses as he does so. Alceste and the women in Chaucer's audience, therefore, are women who "read like men." Chaucer's Clerk, by contrast, is a man who "reads like a woman." He, too, is a reader, a reader and translator of Petrarch (who in turn is a reader

---

[17] Dinshaw, *Sexual Poetics*, 49, *emphasis hers*.

[18] Ibid., 52.

[19] Ibid., 54.

[20] Ibid., 70.

of Boccaccio). Moreover, he is a reader who "is profoundly concerned with the social effects of literary activity."[21] The Clerk's reading of the story of Griselda opens up the multiplicity of audience which Dinshaw argues is the first stage in avoiding totalizing patriarchal reading strategies: he imagines how Griselda feels, identifies with her, and shows up the violence that male "translation" can cause. The Clerk's relationship to Petrarch is a fictionalization of Chaucer's own relationship with his sources, of course, and Dinshaw suggests that through the Clerk, Chaucer can explore new methods of reading that escape and question the patriarchal hermeneutic. Against Petrarch's allegorization of the Griselda story— which discounts or explains away the suffering Griselda undergoes in favour of a totalizing, complacent allegorical meaning—the Clerk insists on bringing to the fore the particularity of Griselda's experience. Rather than "reading" Griselda allegorically or figuratively, that is, the Clerk "reads" her literally, refusing to subsume the details of the narrative within a redemptive moral. The Clerk reads "like a woman," because he reads with an "eye to what is left out of the very reading he is performing."[22] Dinshaw also argues, like Robertson, that there are readers *within* the individual tales as well as within the *Canterbury Tales* as a whole. Griselda is not only a "text" read by the Clerk but a reader as well: she "reads" herself allegorically, "as a religious symbol, moral allegorical image."[23] The rioters of the Pardoner's Tale are poor readers, since they read everything too literally, and it is their inability to understand that Death is a personified concept and not a literal person which leads to their deaths. The knight in the Wife of Bath's Tale is a "brash reader," for his rape of the maiden parallels the way in which an ignorant reader "violat[es] and manhandl[es] secrets more properly left veiled" in a text.[24]

In these final examples, we can see the way in which Dinshaw slips almost imperceptibly from one level to another of Chaucer's exploration of the reading process and the problematics of audience interpretation. Unlike Criseyde, whom we actually see reading, or the Wife of Bath, who interprets and re-tells the works she has been read out of Jankyn's book, or the Clerk, who clearly engages with Petrarch's poem (to the point of citing the poet by name), the knight of the Wife of Bath's Tale and the rioters of the Pardoner's Tale are not *actual* readers. We do not see them reading texts, or interpreting doctrines they have heard. Instead, they are *metaphorical* readers. This is the third level of Dinshaw's understanding of Chaucer's audience: as well as the actual readers of Chaucer's works, as well as the readers depicted within the stories and tales, the characters and events function as a theoretical exploration of the workings of the act of reading. In this, Dinshaw's interpretation adopts much the same framework as Robertson's: both see Chaucer's characters as metaphorical "readers" of the world around them.

---

[21]   Ibid., 133.

[22]   Ibid., 154.

[23]   Ibid., 146.

[24]   Ibid., 128.

Both, for example, describe the rioters of the Pardoner's Tale as overly literal "readers," concerned only with the "letter of the text" and who deny the spiritual or figurative understanding of the world. However, while Robertson divides these metaphorical readers into "good readers" and "bad readers," and sees them as exempla teaching the proper ways of reading, Dinshaw is more interested in the way in which the concept of interpretation is figured as gendered in Chaucer's characters and stories—although she too implicitly codes her categories in moral terms: "good readers" read like women, and "bad readers" read like men.[25]

Dinshaw takes as her starting point the medieval patristic theories of the hermeneutic process, and notes that descriptions of these are often gendered. She writes that the "variety, range, and popularity in the Middle Ages of works which represent literary activity by means of gendered models argue for the fundamental nature of this correlation between the use and interpretation of language, on the one hand, and the social relations and organization of gendered bodies, on the other hand."[26] Medieval writers describe texts, especially allegorical ones, in gendered terms. The (male) reader, seduced by the pleasing literal level of the text, must remove this veil in order to access the truth—"a body figuratively represented as female."[27] At the same time, the literal level of the text is associated with the feminine, the carnal, and the fleshly, and its misleading seductions must be discarded or avoided if one is to reach the truth. The story from Deuteronomy of the beautiful captive women was used by St. Jerome, and throughout the Middle Ages, as an allegory justifying the reading of pagan texts. Texts were figured as female bodies, written upon, decorated, and used by male scribes and readers. Dinshaw shows that terms for reading, interpretation and writing overlap with terms for the acts of love, courtship or sex: the language of hermeneutics and the language of eroticism invariably intertwine. Because of this, "erotic models of literary activity provide us with some broadly based ways to read power relations between *auctores*, narrators, and readers."[28] Because the two discourses, eroticism and hermeneutics, are so similar, and because the acts scribes or readers perform on texts are described in terms of the acts men perform on female bodies, narratives of the relationship between men and women can be used allegorically to represent the interpretative process—and this, Dinshaw argues, is precisely what Chaucer does. Moreover, this exploration is political: Dinshaw suggests that Chaucer engages with the received terms of the patristic tradition in order to explore the consequences for literary tradition, but also to discern the "effects on lived lives"

---

[25] Geoffrey Gust criticizes this kind of moralizing in Dinshaw's scholarship, because he sees it as the critic reading Chaucer's characters as though they have "lives of their own": Geoffrey Gust, *Constructing Chaucer: Author and Autofiction in the Critical Tradition* (New York: Palgrave Macmillan, 2009) 127–9.

[26] Dinshaw, *Sexual Poetics*, 14.

[27] Ibid., 21.

[28] Ibid., 15.

Carolyn Dinshaw (1957–): The Gendered Reader 119

of a hermeneutic framework which envisions literary endeavour as "masculine acts performed on feminine bodies."[29]

Therefore, while some of Chaucer's characters are themselves literal audiences or readers—Criseyde, the Clerk, Alceste and Cupid—others allegorically enact the hermeneutic process in their narratives. Dinshaw, through the image of the captive barbarian woman, links the transfer of women, which forms the basis for Lévi-Strauss's anthropological paradigm of society, with the transfer of texts from reader to reader. Constance, in the Man of Law's Tale, is a figure of the movement of stories (and, indeed, her story begins with a literal enactment of the same thing, as the story of her beauty travels with the merchants), while Griselda, in the Clerk's Tale, in her "translations" from her father to Walter and back again, becomes an allegory for the translated text. The Clerk, in emphasizing the violence done to Griselda and the suffering she undergoes, metaphorically raises the question of the violence of translation—the way in which "*translatio* can indeed function to exclude, to turn away from something."[30] The story of Griselda, therefore, and the way in which the Clerk reads both the text of Petrarch's tale of Griselda and Griselda herself, give Chaucer a way of investigating and questioning the hidden implications of traditional theories of translation.[31]

The Wife of Bath, too, as well as being a reader of texts, is herself a metaphor for textuality: she is "glossed" by her lovers in the way a text is glossed, and both kinds of glossing work to limit and constrain the feminine/the text. The Wife can be interpreted to represent the "desire" of the text—its movements, its sliding, its ambiguity—which, like feminine desire, cannot be fully controlled or restrained by the reader. In the Wife's Tale, furthermore, there is another level of metaphorical reading: the raping knight can be taken to represent the violent, ignorant reader who reads only for the carnal, literal level of the story, and who is later taught to "unveil" the text properly to access the truth beneath, to see beyond the "ugly hag" of difficult understanding to gain a true appreciation of the beautiful body beneath. The Wife of Bath, Dinshaw argues, thus presents through her tale an idealized re-casting of the patriarchal hermeneutic, one which does not challenge the terms of that hermeneutic but nonetheless leaves space for feminine desire (and literal reading). Finally, Dinshaw reads the Pardoner as embodying a radical rethinking of the patriarchal hermeneutic, a suggestion that the traditional, fundamental division between "surface" level and "inner" meaning is an illusion:

> Put in hermeneutic terms, the Pardoner's clothed body suggests that the existence of the letter of the text does not at all ensure the existence of a spirit, a truth beneath it. In fact, the Pardoner opens out another—unnerving—possible

---

[29] Ibid., 25.

[30] Ibid., 154.

[31] In this reading of Griselda as an allegorical figure, Dinshaw comes perilously close to doing the very thing she praises the Clerk for not doing—de-individualizing Griselda and removing the particularity of her suffering.

120   *Twentieth-Century Chaucer Criticism*

hermeneutic significance of the image of the body swaddled in veils: there is perhaps *nothing* underneath those cloaks of representation. There might be nothing but veils and letters covering a fundamental absence, a radical lack of meaning or truth.[32]

The Pardoner's physical lack—his eunuchry or homosexuality—figures a hermeneutic lack: it exposes the flaw in the patriarchal metaphor of the feminine text by suggesting that underneath the captive woman's literal clothing or carnality there might be nothing meaningful at all. In other words, the "emptiness" beneath the Pardoner's clothing figures the suggestion that texts might be nothing but endless plays of signifiers, with nothing beneath—no signified, no point of origin, no "truth." In this way, throughout the *Canterbury Tales* Chaucer figuratively and allegorically explores the hermeneutic process through his equation of female characters with the (traditionally) feminine text, acted upon by male characters and male readers. The Pardoner, as the only male character to fill this allegorical role as text, calls the entire metaphor into question, and enables Chaucer to envision a hermeneutic which does not depend upon a gendered metaphor. The characters in the *Canterbury Tales* are not one-dimensional—they work at the literal level of the tales as well, as individuals with psychology and "interiority"—but they also function as "embodiments or reifications of patristic images and hermeneutic ideas," and are thus used to explore, analyze, and undercut those patristic theories of hermeneutics.[33]

Dinshaw's concept of audience, therefore, undergirds her interpretation of Chaucer. Her understanding of all reading, and all readers, as fundamentally gendered leads her to perform an analysis of the way in which Chaucer presents the gendered nature of reading, and questions or challenges the models he has received from the hermeneutic tradition. Dinshaw's image of Chaucer's real audience is multiple and diverse. It arises out of the question of how reading might be different for a man as for a woman. This, in turn, leads her to a consideration of the way in which Chaucer presents the practices of reading, and to an understanding of the medieval depiction of those practices as gendered. Reading—especially as it is presented in the Middle Ages—is figured as gendered, and thus all reading is essentially political. How an audience reads is determined ideologically, which Dinshaw describes in terms of gender: "masculine" reading and "feminine" reading are essentially ideological stances, practices which either include or ignore marginalized and repressed figures. Chaucer's depiction of this ideological valence of reading in his works, therefore, is read as a challenge to his audience: Chaucer's readers are encouraged to reconsider their own reading practices in light of the allegories of reading given through the characters of the stories. This turn, interestingly, puts Dinshaw in line with Robertson in many ways, for it means that she assumes, like Robertson, that Chaucer's audience would read his

---

[32] Dinshaw, *Sexual Poetics*, 157.
[33] Ibid., 26.

Carolyn Dinshaw (1957–): The Gendered Reader   121

works at several levels, both literally and allegorically. The idea that Chaucer's own works allegorically figure a reading process which his audience itself enacts in deciphering that allegory likewise parallels Robertson in many ways, as do the moral valuations Dinshaw puts on "good" and "bad" reading practices.

The Erotics of Reading

This understanding of reading as invariably gendered, which runs throughout *Sexual Poetics*, turns, in *Getting Medieval*, published a decade later, into a fully-developed theory of reading and interpretation dependent upon concepts of eroticism and sensuality. As Dinshaw shows in her discussion of medieval hermeneutic theories in *Sexual Poetics*, metaphors for the reading process are almost always eroticized. In *Getting Medieval*, she turns these erotically-laced metaphors to her own use. She proposes a theory or method of interpretation that is explicitly eroticized, one that depends upon metaphors of touching and bodily contact. This approach draws on the theories of Roland Barthes and Homi Bhabha. Interestingly, however, as we have seen, this metaphor is also profoundly medieval, for its eroticism gestures towards the eroticism Dinshaw traces in the medieval metaphor of the text as a veiled woman. The "queer historical touch," as Dinshaw calls it, is both diachronic and synchronic: it is a "desire for bodies to touch across time" but also a way in which the disparate political entities in the present-day United States can form coalitions and communities.[34] This method of reception of medieval texts—"touch" as a metaphor for reading and analysis—depends upon some radical assumptions in terms of audience.

For example, this theory of "touching" shows that Dinshaw's understanding of Chaucer's audience is multiple not only synchronically but diachronically. Her concept of audience includes not just men *and* women, but medievals *and* moderns. The discussion of "reading like a man" in *Sexual Poetics* clearly shows this multiplicity of audience. In her category of "readers," Dinshaw includes modern readers such as Donaldson and Robertson—and herself—alongside medieval "readers" such as Troilus and Pandarus and the aristocratic women at court; men such as Pandarus or Donaldson and women such as Criseyde and herself; "real" readers such as modern critics and medieval courtiers, and fictional "readers" such as Alceste, Cupid, and Troilus. More importantly, she explores the unique, particularized, individual reading practices of each. Dinshaw's multiple audience thus includes a cross-historical dimension: medieval and modern individuals are equally readers of Chaucer, just as men and women are.

Dinshaw's metaphor of reading as "touch" suggests a method of analysis which is emotional, emotive, and affective. Unlike the scholarly, intellectual methodology of Robertson's approach to the past, or Donaldson's detailed close reading techniques, Dinshaw aims to make "histories"—and the plural is important here—

---

[34] Dinshaw, *Getting Medieval*, 3, 54.

122   *Twentieth-Century Chaucer Criticism*

"manifest" through "juxtaposition" alone.[35] This "juxtaposition" is not merely emotional but overtly erotic: queer history "creates a relation across time that has an affective or an erotic component," and historians, through writing, "'touch' bodies across time."[36] Perhaps it is this erotic component of the kind of history Dinshaw performs which makes it "feminine reading" or "queer history": feminist theorists have long argued that female bodies, queer bodies, touch themselves and each other in ways that normative, male bodies do not.[37] The metaphor of "touch" carries different connotations from the usual metaphors for interpretation. Instead of "devouring" a novel or "absorbing" a text, "digesting" an argument, "taking in" a movie, or "grasping" a theory, "touch" indicates a connection which does not depend upon one entity subsuming the other. It aims, according to Dinshaw, to intimate a theory of reading which is not exploitative or appropriative, but which attempts to understand a text while leaving that text its own identity, voice, and being. In this theory of reading, neither text nor reader is dominant or exclusively controlling; instead, each shares in the creation of interpretation through "touch."

As we can see, another assumption about reading is present here: that reading or history is a connection between two *individuals*, the individual in the present and the text, character, or person from the past. The modern historian does not try to "touch" some larger-than-life entity like "the medieval mind"; instead, she desires to touch one medieval individual in all that individual's particularity and specificity. Likewise, her own individuality and historical situatedness is both ever-present and theoretically significant. Dinshaw, more than any other author studied in this thesis, turns her own situation (in her case, as a "marginalized" individual) to theoretical purpose. In *Getting Medieval*, she uses her identity as a queer academic to make connections with medieval figures such as Margery Kempe or John/Eleanor Rykener. She also uses the attacks on her National Endowment for the Humanities-supported summer institute "Sex and Gender in the Middle Ages" as a springboard for a discussion about gender and medievalism in American society. In the article "Pale Faces" Dinshaw turns to another aspect of her own identity, her descent from an East Indian paternal heritage, to discuss the concept of "paleness" and its attendant racial and physiological connotations, in both medieval and modern society. She opens another article, the article "New Approaches to Chaucer," with the sub-heading "Chaucer at Ground Zero" and the sentence, "This essay was begun on the day that the last load of debris was removed from the site of the World Trade Center disaster of September 11, 2001"—

---

[35]   Ibid., 12.

[36]   Ibid., 50, 47.

[37]   Although Dinshaw only explicitly uses Luce Irigaray's theory of mimicry (see Dinshaw, *Sexual Poetics*, 115–16), the concept of "touch" as a specifically "feminine" method of reading seems to draw some of its affective metaphorical force from Irigaray's descriptions of women's bodies in *Ce Sexe Qui N'est Pas Un* as entities which are never single, but always touching, always multiple: see Luce Irigaray, *This Sex Which Is Not One*, trans. Catherine Porter (Ithaca: Cornell University Press, 1985).

here, Dinshaw's situation as an American academic in New York post-September 11th works as a ground and basis for a study of racism and religion in Chaucer's Man of Law's Tale. These emphases on the individuality and situatedness of both the reader and the "read" (the medieval text, character or individual) go hand-in-hand with the multiplicity of audience Dinshaw envisions. Audiences both present and past are imagined as individual, singular, and unique. The task of the modern historian or reader is to "touch" and understand that past individual without misrepresenting, misreading, or destroying that person's uniqueness. The uniqueness of the reader's situation and identity in the present become tools in that process of touching without exploitation or appropriation.[38]

Trans-historical Criticism

The concept of "touching," therefore, places Dinshaw in an interesting position with reference to the other critics in this study. Up to this point, I have categorized critics according to their attitude to history, or the distance between modern and medieval audiences: Kittredge and Donaldson both collapse historical distance, positing a universalized, timeless audience for Chaucer, while Lewis and Robertson emphasize the historical distance between medieval and modern times, and argue that the medieval interpretation is the only correct one. Dinshaw would be allied with Kittredge and Donaldson, since she would not maintain that a medieval response is the only "right" response; however, she would insist on the historical distance and the distinctness of readers medieval and modern. Dinshaw clearly differentiates Chaucer's medieval audience from his modern audience, and an awareness of this historical distance informs her criticism. Thus she characterizes the audience of *The Legend of Good Women* as a "courtly audience," conservative in their tastes and desirous of "simplicity and closure," along with conventional morality, in the stories they read or listened to.[39] This image of Chaucer's medieval audience greatly affects Dinshaw's interpretation, for she reads *The Legend of Good Women* as Chaucer's performing an exercise in writing such a conventional story, and demonstrating the ideological problems with the genre. Alceste and the God of Love, in *The Legend*, are, for Dinshaw, representations (albeit exaggerated) of Chaucer's real readers. Dinshaw thus reads *The Legend of Good Women* biographically and historically, as Chaucer's response to a real demand placed upon him by his audience. In other instances, too, Dinshaw uses the historical circumstances of Chaucer's actual audience to inform her readings: this audience would have been "comfortably familiar" with

---

[38]   See below for a critique of the problems of this methodology of "touching"—if it can be called a methodology at all, since Dinshaw does not clearly describe her methods nor explain how other people might replicate them.

[39]   Dinshaw, *Sexual Poetics*, 66–7. Cf. Carolyn Dinshaw, "Chaucer's Queer Touches/ A Queer Touches Chaucer," *Exemplaria* 7.1 (1995) 90.

124 *Twentieth-Century Chaucer Criticism*

episodic romances and hagiographies, and thus would have been less bewildered than a modern audience by the disorderly Man of Law's Tale. The Cook's Tale is contextualized with reference to a real court case from medieval London, and she notes that the discourse of the Pardoner's Tale, with its Lollard references and overtones, picks up on "a lively issue current among Chaucer's audience."[40] More importantly, Dinshaw turns to a wealth of medieval writers and thinkers to develop her readings, including St. Augustine, Richard of Bury, Robert of Basevorn, Ranulph Higden, Peter Abelard, Guibert of Nogent, Alain de Lille, Thomas Aquinas, Giovanni Boccaccio, Francesco Petrarch, Dante Alighieri, John Gower, John Wycliffe, and Christine de Pizan. The entire argument of *Sexual Poetics*, in which Dinshaw juxtaposes sexuality with textuality and considers the ramifications of interpretation and hermeneutics in terms of gender politics, depends upon a medieval image of hermeneutic practice: the idea of the literal level of the text as feminine, the reader as masculine, unveiling or stripping the carnal text to reveal the spiritual truth beneath.[41] Dinshaw thus contextualizes her reading of Chaucer both in terms of the actual history of England in Chaucer's time and in terms of the writings he and his audience would have known, the overarching metaphor she uses (the erotic text) is medieval, and she often draws on historical information about Chaucer's medieval audience to ground her interpretation.[42]

At the same time, however, Dinshaw's project is cross-historical, since it aims to cross the historical distance between then and now, to place medieval and modern responses side by side and make them comment upon one another, make them "touch." Alongside Augustine, Boethius and Boccaccio, Dinshaw draws on modern feminist theorists (Luce Irigaray, Julia Kristeva, Gayle Rubin, Sandra Gilbert, Susan Gubar, Simone de Beauvoir, Judith Butler), modern psychoanalytical theorists (Sigmund Freud, Jacques Lacan), and modern philosophers (Paul Ricoeur, Jacques Derrida). Much of the argument of *Sexual Poetics* depends upon the anthropological theories of the exchange in women developed by Claude Levi-Strauss, while *Getting Medieval* draws heavily on the approaches of Roland Barthes and the post-colonial theories of Homi Bhabha. As the page devoted to him in the bibliography of *Getting Medieval* attests, Michel Foucault also looms large in Dinshaw's theoretical grounding. As a result of this wide-ranging assemblage of theories both medieval and modern, Dinshaw's prose often contains an eclectic mix of terms: psychoanalytical terms such as "fetish," "radical desire," "psychological valence" or "substitute objects" are found in the same paragraph as medieval words such as "relics," "cupiditas" and "caritas."[43] The Pardoner's

---

[40]   Dinshaw, *Getting Medieval*, 115.

[41]   Dinshaw, *Sexual Poetics*, 14, 21 and throughout; cf. McAlpine, "Catching the Wave," 601.

[42]   See, however, Dinshaw's later critique of the historicist project: "there is no pure moment of contemporaneity within which to situate Chaucer's texts." Dinshaw, "New Approaches," 275.

[43]   Dinshaw, *Sexual Poetics*, 159.

Carolyn Dinshaw (1957–): The Gendered Reader 125

belief that his relics and documents can incorporate him into the group of pilgrims and the community of Christianity is described, some would say anachronistically, as a "fetishistic belief"; and Dinshaw compares the Pardoner to Oscar Wilde.[44] Dinshaw, obviously, has no compunction about using modern theories or terms to illuminate medieval literature. Indeed, even her chapter headings reflect this merging of medieval and modern: Dinshaw pilfers from pop song lyrics and titles for her chapter titles and sub-titles—"Good Vibrations," "Don't Leave Me This Way," "(You Make Me Feel) Mighty Real."[45]

Despite this cross-historical approach, Dinshaw insists on maintaining the distinctions between periods, on maintaining their integrity as separate "bodies." Dinshaw would not subscribe to a concept like "universal human nature" in the way that Kittredge, Donaldson, and, occasionally, Lewis do, in part because her political project is to change society and the way in which people view gender. Characteristics and attributes which have formerly been viewed as part of "human nature"—such as heterosexuality or the inferiority of women—are argued by Dinshaw to be historically contingent and culturally inflected. Nevertheless, because she believes that both medieval and modern societies are structured and conditioned by patriarchy, Dinshaw would consider many aspects of human nature to be constant from medieval times to now. Especially in terms of the way in which language and interpretation works, Dinshaw argues, "there is a continuity of such patriarchal thinking about signifying ... modern articulations are inflections of a very long patriarchal tradition of understanding language and literary activity."[46] Difference, Dinshaw writes, "in our male-dominated culture, is always gendered feminine."[47] Likewise, the exchange in women described by Levi-Strauss was operative in both medieval and modern societies, and "constitutes society as we know it."[48] Levi-Strauss "belongs in a long ideological tradition of which [Chaucer's] Man of Law is an early, card-carrying member," Dinshaw states, and because of this long ideological tradition, ideas which are really historically situated can seem universal.[49] The modern "story" of psychoanalysis, with its "myth of original loss and the desire for restitution," is similarly part of the same tradition as Christianity, which is informed by the same originary myth.[50] In the same way, the castration anxiety Dinshaw describes with reference to the

---

[44]   Dinshaw, *Getting Medieval*, 159, 161; 125.

[45]   Ibid., 100, 165, 136. Likewise, Dinshaw used a handout with a picture of k.d. lang and Cindy Crawford on the cover of *Vanity Fair* as an introduction to a paper about the Pardoner and Chaucer: Dinshaw, "Chaucer's Queer Touches," 75.

[46]   Dinshaw, *Sexual Poetics*, 16.

[47]   Carolyn Dinshaw, "Quarrels, Rivals, and Rape: Gower and Chaucer," *A Wyf Ther Was: Essays in Honour of Paule Mertens-Fonck*, ed. Juliette Dor (Liege: Department of Language and Literature, Liege, 1992) 115.

[48]   Dinshaw, *Sexual Poetics*, 56.

[49]   Ibid., 96.

[50]   Ibid., 165.

126   *Twentieth-Century Chaucer Criticism*

Pardoner is neither "universal" nor "natural," but "it does accurately account for the cultural construction of gender and the gendering of culture in Western patriarchal society."[51] Dinshaw, therefore, occupies a distinctive position with regards to historicity and historicism. In principle, she would oppose the concept of a "universal human nature" to which Kittredge and Donaldson subscribe. In practice, since medieval society and modern society are both patriarchal and heterosexual, she would argue there are many continuities and commonalities between then and now. At the same time, Dinshaw is extremely concerned with historicity and the specificity of particular historical moments, because through a demonstration of medieval workings of power and social influence she can show that aspects of modern American society are not "universal" or "natural" but similarly historically contingent and situated.

Political Literary Criticism

Dinshaw's cross-historical project, therefore, goes beyond the use of modern theories to inform readings of medieval literature. She also wants to use medieval theories and attitudes to inform a reading of modern society. She asks, "How does Chaucer matter now? How does reading Chaucer's texts relate to the world in which we live?"[52] Her project is as much an analysis of modern society as it is a reading of medieval texts: in *Sexual Poetics*, as discussed above, she devotes part of a chapter to the critics E. Talbot Donaldson and D.W. Robertson, and analyzes both in the same terms in which she analyzes Pandarus, Troilus and the narrator of *Troilus and Criseyde*. She argues that a "medieval philosophical tradition" informs "modern theoretical preoccupations and formulations," and thus although Chaucer's literary concerns "may sound quite modern," the reality may instead be that the critical literary theory of the present is "quite medieval."[53] In another instance, she suggests that the Man of Law's Tale "crucially corrects" Edward Said's *Orientalism*.[54] In *Getting Medieval* she juxtaposes studies of *The Book of Margery Kempe*, the Pardoner's Tale, and medieval legal documents with studies of the modern novel *Margery Kempe* by Robert Glück, United States Congressional debates on the role of Medieval Studies in universities, and the Quentin Tarantino movie *Pulp Fiction*. She explicitly places her study of the Man of Law's Tale in the context of post-September 11th America, implying that the racial, religious and geographical issues of Chaucer's time offer a way to comment on similar issues in

---

[51]   Ibid., 167.

[52]   Dinshaw, "New Approaches," 271. Dinshaw's asks the same kinds of questions with reference to Margery Kempe: Carolyn Dinshaw, "Margery Kempe," *The Cambridge Companion to Medieval Women's Writing*, ed. Carolyn Dinshaw and David Wallace (Cambridge: Cambridge University Press, 2003) 236.

[53]   Dinshaw, *Sexual Poetics*, 17.

[54]   Dinshaw, "New Approaches," 273.

Carolyn Dinshaw (1957–): The Gendered Reader 127

our own time. This juxtaposition, this use of modern theories to inform medieval texts, and, conversely, medieval stories and characters to analyze modern society, Dinshaw dubs "queer history." The "queer historical impulse," she writes, on the first page of the introduction to *Getting Medieval*, is "an impulse toward making connections across time between, on the one hand, lives, texts, and other cultural phenomena left out of sexual categories back then and, on the other, those left out of current sexual categories now."[55] In this concept she is drawing heavily on Roland Barthes, seeing in his work a "queer historical touch," a desire for "bodies to touch across time."[56]

The impetus behind Dinshaw's project is highly political, but it works on two levels. On one level, she acknowledges the validity and importance of gay history such as that done by John Boswell in his book *Christianity, Social Tolerance, and Homosexuality*, in arguing for and tracing a community of homosexual individuals throughout history. She is interested in continuing this project, in "making relations with the past," making "affective connections" across time with people in similar situations or with similar identities, who share a "marginality, a queer positionality."[57] Late twentieth-century novelists such as Robert Glück and Allen Barnett who draw on medieval figures like the Pardoner or Margery Kempe for inspiration are attracted to them because of their "shared marginality, their shared uncategorizability."[58] Likewise, Dinshaw links herself and Margery Kempe, stating "Margery and I are both queer—in different ways, in relation to our very different surroundings—and are thus queerly related to one another."[59] In the same way, John/Eleanor Rykener, a figure described in a medieval court case (a man who dressed as a woman and made a living as a prostitute) "haunts" the normative fourteenth-century culture of medieval London in a way comparable to the way in which Dinshaw herself "haunt[s]" the "normative household in current United States culture."[60] This historical project, of discovering individuals like oneself in the past, can help create selfhood and identity for queer historians such as Dinshaw in the present.

On another level, however, Dinshaw critiques projects such as Boswell's, and advocates a different sort of "queer" history. Rather than attempting to find homosexuals (defined in modern terms) in medieval society, and thus create a cohesive history of gay identity, she wants instead to demonstrate how all such definitions and categories are historically situated and contingent. By analyzing the ways in which medieval culture defined and differentiated its marginal figures,

---

[55]   Dinshaw, *Getting Medieval*, 1.

[56]   Ibid., 3; cf. 12. Dinshaw is also benefiting from Homi Bhabha in developing a theory that will allow "the possibility of contact between linguistic fragments across time"; Dinshaw, *Getting Medieval*, 21.

[57]   Dinshaw, *Getting Medieval*, 11, 39; cf. 21–2.

[58]   Ibid., 114; cf. 141.

[59]   Ibid., 158; cf. Dinshaw, "New Approaches," 274.

[60]   Dinshaw, *Getting Medieval*, 138; cf. 142.

128 *Twentieth-Century Chaucer Criticism*

she can show how modern American culture forms its own marginalizations in similar terms and deploys similar strategies—and thus that those definitions and categorizations are not "universal," "natural" or "essential." What she calls "queerness" is always defined in relation to "normal" society, and the dominant culture uses such definitions and exclusions in forming and maintaining its own identity and community. So, for example, by demonstrating the equivocal nature of medieval discourses of persecution (of heretics, of sodomites), Dinshaw can "deligitimate" modern Western discourses which claim that "religious and sexual discrimination now in the United States or the United Kingdom are based on simple historical precedents."[61] Moreover, and importantly for a medievalist, one of the "queer" categories against which modern American society defines itself is "the medieval": in the movie *Pulp Fiction*, the slang phrase "getting medieval" is used to designate everything modern American society considers itself not to be—brutal, violent, undemocratic. As Dinshaw shows in her analysis, "medieval" stands in for a slew of undesirables—blacks, hicks, sodomites, perverts. In thus rejecting the medieval, the modern United States protects itself from the challenges and questioning that a recognition of the historical contingency of so-called "universal" values would bring. Likewise, in the rhetoric deployed after the attacks on the World Trade Center on 11 September 2001, the concept of "the medieval" was evoked as a way of differentiating the "backward" terrorists from "modern" America. Dinshaw proposes appropriating and inverting the phrase "getting medieval" to mean "making partial connections between incommensurate entities," for example between marginalized medieval figures and modern political advocates for sexual freedom and academic freedom of speech.[62] The Pardoner, for example, can "offer an image now of the queer historian" in the way in which he "tot[es] his relics of lives past and flash[es] them before a desiring public."[63] And in the spirit of Margery Kempe, Dinshaw calls for "preaching," for political action "in which such abjected figures as queers and scholars of early periods are armed and empowered in the fray of the culture wars."[64] Dinshaw's concept of Chaucer's audience, therefore, emphatically includes *herself*, and her role as "audience" is crucial to her engagement with contemporary politics.

In her work, Dinshaw clearly wants to turn the past to political purposes of present, in a way that could be seen as appropriative or exploitative. Dinshaw's "touches" are deliberate and calculated, and in many ways self-interested: by "touching" specific people and incidents in the past, she can question and unsettle the certainties and complacencies of American society in the present, and thus advance her own political goals. "I have my agenda too," she writes, "My Middle Ages, informed as it is by primary and secondary materials, is nonetheless as

---

[61] Ibid., 38.
[62] Ibid., 54; cf. 206.
[63] Ibid., 142.
[64] Ibid., 182.

Carolyn Dinshaw (1957–): The Gendered Reader   129

political."[65] The last line of her article "Quarrels, Rivals, and Rape," which analyzes the critical history of the supposed "conflict" between Gower and Chaucer in terms of violence against the feminine, is "Over my dead body"—indicating the vested interest Dinshaw and, she would argue, all women, have in such structures of gender in the Middle Ages and now.[66] Dinshaw, therefore, treads a fine balance between "touching" and "appropriating".[67] The distinction between the two seems to lie in the integrity of the entity being touched. If the medieval text or figure is not misrepresented, distorted, or misread by the reader in the present, then her use of it for political purposes is justified; if the reading does not respect the integrity or essence of the medieval individual, such a reading becomes an appropriation or an exploitation. To use the terms of the metaphor, if the "touching" leaves the "body" of the other whole and unique, able to speak for itself, then the touching is acceptable. If the "touching" compromises or fails to respect the integrity of the other, or silences it in any way, the reading becomes rape. Yet Dinshaw does not explain or theorize how such raping readings might be avoided. In many ways, *any* interpretation, any analysis, usurps a text's "voice," and is predicated upon its fundamental inability to speak for itself. Nor does Dinshaw theorize about who should judge whether a text is "distorted" or "appropriated." Dinshaw's explicit interest in the marginal, the abberant and the queer also runs the risk of providing a distorted—possibly appropriative—image of medieval society: Derek Pearsall accuses her of using historical details only when they suit her argument.[68] The selectiveness she practises in choosing particular individuals to study, while it has benefits in terms of emphasizing and retaining their individuality, and in providing a corrective to totalizing views of "normal" society, also comes dangerously close to the possibility that it is merely inverting another oppressive opposition. In promoting the "marginal" at the expense of the "normal," she runs the risk of being as oppressive as those who do the opposite.

Dinshaw's cross-historical attitude, then, is of an entirely different breed from Kittredge's or Donaldson's. Far from being a complacent confidence in the universality of human nature, it is a highly political, radical, and aggressive weapon with which to fight modern culture wars, both in academia and in society at large. I suggest that Dinshaw's concept of audience is crucial to this political project. Her vision of Chaucer's audience is emphatically, forcefully multiple. It includes both medieval and modern individuals, and yet the historical situatedness

---

[65]   Carolyn Dinshaw, "Getting Medieval: *Pulp Fiction*, Gawain, Foucault," *The Book and the Body*, ed. Dolores Frese and Katherine O'Brien O'Keefe (Notre Dame: University of Notre Dame, 1997) 125.

[66]   Dinshaw, "Quarrels, Rivals," 122.

[67]   Indeed, in the article "Chaucer's Queer Touches" Dinshaw explicitly advocates "appropriat[ing]" the "shock" and "power" of the queer Pardoner in the *Canterbury Tales*, which she argues Chaucer himself in the end deploys "in order to promote heterosexuality in [his] audiences": Dinshaw, "Chaucer's Queer Touches," 79.

[68]   Pearsall, "Review," 137.

130   *Twentieth-Century Chaucer Criticism*

of these individuals is not obscured: Dinshaw is as concerned to detail the historical difference between modern and medieval times as she is to point out the similarities and connections.[69] These medieval and modern audiences are in turn similarly multiple, including both mainstream and marginalized groups (modern academics and medieval Lollards; fourteenth-century courtiers and twentieth-century gay novelists). In Dinshaw's own words, "the historian's interest is in diversity—diversity of conceptualizations *within* each period, in fact, as well as *between* medieval and present day."[70]

Dinshaw also proposes a theory of reading and reception which is radically different from that of the other critics studied so far, and which rests upon considerably different assumptions about Chaucer's audience. Donaldson, for all his falling in love with Criseyde, never quite envisions sleeping with her—and yet this is exactly what the eroticism of Dinshaw's metaphor of reading as "touching" insinuates. The final chapter will return to a more conventional concept of reading. Lee Patterson, like Dinshaw, maintains a sense of the multiplicity of audience, and of both the reader's historical situatedness and the historical specificity of the text. Like Dinshaw, he advocates using the "otherness" of medieval literature for explicitly political goals in the present. Patterson, however, returns to a less radical concept of reading and a less radical sense of audience: rather than taking Chaucer's readers to bed with him, he insists on leaving them where they originated, in the historical documents which provide the sole traces we have left of them.

---

[69]   See Dinshaw, "New Approaches," 272–3; 275; cf. Dinshaw, "Chaucer's Queer Touches," 78.

[70]   Dinshaw, "New Approaches," 273; *emphasis hers*. See also Carolyn Dinshaw, "Pale Faces: Race, Religion, and Affect in Chaucer's Texts and Their Readers," *Studies in the Age of Chaucer* 23 (2001) 21, 41.

Chapter 6

Lee Patterson (1940–):
The Subjective Reader

Criticism in the 1980s and 1990s turned political. Carolyn Dinshaw, as we have seen, uses her inclusion of modern readers in Chaucer's audience for explicitly political purposes. She is interested in medieval times and people not only for themselves, but for what they can tell us about our society now. In studying the ways in which medieval society defined the marginalized, the "normal," and the transgressive, she can point to similar structures of power or marginalization in twentieth-century American culture. Dinshaw, in this movement towards the political, was in many ways typical of her generation. Towards the end of the 1980s, several works of "politicized historicist criticism" were published.[1] This "politicization" is a crucial feature of the entire post-structuralist movement, which includes queer, feminist and Marxist scholars as well as a group of scholars loosely associated with New Historicism. In this chapter I wish to turn to New Historicism and focus on a key figure, Lee Patterson, whose complicated relationship to the New Historical movement is illuminating in terms of its concept of audience.[2] In many ways, Patterson and Dinshaw have more in common with each other than they do with any of the scholars studied earlier in this thesis. Both use detailed historical evidence, both draw on modern theories for interpretative frameworks and approaches, both display an unquestioning fidelity to the New Critical technique of close reading. Both are unapologetically political: indeed, Patterson dedicates his first book to a politician, and opens his second book with a discussion of the contemporary state of American society, academia, and politics.[3] Both Patterson and Dinshaw call for academics to "stand against" what Patterson

---

[1] This term is Elizabeth Scala's: Elizabeth Scala, "Historicists and Their Discontents: Reading Psychoanalytically in Medieval Studies," *Texas Studies in Literature and Language* 44.1 (Spring 2002) 125.

[2] Other figures could have been chosen: Ethan Knapp lists Patterson among a group of New Historicists including Paul Strohm, David Aers and David Wallace; Ethan Knapp, "Chaucer Criticism and Its Legacies," *Yale Companion to Chaucer*, Seth Lerer ed. (New Haven: Yale University Press, 2006) 349. However, Patterson is exemplary because he theorizes most explicitly about his literary critical practice and its place in the history of criticism.

[3] Lee Patterson, *Negotiating the Past: The Historical Understanding of Medieval Literature* (Madison: University of Wisconsin Press, 1987) xiv; Lee Patterson, *Chaucer and the Subject of History* (Madison: University of Wisconsin Press, 1991) 3–13; cf. Lee

calls "the culture industry," which "imposes upon us all homogenized identities that can be resisted only by an insistence on heterogeneity and specificity"[4] and what Dinshaw calls "the increasingly conservative cultural climate in the United States."[5] In addition to this explicit call to politicization, both ultimately deny the possibility of absolute "objectivity" in scholarship: the writing of history is governed, inescapably, "by values and commitments that are in the last analysis political."[6] Scholarship, then, is always necessarily *implicitly* political, and for both Dinshaw and Patterson, is *explicitly* political as well. For scholars of this generation, historical scholarship is a weapon to be used in the culture wars: most would fully concur with Patterson's comment that "while historical knowledge may be a frail instrument with which to confront the vast economic and social forces that are shaping and misshaping our world, it is not finally to be scorned."[7]

In many ways, both Patterson's and Dinshaw's images of Chaucer's audience arise out of this broadly political attitude. According to them, since all reading and all scholarship is political, all audiences are inherently subjective. Each reader approaches a text from a particular position, and reads it according to particular ideologies, interests and biases. There is no such thing as an objective, or disinterested, audience. For Dinshaw, this subjectivity is often of a personal nature, which one could call intra-subjectivity: she is interested in the aspects of subjectivity which are internal, aspects of a person's identity. She traces the way in which identity—one's gender, sexual orientation, and race—influence one's individual response to texts and to society at large. For Patterson, by contrast, subjectivity is first and foremost a historical phenomenon: every audience, every reader, is conditioned by a unique historical situation. This kind of subjectivity can be called inter-subjectivity. It is more concerned with the way in which one is subject to one's society and culture than with one's inner identity. Patterson believes that no one can escape one's time or place into a realm of ahistorical, universal objectivity. The most one can do, in providing a historically sensitive interpretation of a text from another era, is to try to control for one's own historical situatedness by taking it into account when drawing conclusions about another time. A similar distinction between Dinshaw and Patterson is at work when it comes to the heterogeneity of

---

Patterson, "The Return to Philology," *The Past and Future of Medieval Studies*, ed. John Van Engen (Notre Dame: University of Notre Dame Press, 1994) 231–44.

[4] Patterson, *Subject*, 425.

[5] Carolyn Dinshaw, *Getting Medieval: Sexualities and Communities, Pre- and Postmodern* (Durham: Duke University Press, 1999) 37.

[6] Patterson, *Negotiating*, x.

[7] Patterson, *Subject*, 12. For discussion of Lee Patterson's politics, as well as those of other New Historicists such as David Wallace, see Britton Harwood (who, in fact, criticizes Patterson for not being political enough): Britton J. Harwood, "The Political Use of Chaucer in Twentieth-Century America," *Medievalism in the Modern World: Essays in Honour of Leslie J. Workman*, ed. Richard Utz and Tom Shippey (Turnhout, Belgium: Brepols, 1998) 379–92.

audiences. Both Dinshaw and Patterson envision Chaucer's audience as multiple and heterogeneous, but Dinshaw is more interested in the intra-subjective aspects of that heterogeneity—readers' identity as men and women, straights and queers, and so on. Patterson is interested in the inter-subjective aspects of multiplicity— the ways in which different readers have read Chaucer in different social situations throughout time. The corollary of multiplicity is specificity, and both Dinshaw and Patterson focus their analysis on specific readers and individuals, as opposed to a generalized "audience" or universalized "reader." Once again, Dinshaw chooses her specific readers for their personal, intra-subjective qualities (the maleness of Robertson and Donaldson, the queerness of Margery Kempe or Robert Glück), whereas Patterson chooses specific readers located in a particular, particularly analyzable, time. The image of Chaucer's audience prevalent by the end of the twentieth century, then, as represented by Dinshaw and Patterson, has three main characteristics: heterogeneity, subjectivity, and specificity.

Historical Criticism

The main difference between Patterson's and Dinshaw's concepts of audience, therefore, has to do with their different definitions of historicity. Indeed, this conflict has been made explicit in their writing: a contemporary of Dinshaw's, Patterson has contested the more ahistorical or presentist aspects of the kind of criticism she performs (her use of psychoanalytical theory, for example).[8] Patterson, like Dinshaw, draws on modern theories in his analyses of medieval texts—the concept of subjectivity, a Foucauldian analysis of power—but he tends to subordinate those modern theories to medieval evidence. In Patterson's work, unlike in Dinshaw's, a "historical" theory—one that uses concepts and terms used in medieval times—is generally preferred to a modern theory. Over the course of his career Patterson seems to have become increasingly convinced that modern ideas or approaches are acceptable only if they explain phenomena for which medieval individuals had no discourse. This preference is most clearly visible in Patterson's changing attitudes to the Pardoner's Tale, discussed more fully below: while Patterson at first was happy to base a reading of the Pardoner's Prologue and Tale on twentieth-century theories such as psychoanalysis, later in his career he rejected his own earlier interpretations in favour of one based on medieval, rather than modern, discourses and theoretical frameworks.

Patterson believes that it is the task of the scholar of history to discover, as far as possible, actual medieval responses. He asks, "How did medieval readers read medieval poetry?" and states that this question "is at the center of the entire historicist project, acknowledging as it does that literary meaning is not an atemporal constant

---

[8]   See the criticism of Dinshaw's work in Lee Patterson, "Chaucer's Pardoner on the Couch: Psyche and Clio in Medieval Literary Studies," *Speculum* 76 (2001) 658.

134 *Twentieth-Century Chaucer Criticism*

but a historical variable."[9] In his description of the New Historical project for the student readers of Beidler's collection of contemporary criticism, Patterson writes, "One goal of historical criticism is to reconstruct a text's original meaning"—that "original meaning" being the meaning the text would have had for its original audience.[10] This reconstruction of the "medieval" meaning of a text then guides the critic in forming his/her own interpretation of the literature. Again, we see the "audience function" at work: some possible interpretations are eliminated on the basis of the way in which a medieval audience would have interpreted the text. So, for example, in response to what he sees as restrictive readings such as D.W. Robertson's, Patterson writes, "our reading of this [fifteenth-century] text must be as capacious as it itself shows medieval reading to have been."[11] Like the other historicist critics in this thesis, Lewis and Robertson, Patterson advocates reading a text "on its own ground"—that is, as a medieval audience would have read it—although he is perhaps less sanguine than they about the ability of the modern historian to reconstruct that "ground." He writes,

> To acknowledge that absolute objectivity is impossible does not mean that no interpretive procedures are more reliable than others. To say that one cannot read a medieval text "on its own ground" (a position with which virtually every scholar would agree) does not mean that one is entitled to ignore evidence of what that ground might have been. ... Not even to inquire what Chaucer might plausibly be thought to have meant by the Pardoner's Prologue and Tale, nor how a contemporary reader might plausibly have understood it, is—to adapt Robert Frost's comment on writing free verse—like playing tennis with the net down.[12]

Patterson characterizes modern scholars as "eavesdroppers" on a conversation meant initially for another audience, and that audience's response is what "we must painstakingly try to reconstruct."[13] This metaphor of "eavesdropping" is an interesting image in terms of the assumptions Patterson holds about audiences: he includes the modern reader in his image of audience, but pushes that reader as far to the edge of the audience as possible. Not even "in the room" with the "real" audience, the modern audience's role is acknowledged, but is minimized as much as possible.

---

[9]   Patterson, *Negotiating*, 115.

[10]   Lee Patterson, "'Experience Woot Well It is Noght So': Marriage and the Pursuit of Happiness in the Wife of Bath's Prologue and Tale," *The Wife of Bath: Case Studies in Contemporary Criticism*, ed. Peter G. Beidler (Boston: Bedford Books of St. Martin's Press, 1996) 133; cf. Lee Patterson, "The Disenchanted Classroom," *Exemplaria* 8.2 (1996) 532–3.

[11]   Patterson, *Negotiating*, xii.

[12]   Patterson, "Chaucer's Pardoner," 679.

[13]   Ibid., 678.

In many ways, and in ways that are interesting in terms of institutional history and university history, the theoretical trajectory of Patterson's career is a mirror image of Dinshaw's.[14] Carolyn Dinshaw studied at Princeton under D.W. Robertson and John Fleming, and over the course of her career steadily moved away from these historicist beginnings to an approach which, while maintaining its reliance upon historical evidence and detail, nonetheless displays more and more concern with modern-day affairs, and is less and less willing to privilege medieval interpretations at the expense of modern ones. Lee Patterson, by contrast, studied at Yale under E. Talbot Donaldson. He considered himself fully a New Critic, and only gradually turned to historicism.[15] In a paper given at the 2004 International Congress of Medieval Studies at Kalamazoo, Michigan, for a session on D.W. Robertson, Patterson describes his slow conversion towards Robertson-inspired historicism, if not to a fully-fledged Robertsonian approach. Having started out at Yale trained in the techniques of New Criticism, he had little expertise in the "historicist" tools of philology, paleography, or textual criticism. "It was Donaldson's edition of Chaucer's Poetry, with its apparently effortlessly established text and its deceptively slight commentary, that I knew," Patterson writes. "Moreover, since Robertson was the Great Satan at Yale, none of us read any [of his work]."[16] Upon graduating from Yale, Patterson moved to the University of Toronto, whose medieval program was resolutely Latinate and historically based, and it was only there that he read *A Preface to Chaucer*.[17] While he disagreed with much of it, over the following years he came to the realization that if he were to contest its conclusions, he had to do so on its own, historicist, terms, rather than retreating into what he calls his "cozy New Critical enclave"—and that in order to do so, he had to develop a historicism different from Robertsonian historicism.[18] In the anti-Vietnam, anti-American atmosphere of Canada in the early 1970s, Patterson also became interested in Marxism, and was actively involved in politics: he was an organizer and campaign manager for the New Democrats, Canada's socialist, left-leaning political party. He began to search for a way to combine his political ideologies with his scholarship, especially his burgeoning desire to find a historicist, yet non-Robertsonian, approach to literary criticism.[19] Patterson moved from Toronto to Johns Hopkins University, then to Duke, and finally returned to

---

[14] For a brief critical biography, see Rosalyn Rossignol, "Patterson, Lee," *Chaucer: A Literary Reference to His Life and Work* (New York: Infobase Publishing, 2007) 524–5.

[15] Lee Patterson, "Remainders and Reminders," *Unquiet Spirits: D.W. Robertson's Remains in Medieval Studies Now*, chair Wesley Yu, International Congress on Medieval Studies (Kalamazoo: Princeton Program in Medieval Studies, July 5, 2004). I am grateful to Professor Patterson for sending me a copy of this paper.

[16] Ibid.

[17] Lee Patterson, *Temporal Circumstances: Form and History in the Canterbury Tales* (New York: Palgrave Macmillan, 2006) 2.

[18] Patterson, "Remainders." See also Patterson, *Negotiating*, 115.

[19] Patterson, *Temporal Circumstances*, 3.

136 *Twentieth-Century Chaucer Criticism*

Yale as Frederick W. Hilles Professor of English. Over the course of his career he developed more fully this "different" historicism, until he has come to be seen as one of the leading "New Historical" critics in the field.[20]

Lee Patterson's gradual self-definition as a New Historicist seems to have come, at least in part, because of the changes he himself initiated into the movement. In his 1987 survey of trends in Chaucer studies and literary criticism as a whole he is hesitant to identify himself as a New Historicist. At a time when other medievalists such as Anne Middleton and Paul Strohm were calling themselves New Historicists, Patterson refused to adopt the epithet for himself. Medievalists such as Patterson were reluctant to identify themselves fully with the New Historicism coming out of Renaissance studies, some calling themselves instead "New Philologists" in an attempt to differentiate themselves from the Renaissance scholars with whom they disagreed.[21] Patterson lauds the new approach of some Renaissance New Historicists, such as Stephen Greenblatt, for their skillful combination of deconstruction's understanding of textuality with a social and cultural awareness drawn from Marxism. He also takes Greenblatt and his colleagues to task, however, for their over-emphasis on a totalizing, Foucauldian vision of power. In the understanding of the Renaissance New Historicists, Patterson says, power comes to be such a pervasive and overriding cultural phenomenon that it is difficult to consider the possibility of change within the structures of society they describe:

> New Historicism discloses a world strangely drained of dynamism, in which every effort to enact change issues in a reaffirmation of the status quo, and where the continually renegotiated antagonisms of Renaissance culture are always already inscribed within a space of stasis. It arrives, in fact, at a paradox: on the one hand Renaissance culture is an arena of social contradictions engaged in ceaseless strife, and yet on the other hand, nothing happens.[22]

Patterson likewise objects to the Renaissance New Historicists' over-emphasis upon the structures of culture and society, at the expense of individual subjectivity. As he points out, despite the fact that Stephen Greenblatt's most influential work, *Renaissance Self-Fashioning*, is ostensibly about the development of the individual self (as the title indicates), over the course of the work the individual comes to seem completely unfree, an ideological product of social power structures rather than an autonomous being. With a New Historical concentration on structural power to the exclusion of all other considerations, "the individual [in Renaissance

---

[20]   See the comments in Scala, "Historicists," 110; Corinne Saunders, ed., *Blackwell Guides to Criticism: Chaucer* (Oxford: Blackwell, 2001) 177; Gillian Rudd, *The Complete Critical Guide to Geoffrey Chaucer* (London: Routledge, 2001) 170.

[21]   See Patterson, "The Return to Philology," 231–44; see also the special edition of *Speculum* 65.1, 1990.

[22]   Patterson, *Negotiating*, 63; cf. xi.

society] disappears because the historian stops looking for him."[23] Patterson's goal, then, is to reinstate the individual within the workings of power. This will become important in terms of his concept of audience. The relationship between the individual and society is, in many ways, similar to the relationship between an individual reader or listener and the audience as a whole. Just as Patterson tries to restore the position of the individual in the New Historicist understanding of power relations, so he tries to reinstate the individual reader into the sometimes totalizing historicist concepts of the audience and the "medieval mind."

Patterson, then, attempts to rehabilitate New Historicism for medievalists. He adopts many of the strengths of New Historicism while compensating or correcting for its weaknesses. Alongside an understanding of the structures of power and discourse at work within a culture or society, he insists on a recognition of the force of individual subjectivity; within the Foucauldian structures of power and ideology he posits the possibility of change and challenge; and against the Renaissance scholars' narrative of a radical break in history between the medieval period and the Early Modern period, he demonstrates the way in which so-called "modern" concepts such as individuality, subjectivity and psychology can be found in the Middle Ages. Thus, while Patterson explicitly positions himself as a "historian" in *Negotiating the Past* in 1987, he is reluctant to identify himself fully as "New Historicist." By 1996, however, he is comfortable enough with the term "New Historicist" to agree to be the representative of New Historicism for Peter Beidler's collection of case studies on the Wife of Bath's Tale. Other scholars have recognized Patterson's role as a leading New Historicist critic: Elizabeth Scala calls Patterson an "exemplary (in every sense of the word) historicist critic," while Caroline Saunders's anthology of Chaucer criticism classifies Patterson's study of Chaucer as clearly New Historicist.[24] This recognition testifies to the extent to which Patterson has re-defined the term New Historicism through his own work and his own place in the movement.

Patterson's historicism is inextricably tied to his concept of audience. If the goal of literary criticism is to come as close as possible to understanding the meaning of Chaucer's works as they would have been understood by Chaucer's original audience, then—if one is to "eavesdrop" effectively—that audience itself must be detailed and understood as fully as possible in its unique historical moment. At first glance, therefore, Patterson's New Historicism does not always appear very different from the "old" historicism practised by scholars such as C.S. Lewis or D.W. Robertson. Patterson puts Chaucer's works in their "historical context," detailing for the modern reader the social and cultural conditions and knowledge which a medieval reader would take for granted in reading Chaucer's works. So, for example, in the collection of articles on the Wife of Bath, Patterson's contribution is to examine the role and position of widows and wives in medieval society, and to read the Wife of Bath on those terms. Instead of viewing Alison

---

[23] Ibid., 67.

[24] Scala, "Historicists," 110; Saunders, *Chaucer*, 177.

138   *Twentieth-Century Chaucer Criticism*

as a "protofeminist, launching a no-holds-barred attack on certain medieval pieties about male supremacy," Patterson concludes Chaucer's readers would probably have considered her as "a typical widow on the make" since "Chaucer was reproducing the conventions and, to a large extent, the social realities of his day" in her characterization.[25] The Miller, too, is read with reference to the real conditions under which medieval millers and peasants lived and worked. Likewise, when Patterson studies Thomas Hoccleve, he explains the writings in terms of the conditions of life under the Lancastrians, and the bureaucratic context of Westminster and London; the Prioress's Tale is read with reference to the historical dealings in Christian Europe with Jewish communities; the Parson's Tale is put in the context of the Fourth Lateran council and the increase in confession and penance. Near the beginning of *Chaucer and the Subject of History*, Patterson gives a detailed outline of the historical context in England at the time, before launching into his analysis of Chaucer's works. Like Robertson, Patterson reads both *Troilus and Criseyde* and the Knight's Tale in terms of the political situation in England and the court during the 1380s: the Parliament in which Criseyde is exchanged for Antenor is considered as a reflection on the Wonderful Parliament of 1386; the description of the tournament in the Knight's Tale may have been influenced by a tournament held by Richard II. The Wife of Bath's Tale is explained in terms of "folk rituals" of wooing and courtship.[26]

Subject to History

This traditional historicism, however, is underpinned and woven through with the preoccupations and imperatives of New Historicism—preoccupations themselves based upon assumptions about audiences and the ways in which they work. The titles of Patterson's two main works, *Negotiating the Past* and *Chaucer and the Subject of History*, contain puns which are subtly indicative of the values Patterson wishes to embrace. "*Negotiating the Past*" can be taken two ways: first, that the historian must "negotiate" the past as one negotiates a difficult landscape— "negotiate" here would suggest "navigate" or "tread carefully." The past is not an easily-defined metanarrative against which one can analyze literary works, but contains its own attendant pitfalls, obstacles and traps. Past audiences are multiple and heterogeneous, not monolithic. They do not provide a two-dimensional "backdrop," like a stage setting, against which one can show a literary work in relief. Instead they are landscapes one must negotiate, and the literary work is only one feature of the landscape among many. Second, the historian must "negotiate" *with* the past in writing history: the past is a separate entity which must be respected as such, but the historian him/herself plays a major role in "creating" history. Historians, in other words, collaborate with the facts/details/documents of the past

---

[25] Patterson, "'Experience Woot Well'," 133, 137.

[26] Patterson, *Subject*, 294.

Lee Patterson (1940–): The Subjective Reader 139

in writing history—the past is not a passive object simply waiting to be found or unearthed by the historian. Each individual, each reader, of Chaucer's works contributes a slightly different reading to the generalized "medieval perspective," and the historian must negotiate with each particular reading—or whatever evidence of it she can find—before developing any generalizations. The title of Patterson's second major work, *Chaucer and the Subject of History*, contains even more meaningful puns. First, at the most literal level, the work is about the way in which Chaucer himself deals with the subject or "topic" of history—the Greek and Roman classical history he has inherited. Second, Patterson, as a historicist, wants to understand Chaucer in his own historical context, so his book deals with Chaucer's writings and the "topic" or subject of *medieval* history—the way in which Chaucer, like all of us, is *subjected* to his own historical moment. Third, as I have indicated above, Patterson is interested in studying subjectivity and individualism within the structures of society and power, and so the book is about Chaucer, his characters and his audience as *subjects*, acting and active individuals who may be created by but who also react against the structures and systems of the society around them. It is also about them as *subjects* in a more technical sense, as beings who are subjected to the structures of grammatical, political or social systems. And finally, Patterson's approach emphasizes an awareness of the historian's own role in the creation of history, and so *Chaucer and the Subject of History* is implicitly also about the way in which Chaucer is *subject* to our historical moment today—the way in which we create, contain and constrain his writings by subjecting him to our analysis and criticism. In this framework the modern historian's role as an audience of Chaucer must be acknowledged and accommodated. The historian's own subjectivity will colour his reading of Chaucer and his understanding of medieval times, and must be reckoned with if he is to provide a responsible interpretation.

This conflicted, problematic relationship with historicity, the tension between the temptations of a modern response and the difficulty of discovering a medieval one, is seen most clearly in Patterson's changing analysis of the Pardoner's Tale. (That Patterson discusses the way his views have changed—that the narrative of the way in which Patterson came to believe his original conclusion was wrong becomes proof in that very analysis—itself speaks to his commitment to understanding subjectivity, his own as well as others'.) Patterson's first published study of the Pardoner's Tale was in the article "Chaucerian Confession, Penitential Literature and the Pardoner," which was reprinted, with some modifications, as Chapter 8, "The Subject of Confession: The Pardoner and the Rhetoric of Penance," in *Chaucer and the Subject of History*. While Patterson argues in this article for a "medieval" context or reading of the Pardoner's Tale—as being grounded in (and therefore interpreted through) penitential and confessional rhetoric—he nonetheless provides a very Freudian reading of the Old Man and of the Pardoner himself. He calls the Pardoner's performance an enactment of an "Oedipal drama

140   *Twentieth-Century Chaucer Criticism*

that has castration as its central event and ultimate penalty."[27] Of the Old Man's self-description speech, he writes,

> These lines articulate the desire for penitential conversion in terms that are unavoidably Oedipal ... the act imagined here is a transaction conducted not with the Divine Father who sits in judgment but with the Mother Earth who is the chthonic, and unsanctified, source of life. ... The moment of fulfillment is thus imagined not as atonement with the Father but as reunion with the Mother, a return to primal oneness that the entrance into the fallen world of history has ruptured. And the confrontation with which the performance as a whole concludes provides the aetiology of this severance ... the Pardoner is threatened with castration.[28]

In another place Patterson cites Barthes, commenting that "to the masculinist mind, 'castration is contagious' ... the compulsions of the Pardoner become those of his audience."[29] Yet Patterson's discomfort with this interpretation is obvious (not in the least because of the thickening of his rhetoric at these moments). His interpretation becomes almost excessive in these sections: he provides multiple layerings of justification for his psychoanalytical interpretation, invoking everything from Chaucer's knowledge of the Oedipal/Theban story, to the medieval tradition which linked Judas with Oedipus as a figure of despair, to the role of despair in the problematics of confession, to the universal nature of the Oedipal myth, "that area of human experience in which the Oedipal drama takes place, a drama in which all male readers, at least, are implicated."[30] The "audience function" is being used rather awkwardly here to justify a Freudian reading: because Chaucer's medieval audience would have known all of these things (the Theban myth, the tradition of Judas, etc.), the logic runs, a Freudian reading is allowed, even though a medieval audience would not have had Freudian concepts of psychology or a Freudian understanding of sexuality. Finally, Patterson implies that while such a reading may not be wholly medieval it meets a modern need to understand the problem of self-representation as "a rift or split endemic to a symbolic order that is itself the effect of a primal repression—a repression, moreover, that is both a disabling castration and the means by which the male subject is constituted."[31] Here the definition of audience—first restricted to the original medieval audience— changes to allow a specific reading. The "audience function" is redefined on new terms in order to enable a Freudian reading. Even with this excess of justification, however, Patterson is hesitant to present the psychoanalytic reading as definitive, uncomfortable, perhaps, with this redefinition of the "audience function." He

---

[27]   Ibid., 372.

[28]   Ibid., 411–12.

[29]   Ibid., 410.

[30]   Ibid., 418–19.

[31]   Ibid., 407.

doubts his own interpretation: "Is the staff really phallic? Are we right in thinking that the hair clout invokes the mother's pubic hair ... ? There is no definitive answer to these questions."[32]

The unease with the modern, psychoanalytical reading which comes through in the earlier study becomes full-blown in Patterson's later study of the Pardoner's Prologue and Tale, "Chaucer's Pardoner on the Couch: Psyche and Clio in Medieval Literary Studies."[33] In this article, Patterson performs a devastating analysis of psychoanalytical criticism, regretting his earlier dependence on the psychoanalytical approach. He says, rather ruefully, that "we start our intellectual lives under the spell" of Freud, and that the language and assumptions of psychoanalysis pervade our modern culture and our ways of thinking.[34] His own subjectivity as a modern reader, his subjection to the discourses and assumptions of our society, was not sufficiently controlled for in his earlier reading. The article "Chaucer's Pardoner on the Couch" is, accordingly, a "palinode," a "retraction resembling Chaucer's own selective rejection of some of his works." Patterson writes that in his earlier works he succumbed to the "allure of psychoanalytic interpretation," and, as a result, the "seeming persuasiveness" of the psychoanalytical approach "foreclose[d] access to relevant medieval materials and contexts."[35] The suggestion of the Pardoner's castration or homosexuality, the Old Man's comment that he wished to return to Mother Earth, the Pardoner's concern with language and the "real," and the Host's threat to castrate the Pardoner, all provide enticements to a Freudian/Lacanian reading for "the modern reader, for whom sexual identity is the crucial determinant of selfhood."[36] Patterson, having succumbed to this temptation in his earlier analysis, corrects it in his later article with a properly medieval interpretation. In other words, he modifies the intuitive response of a modern audience—which is to invoke Freud—with extensive research and reading designed to discover the medieval audience's response. His second reading of the Pardoner's Tale is dependent not on modern psychoanalytical theory but on the medieval discourse of spiritual reform (both orthodox and Lollard). He asks, "What would a reader in fourteenth-century England have assumed about this figure [of the Pardoner], whom the narrator introduces as either a gelding or a mare? Did such terms imply literal or symbolic effeminacy? And if symbolic, symbolic within what system of signification?"[37] Ultimately, he argues that the answer is religious, not sexual— that a medieval audience would have seen both the Pardoner and the Old Man

---

[32] Ibid., 418.

[33] Patterson, "Chaucer's Pardoner." This article in many ways pre-empted the criticism leveled by Elizabeth Scala, who writes that despite Patterson's and other New Historicists' hostility to psychoanalysis, they were in fact profoundly psychoanalytical in their assumptions and discourse.

[34] Ibid., 639.

[35] Ibid., 656.

[36] Ibid., 657.

[37] Ibid., 668, 659.

142   *Twentieth-Century Chaucer Criticism*

not in sexual terms but in religious terms, as figures who were *spiritually* sterile. "The Pardoner," he writes, "as a simoniac who both sells spiritual goods and fails to sow God's seed in the field of holy mother church ... would have been seen by a contemporary audience as impotent twice over." Patterson concludes that the Pardoner's Tale is, "in short, a tale not about sex but about religion."[38] In this article, more than any other, we can see Patterson's use of the "audience function" in forming his interpretations. After a thorough consideration of the role of Freudian discourse in our society, he ultimately excludes interpretations based on that discourse because a medieval author and audience would have been situated within a different discursive framework. Patterson uses the "audience function" to close down the possible interpretations of the text and to determine the "meaning": the Pardoner's Tale "is about" religion, not sex, because that is what a medieval audience would have understood it to be about. In his changing understanding of the Pardoner's Tale, therefore, Patterson shows a clear preference for reading the tale as a medieval audience would have read it. He takes his own historicity and subjectivity into account to correct for the biases and presuppositions of a modern audience.

The Historian's Role

This awareness of the historian's own historicity and subjectivity is crucial to Patterson's philosophy. He writes at the close of the article retracting his earlier use of psychoanalysis, "The point is *not* to abandon psychoanalytic theory, but to approach it with a full awareness of its own historicity, of its place in the current state of the fields of psychology and psychiatry, and of its intellectual coherence and (especially) evidentiary support."[39] Patterson's awareness of his own position in post-Freudian modernity, and his own conditioning by an intellectual culture shot through with psychoanalytical discourse and modes of thought, make possible the imaginative step which enables him to envision a medieval response. Only when one is aware of one's own assumptions, intuitive responses and biases can one imaginatively move outside of them, and approach an understanding of the mindset of another era. This emphasis on the critic's own historicity permeates Patterson's writings. So, for example, at the opening to *Negotiating the Past*, he writes, "While wanting to do justice to the otherness of a distant past, the historian is unavoidably conditioned by his own historical situation; while concerned to incorporate and understand as much of the material relevant to his chosen problem as he can, he is also aware that that material is never raw data but rather produced by elaborate processes of interpretation."[40] History is not "raw data" against which

---

[38]   Ibid., 673.

[39]   Ibid., 679.

[40]   Patterson, *Negotiating*, ix. Cf. Patterson, *Negotiating*, 44: "The appeal to 'history' so commonly made in current critical discourses of all varieties is necessarily always to a

a literary text can be interpreted, but itself requires interpretation, and the historian must remain aware of his/her own role in the interpretative process.

Patterson's image of Chaucer's audience, then, is multiple historically. The responses of modern and medieval readers to Chaucer's works are different, and while Patterson is more interested in the medieval readings, the modern ones must be taken into account in the historian's analysis. To put it another way, Patterson limits the "audience function" to the medieval audience—only the medieval audience should be used in determining which interpretations are permissible—but the assumptions and conditioning of the modern audience must be acknowledged and controlled for in the historian's reconstruction of his or her image of the medieval audience. Furthermore, these two distinct audiences are themselves also heterogeneous. In searching for an authentically medieval response one must not fall into the trap of believing that all individuals in the Middle Ages would have responded to a story or read a text in the same way. Rather than attempting to provide overarching descriptions or theories about medieval culture or medieval mindsets which, for the most part, ignore exceptions as aberrations or irrelevancies, when attempting to understand the interrelations of power, hegemony and individual subjectivity Patterson focuses precisely on those exceptions, aberrations, and specific, unique instances. These particular readings and examples provide crucial insight into our image of the negotiations and strategic maneuverings which create the overall culture. Patterson explicitly calls for an approach which "both proscribe[s] recourse to absolutizing, totalizing schemes and redirect[s] our attention to the specific, the particular, the local, and the contingent."[41]

Crucially, this technique is central to Patterson's understanding of Chaucer's audience, as well as to his approach to history in general. Instead of developing an overall image of medieval society, as Lewis does in *The Discarded Image* or Robertson does in *Chaucer's London*, and then deducing from this image the way in which Chaucer's readers would have been likely to read, Patterson focuses on the actual reading practices of particular, specific readers. This is not a particularly new technique: both Lewis and Kittredge turned to Lydgate, Hoccleve, and Chaucer's other followers and imitators for evidence about the way in which contemporaries interpreted Chaucer's work. New Historicists such as Patterson, however, came to the realization that scribes of medieval texts were themselves readers of the texts they copied and, in their emendations and

---

reconstruction fabricated according to processes of interpretation that are identical to those applied to the 'not-history' of the literary text. Whether we rely upon previous texts, social and political formations, or a period consciousness, we are turning not to 'extrinsic data' in the sense of something instantly apprehensible and self-evidently meaningful, but rather to a mass of material, almost all of it textual, that requires interpretation before it can enter into the process of historical understanding."

[41] Patterson, *Subject*, 425; cf. Lee Patterson, "On the Margin: Postmodernism, Ironic History, and Medieval Studies," *Speculum* 65.1 (1990) 90.

144 *Twentieth-Century Chaucer Criticism*

annotations, interpreters as well. Each recopying of a text is potentially a *reading*: if the scribe or copyist did not understand a section, or disagreed with it, or had a particular interpretation which he felt could be more fully expressed, he might make changes to the text he was copying. These changes could range from a word (replacing one word for one that was not understood or was unclear) to a sentence or paragraph (moving a section, rewriting a section to give it a different slant or interpretation) to entire texts (excerpting texts from their original contexts to place them in a new work; compiling texts with others which would provide implicit commentary on them). As well, specific books and manuscripts were owned by individuals, and those people, too, were individual readers who provided evidence of their reading practices in their annotations, habits of collection, and quotations. Every scrap of marginalia, every scribal change, every gloss, every commentary becomes potential evidence for a particular reading of a text. The old practices of codicology and palaeography become newly useful in an approach which insists upon the specific and detailed in understanding Chaucer's audience. Likewise, wills and lists of library collections, formerly useful primarily in tracing a book's provenance, demonstrate ownership and hence almost certainly readership, and conclusions about a work's specific readers can likewise be drawn from these.

Specific Readers

The best instance of this concept of the audience as specific and individual in Patterson's work is in his article "Ambiguity and Interpretation: A Fifteenth-Century Reading of Troilus and Criseyde," reprinted as chapter four of *Negotiating the Past*. In this study, Patterson challenges Robertsonian readings of *Troilus and Criseyde* not on New Critical grounds (by reference to "the poem itself"— which he calls "both polemically evasive and theoretically indefensible"), but on exegetical criticism's own "turf," historicism and the history of reading.[42] Rather than deducing medieval reading practices from the protocols for reading set out in medieval textbooks of exegesis and biblical criticism, as Robertson does, he proposes studying evidence of the actual individual instance of reading as given in a fifteenth-century treatise which quotes *Troilus and Criseyde*. Since the treatise directly cites *Troilus and Criseyde*, we know the scribe of the treatise read Chaucer, and we can deduce important things about his method of reading from the use to which he puts the quotation, the interpretation he gives the tale, and the moralization (if any) he draws from it. In Patterson's words, this treatise provides evidence of "an inescapably individual moment of literary reception, a moment whose specificity is palpable and whose significance, while necessarily open to debate, raises questions that have an immediacy that the modern reader cannot evade."[43] This "palpable specificity" which Patterson searches for in discovering

---

[42] Patterson, *Negotiating*, 115.

[43] Ibid., 116.

medieval methods of reading is what distinguishes him from earlier historicists such as Lewis and Robertson, who discard the specific in favour of the general. Since the treatise Patterson studies, called *Disce mori*, was owned by Syon Abbey, and was possibly compiled there, we know that its audience was "not only a feminine and conventual audience, but ... one subject to the particular temptations offered by a foundation, such as Syon, in which both men and women were in residence."[44] The scribe or compiler incorporates a passage from Chaucer's *Troilus and Criseyde* into a discussion of the "Seven Tokens of Carnal Love"; he then recommends that his readers seek out the story of Troilus, Criseyde and Diomede if they want to know more. Patterson argues that while it is clear that *Troilus and Criseyde* could be read allegorically, as D.W. Robertson maintains, and that some medieval readers would have indeed read it that way, "this conclusion, although comfortable, is only part of the story: it suggests how David of Augsburg [a medieval exegete] would have read the poem (had he allowed himself to read it at all) but not how our fifteenth-century reader actually did read it."[45] Instead, as Patterson shows through a close analysis of the changes the scribe made to his sources, the fifteenth-century reader read *Troilus and Criseyde* as "fully real," not allegorical: "our reader categorized *Troilus and Criseyde* as a text to be read literally ... as describing a psychological reality, the conflict and bewilderment brought on by love."[46] This Syon reader not only appreciated the psychology of the poem, but read with an attention to and appreciation of its literariness. He ignored obvious possibilities for exegetical or thoroughly allegorical readings. Instead, he shows "an attention to the texture of the poem and a respect for the psychological reality of the characters that sharply mark [his reading] off from fully fledged spiritualizations."[47] By focusing on a specific instance of reading, a specific individual reader, Patterson applies important correctives to D.W. Robertson's image of Chaucer's audience. Patterson's vision of Chaucer's audience is multiple—*this* specific reader may have read *Troilus and Criseyde* psychologically and literally, but that does not mean all medieval readers would have. Some readers—readers such as David of Augsburg, who wrote the original treatise the Syon scribe was copying—might have been perfect exegetes, but this does not mean that all medieval people read exegetically or allegorically. Patterson refuses to be constrained by overarching theories about the "medieval mind" or "the medieval approach." Instead, his interpretation is grounded in specific, individual examples of reading practices which may themselves be multiple, varied, diverse and contradictory.

Patterson also develops his image of medieval reading practices, and his image of the medieval audience, through his recognition of Chaucer himself as a reader. Chaucer was a reader of earlier stories which he used and adapted for his own purposes, just as the Syon reader used and adapted *Troilus and Criseyde*.

---

[44] Ibid., 118.

[45] Ibid., 145.

[46] Ibid., 147.

[47] Ibid., 147.

146   *Twentieth-Century Chaucer Criticism*

As such, he is a "specific reader" who can give insight into medieval reading practices. Patterson, therefore, incorporates Chaucer himself into the "audience function." Chaucer's own methods of reading aid in constructing the delineations of the "audience function," which can in turn limit or enable interpretations of Chaucer's own works. So, for example, Chaucer's turning of the historical text of the *Thebiad* into a romantic tale suggests that some medieval people—Chaucer, at least—used the erotic and the personal to explain or understand the epic and the historical. This indicates that some medieval readers made sense of large-scale political complexities by personalizing them and bringing them down to an individual level: "just as the failed love of Troilus and Criseyde can presumably teach us about the failure of Troy, so can Theban compulsions be explicated by reference to Anelida and Arcite."[48] Chaucer's reading of Benoit and Guido, in *Troilus and Criseyde*, follows this process of making sense of the historical through the personal. Moreover, Patterson argues that Chaucer suggests that this is the only way of making sense of history, that other methods of historical exegesis have failed: "[Chaucer] encourages us to read his poem as both an attempt to clarify the enigma of the Trojan experience through the experience of his two lovers and as an ironic and knowing tribute to the failures of earlier historical exegesis."[49] Again, the reading practices of a specific individual—Chaucer himself—become visible through Patterson's analysis, and allow him to speculate about medieval reading practices in general: in this case, that some medieval readers read history through the lens of personal individual experience. Chaucer's reading of Theban and classical history, as exhibited in the Knight's Tale, provides further evidence of medieval reading practices. The description of the tournament in the Tale shows that Chaucer read the *Teseida* with contemporary politics in mind, for he juxtaposes the description in the *Teseida* with descriptions taken from contemporary accounts of Richard II's Smithfield tournament. This juxtaposition of a classical text with contemporary events shows that Chaucer thought that the works of the "auctorites" could be used to cast light on present-day politics; in other words, that he read old texts at least in part for their present relevance. His inclusion of this juxtaposition in the Knight's Tale raises the possibility that he may have wished his audience to read in the same way, and opens the door for a reading of the Knight's Tale as a commentary on fourteenth-century chivalry. In this way, Patterson considers Chaucer as an individual reader of other texts, and incorporates Chaucer's reading practices into his idea of the "audience function." Those practices are then turned onto Chaucer's own works as guides to Patterson's own interpretation.

These explorations of specific readers, therefore, give an image of Chaucer's audience as multiple and variable. The audience of the dream poems is not necessarily the audience of the *Canterbury Tales*. Indeed, Patterson posits a movement away from the courtly audience with which Chaucer began his career, to a more bourgeois, broader audience for his final works. Until the late 1380s,

---

[48] Patterson, *Subject*, 64.

[49] Ibid., 126.

Lee Patterson (1940–): The Subjective Reader 147

Patterson maintains, "all of Chaucer's pre-*Canterbury Tales* poetry was almost certainly written within the environment of noble and royal courts and was directed to a court audience." Some tales within the *Canterbury Tales*, such as the Knight's Tale, were also probably intended for a courtly audience.[50] However, as the modest, inexpensive format of fifteenth-century *Canterbury Tales'* manuscripts and their wide provenance show, Chaucer's later audience extended well beyond his original courtly circle. The actual owners of medieval manuscripts, therefore, show that Chaucer's medieval audience was multiple and varied. Moreover, this audience not only comprised several groups, but in all probability differed within itself. Indeed, individual readers themselves may have changed from day to day: "Medieval feelings are rarely any less complicated than modern ones," Patterson writes,[51] and one can hear in this phrase a rejection of D.W. Robertson's view of the homogeneous, "quiet," "medieval mind." Again, in implicit counter to Robertson's approach, Patterson argues, "Unless we accept the notion of a culturally monolithic Middle Ages"—which Patterson clearly does not—"we cannot assume that the habits of one group of readers can simply be extended across the cultural field as a whole."[52] Augustinian methods of reading cannot, in fact, be extended to all medieval society: later medieval historiography, at least as evidenced in the chronicles, in fact directly counters Augustinian principles. Thus Patterson rejects exegetical criticism's insistence on one method of reading for all medieval people, suggesting instead that there may have been a multiplicity of authentically "medieval" methods of reading.

Specific Readers, General Audience

Often, the terms "audience" and "reader" are used as though they were synonymous—as though there were no difference between an "audience" and the "reader." Patterson, however, forces a distinction by focusing on specific readers. There is no general audience for Chaucer, only a conglomerate of readers. The "audience" is multiple and heterogeneous, and it is dangerous for the critic to treat it as a single entity, because the specificity and individualism of particular readers, and the uniqueness of their individual reading practices, will be lost. Despite this emphasis, however, and despite Patterson's stated focus on "the specific, the particular, the local and the contingent,"[53] Patterson's historicist imperative—his limitation of the "audience function" to a medieval audience, whereby the medieval audience's responses are used to determine permissible interpretations—means that Patterson *needs* to generalize. In order to determine what *our* interpretation

---

[50] Ibid., 22; cf. 23, 25, 51–4, 84, 194, 197, 233, 235–6.

[51] Lee Patterson, "'For the Wyves Love of Bathe': Feminine Rhetoric and Poetic Resolution in the *Roman de la Rose* and the *Canterbury Tales*," *Speculum* 58.3 (July 1983) 659.

[52] Patterson, *Negotiating*, 116.

[53] Patterson, *Subject*, 425.

148   *Twentieth-Century Chaucer Criticism*

should be like, at least in its broad outlines, he must generalize from one specific medieval response to some sort of abstract idea of a "medieval response," which will delineate the parameters of possible interpretations.

One would think that Patterson's search for the specific and unique would produce some truly bizarre interpretations of Chaucer, individuals who read Chaucer in a wholly unique or unusual manner. One might expect Patterson to find someone similar to John/Eleanor Rykener, whom Dinshaw discusses: a truly unusual individual who perplexed the medieval courts before whom s/he was tried.[54] Patterson, however, finds no such unusual cases, and no truly bizarre readings of Chaucer's works. And it is not clear how he would deal with them if he did. Patterson's historical imperative becomes problematic when it comes to individual medieval readings which strike us as just plain wrong, bizarre, or obscure. He provides little methodology for determining whether a particular reading is representative or aberrant, nor does he explicitly indicate what a critic should do if he concludes a particular reading is atypical. In the words of Thomas Hahn, Patterson's humanism "pressure[s] him to shut out excess, lack, overdetermination—the non-causal forces or features of the unconscious, of the repressed, of the historical process that underlie or defy reasonable, self-conscious, humanistic analysis."[55] Patterson's approach does not seem to allow much space for excessive or irrational readings.

Patterson's approach also sometimes begs the question of how to deal with cases in which individual medieval readings conflict with or contradict one another. For example, he makes several gestures to the multiplicity of the audience in terms of gender—the aspect of audience multiplicity on which Dinshaw insists—but these have little effect on his criticism. That is, Patterson acknowledges the existence of women readers, and (for the most part) avoids the misogynist assumptions of earlier critics, that the "typical" or "normal" or "universal" reader for Chaucer is male.[56] However, he provides no examples of specific women readers, nor does he consider the ways in which they might read differently from men. At times, his audience seems just as male as Donaldson's—as when he discusses castration anxiety in the Pardoner's Tale, for example, or talks about "masculine listening" as opposed to "feminine speaking" with regards to the Wife of Bath's story about Midas, and slides into an assumption that "the reader" is a man.[57] More importantly,

---

[54]   Dinshaw, *Getting Medieval*, 138–42.

[55]   Thomas Hahn, "The Premodern Text and the Postmodern Reader," *Exemplaria* 2.1, (Spring 1990) 7.

[56]   See exceptions in Patterson, *Subject*, 290, 309, 311, 397, 418.

[57]   Ibid., 407, 410, 287–8. It should be noted that the section on the Wife of Bath in *The Subject of History* is adapted from Patterson, "For the Wyves Love of Bath," 657–8, and that Patterson changed the wording in the later book to make it clear that "the reader" is not a universal male reader but the specific male audience of the Wife of Bath: for example, the sentence "But our habits—or compulsions—as listeners may be equally suspect" becomes

his interpretive framework has little room for the implications that might come from the existence of such readers.

It is this movement from specific to general—from reader to audience—which Patterson struggles to conceptualize, and which is the most problematic aspect of his approach. Dinshaw avoids this problem, especially in *Getting Medieval*, because she is interested primarily in specificity and multiplicity. She feels little need to generalize from specific readings to a prescriptive practice of reading, or to resolve contradictions between the readings of different individuals or groups. Patterson, however, seems caught between two imperatives: first, the imperative to focus on the specific, the local, and the contingent in exploring Chaucer's readership, and second, the historicist imperative to read Chaucer's texts as a medieval audience would have read them. Hesitant to generalize in the way Lewis and Robertson did, unwilling to provide an overarching framework through which all medieval individuals read Chaucer's works, Patterson nonetheless faces the need to generalize if he is to base his own readings on medieval readings.

Patterson seems to deal with this problem in his various articles and books in two ways, and each implies a different vision of audience. The first way Patterson deals with the challenge of the possibility of conflicting readings and major abberations is to envision an audience that is not homogeneous in its composition, but which is not so heterogeneous that it cannot be considered as a group entity. Most of this conceptualization is implicit. In some of his articles, such as "Ambiguity and Interpretation: A Fifteenth-Century Reading of *Troilus and Criseyde*," Patterson's image of the medieval audience allows for multiplicity and heterogeneity but seems to limit these somewhat—the audience is never *too* multiple or *too* heterogeneous. His understanding of the way in which audiences work does not allow for true abberations or "lone wolves." Instead, his image of audience in these cases seems to be based on the assumption that audiences, for the most part, act in a "swarm-like" manner.[58] As opposed to Dinshaw's image of audience in her later works, which allows for a whole medley of weird individuals and variant interpretations, Patterson's image of audience is one in which indivdiuals work like a swarm of bees: they each think they are individuals—and in fact they *are* individuals—but they all end up heading in pretty much the same direction. Whatever the varying, erratic pathways of a particular bee might be, when viewed as a whole system, the swarm "heads in one direction"—the swarm

---

"But the habits—or compulsions—of the Wife's almost entirely male audience. ..." Nonetheless, Patterson's criticism here still depends upon the audience being male.

58   Swarm theory and ideas about "self-organizing systems" have developed as metaphors in the fields of business and organizational behaviour: for example, see Kevin Kelly, *Out of Control: The New Biology of Machines, Social Systems and the Economic World* (New York: Addison-Wesley 1994) 5–28; Margaret J. Wheatley, *Leadership and the New Science: Learning About Organization from an Orderly Universe* (San Francisco: Berrett-Koehler, 1994) 75–99. It should be noted that this metaphor of a swarm as a model for theorizing about Patterson's methodology is mine, not Patterson's.

150 *Twentieth-Century Chaucer Criticism*

as a whole can be shown to have interests and desires which the individuals work together to realize. Individuals may be erratic and unpredictable, but the group as a whole operates in predictable, analyzable ways. Unlike a Foucauldian system, which has an overarching structure which constrains and dictates the way in which individuals act, and unlike Dinshaw's heterogeneous, kaleidoscopic whirl of individuals, Patterson's image of audience here seems to be swarm-like: without any clear leader or directing structure, the individual readers nonetheless move in more-or-less the same direction, and provide more-or-less the same readings. When Patterson analyzes a specific reading, he operates on the assumption that the reading will not be a wild aberration from the norm, but will provide evidence for the general outlines of all medieval readings. His own interpretation is then based on these "general outlines." To return to the swarm metaphor, in following the path of one specific bee, one can estimate the path of the entire swarm; one should not head east, however, if the swarm is heading west. In studying the workings of a particular reading—the Syon reader, for example—Patterson can discern the general outlines of the workings of the audience as a whole. Modern critics do not have to exactly replicate a specific medieval reading in order to remain true to the way in which a "medieval audience" would have read. However, they should not interpret the text in a way that seriously opposes or drastically contradicts the way in which a specific medieval reader reads. Patterson's "audience function" in this instance depends upon an image of the audience as being like a swarm: only in this way can he generalize about the "audience" from specific "readers."

The second way Patterson deals with the possibilities of conflicting or bizarre readings is to tone down the historicist imperative, acknowledge the contradictions, and open up a broad interpretive field into which modern readers can fit their interpretations while acknowledging the variety of medieval response. In this case the audience does not function as a swarm—the individual readers produce readings that are distinctly opposed. However, that very fact, the conflict among medieval readers, is taken into account by Patterson and becomes crucial in forming his own reading. This approach becomes most evident in the article "'The Living Witnesses of Our Redemption': Martyrdom and Imitation in Chaucer's Prioress's Tale." The Prioress's Tale has always been a problem for critics who subscribe to a historicist imperative which maintains that we are to read texts as medieval people do: if that medieval reading is discovered to be happily anti-semitic, most modern readers refuse point-blank to respond in such a fashion. Although Patterson does not explicitly talk about audience in this article, he addresses the problem of modern response to medieval anti-semitism by opening up medieval reading to accommodate this response—in other words, by discovering readings in the Middle Ages which counter, challenge, and call into question anti-semitic readings. The tools he draws on in order to do so are ones developed by Chaucerians over the course of the twentieth century, and thus this article is the culmination, in many ways, of a century of Chaucer scholarship.

Lee Patterson (1940–): The Subjective Reader 151

Building on a Century of Scholarship

First, Patterson implicitly adopts Kittredge's dramatic principle (although he does not call it this). He argues that the Prioress is clearly distinct from Chaucer, and that her Tale is a (dramatic) expression of her own personality, biases, and limitations. He writes,

> The tale is suited with special aptness to the historically specific teller described in the *General Prologue*. This is a tale expressive through many of its details—its sentimental diminutives, its concern with (and interest in) the suffering of the small and the helpless, its simultaneous invocation of and disgust with uncleanness, and its display of an affectivism incompletely subordinate to the discipline of Christian love—of the personality of the woman who tells it.[59]

The Prioress is the dramatization of a certain kind of spirituality in the Middle Ages—one found especially in monastaries and convents—and her Tale is, in a way, a soliloquy expressing that spirituality. Patterson, in Robertsonian fashion, next turns to historical, liturgical and iconographical evidence to discover the sources of the Prioress's story, imagery, and discourse. He traces the details of the Prioress's Tale (the slit throat, the martyrdom, the grain, the exclamations) back to the chronicles of the Jews, which record massacres performed during the Crusades and at various times in European history, and to the Christian re-casting of those events in terms of their own martyrdom and Jewish barbarism. Patterson argues that through "mimesis," these discourses, practices, and images were picked up, mimicked, and reused by different groups and cultures, ending, finally, with Chaucer and the Prioress. In this concept of mimesis, Patterson draws on the feminist theorists, such as Luce Irigaray, on which Dinshaw depends in her early work. In this definition of "mimesis," a disenfranchised group that has no "voice" of its own "mimics" official discourses in such a way as to parody, invert, or call into question the ideologies which support them.[60] Patterson's use lacks the power dimension—the Christians who mimic Jewish discourse are clearly not disenfranchised—but many of the structures used by feminist (and queer, post-colonial and black) theorists are at work in his adoption of the term. Thus he argues that Christians picked up on the Jewish discourses and "mimicked" them, adopting their images and plots but turning them to Christian, even anti-semitic, purposes. Patterson also hearkens back to the Robertsonian/Donaldsonian use of irony. He argues that Chaucer's depiction of the Prioress, and his creation of her tale, is ironic and parodic: that through the excessive anti-semitism of the

---

[59] Lee Patterson, "'The Living Witnesses of Our Redemption': Martyrdom and Imitation in Chaucer's *Prioress's Tale*," *Journal of Medieval and Early Modern Studies* 31.3 (Fall 2001) 513.

[60] See Luce Irigaray, *This Sex Which is Not One*, trans. Catherine Porter (Ithaca: Cornell University Press, 1985) 76.

Tale, Chaucer calls this very anti-semitism into question, and challenges the kind of simplistic thinking the Prioress represents. The reader, through the Prioress's obvious shortcomings, is forcibly distanced from the narrator (in much the same way that Donaldson argues the reader is distanced from the narrator in *Troilus and Criseyde* through an increasing awareness of the problems with his perspective). Because of this gap, the reader is challenged to find meanings in the Prioress's Tale other than the surface meaning, to find in the Prioress's Tale the whole history of Christian oppression of the Jews. As C.S. Lewis complains, however, such a concept of irony runs the risk of allowing the critic to ironize any passage or story he does not like; and so, finally, Patterson turns to his own understanding of a multiple, subjective audience to support his reading. He takes both Chaucer and the Prioress herself as instances of unique *reading*—they are readers and inheritors of the traditional texts of anti-semitism and Christian martyrdom. He shows the ways in which other specific readers of these anti-semitic texts produced readings at odds with a monolithic medieval anti-semitism (for example, the sympathetic depiction of Jewish lament in religious drama, particularly the play *St. Nicholas and the Jew*). In this way Patterson establishes that readings that are not anti-semitic are not anachronistic and are, therefore, options available to a medieval audience.

But was Chaucer such a reader? Patterson uses the readers *within* Chaucer's works—the concept of audience that Robertson and Dinshaw depend upon, that includes Chaucer's characters themselves as readers—to answer this question. He demonstrates that the two "readers" who are socially closest to the Prioress, her two companions the Second Nun and the Nun's Priest, both tell tales which are "readings" of her own tale. He calls these readings "intertextual commentaries" on the Prioress's Tale, arguing that the Second Nun's emphasis on responsible historicity and unsentimentalized martyrdom in her own Tale shows up the sentimentality and lack of historical awareness in the Prioress's, while the Nun's Priest, "in having Chauntecleer both tell and then ignore the legend of St. Kenelm, whose history closely parallels that of the clergeon [in the Prioress's Tale] ... implies that the Prioress no more grasps the effective lesson of her tale than does Chauntecleer his many proofs of the reliability of dreams." The "grain" of the Prioress's Tale, a seed that symbolizes unmediated transcendental signification, is mocked by the Nun's Priest's "disingenuous claim that the reader of his wonderfully multivalent tale should simply 'Taketh the fruyt and lat the chaf be stille'."[61] In this way, Patterson argues for an audience of the tradition of medieval anti-semitism which is conflicted, contradictory, and divided against itself. Through studying individual readers of the texts of this tradition—from the writer of *St. Nicholas and the Jew*, to Chaucer himself, to Chaucer's own characters—Patterson creates an image of a multiple, diverse medieval audience. Into the outlines of interpretation demarcated by this "audience function," a modern interpretation, with a modern awareness of the horrific history of anti-semitism, can comfortably fit. By drawing

---

[61]   Patterson, "Living Witnesses," 511.

on the techniques and approaches developed in a century of Chaucer scholarship, Patterson can develop an interpretation which accommodates both medieval and modern audiences.

Conclusion:
Readers Then, Now, and In Between

The closing years of the twentieth century and the opening years of the twenty-first century have seen exciting developments in the study of Chaucer and his audiences. Reader-response and reception theory have become important sub-fields for Chaucer studies, and it is in these fields that many of the most interesting new developments both in Chaucer studies and in Medieval Studies as a whole have taken place.[1] The old division between "critics" and "scholars" seems to have disappeared, and few scholars today could do without either the close reading techniques inherited from New Criticism or the palaeographical, codicological and philological tools inherited from the more historicist branches of past scholarship.[2] The multiplicity and plurality of Chaucer's audiences—concepts which were relatively revolutionary for the scholars of twenty years ago—are taken for granted, and to speak of "Chaucer's reader," as Kittredge and Donaldson do so confidently, today would almost certainly prompt the question, "which one?" While many scholars would still subscribe to a historicist imperative (that modern interpretations should be based on the way in which a medieval audience read Chaucer's works) most would be acutely aware of just how problematic the definition of that "medieval audience" has become, and how our attempts to describe it are inevitably political and subjective.

Studies in Chaucer's audience have developed in two mutually complementary and overlapping directions in the past five or ten years. First, many scholars have realized that "Chaucer's audience" does not just include medieval people and modern people, but everyone in between, and have built on the isolated early work by Caroline Spurgeon and Derek Brewer in studying those various audiences.[3] These scholars, more than Kittredge, Donaldson, or even Dinshaw, are truly cross-

---

[1]   Ethan Knapp, "Chaucer Criticism and Its Legacies," *Yale Companion to Chaucer*, Seth Lerer ed. (New Haven: Yale University Press, 2006) 351.

[2]   See the comment by Seth Lerer quoted in Joseph Dane, *Who Is Buried in Chaucer's Tomb? Studies in the Reception of Chaucer's Book* (East Lansing: Michigan State University Press, 1998) 195.

[3]   Caroline Spurgeon, ed., *Five Hundred Years of Chaucer Criticism and Allusion, 1357–1900,* 3 vols. (London: Cambridge University Press, 1925); Derek Brewer, *Chaucer: The Critical Heritage,* 2 vols. (London: Routledge and Kegan Paul, 1978). See the update of Spurgeon's work: Jackson Campbell Boswell and Sylvia Wallace Holton, *Chaucer's Fame in England: STC Chauceriana 1475–1640* (New York: Modern Language Association of America, 2004).

156 — Twentieth-Century Chaucer Criticism

historical. From the study of the formation, development and conflicted history of the "Chaucerian community" which Stephanie Trigg performs, to the changing configurations of the reception of Chaucer's body and Chaucer's book done by Joseph Dane, these scholars do not restrict their idea of Chaucer's audience to either medieval audiences or modern ones, but consider Renaissance, seventeenth-century, eighteenth-century, Victorian, modernist, and late twentieth-century responses to Chaucer's works.[4] Seth Lerer's study of Chaucer's fifteenth- and sixteenth-century readers was groundbreaking in many ways, for it studied the way in which those readers both reworked Chaucer's texts and remained faithful, in their terms, to "Father Chaucer."[5] Kathleen Forni and others have examined the way in which the inclusion of apocryphal works in the Chaucer canon affected Chaucer's reception in the sixteenth- and seventeenth-centuries.[6] Thomas Prendergast traces the changing receptions and definitions of Chaucer's "body"—both physical and literary—over the years,[7] while numerous articles and collections of essays have explored the specific responses of particular individuals.[8] Writers

---

[4] Stephanie Trigg, *Congenial Souls: Reading Chaucer from Medieval to Postmodern* (Minneapolis: University of Minnesota Press, 2002); Stephanie Trigg, "Chaucer's Influence and Reception" in Lerer, *Yale Companion to Chaucer*, 297–323; Dane, *Who is Buried?*; Steve Ellis, *Chaucer: An Oxford Guide* (Oxford: Oxford University Press, 2005), 497–543.

[5] Seth Lerer, *Chaucer and His Readers: Imagining the Author in Late-Medieval England* (Princeton: Princeton University Press, 1993); cf. Seth Lerer, "Chaucer's Sons," *University of Toronto Quarterly* 73.3 (Summer 2004) 906–15; Helen Cooper, "Chaucerian Representation," *New Readings of Chaucer's Poetry*, eds. Robert G. Benson and Susan Ridyard (Cambridge: D.S. Brewer, 2003) 12–15.

[6] Kathleen Forni, *The Chaucerian Apocrypha: A Counterfeit Canon* (Gainesville: University Press of Florida, 2001); Kathleen Forni, "The Chaucerian Apocrypha: Did Usk's 'Testament of Love' and the 'Plowman's Tale' Ruin Chaucer's Early Reputation?" *Neuphilologische Mitteilungen* 98.3 (2001) 261–72; Kathleen Forni, "The Value of Early Chaucer Editions," *Studia Neophilologica* 70.2 (1998) 173–80; Joseph A. Dane, "Bibliographical History Versus Bibliographical Evidence: The Plowman's Tale and Early Chaucer Editions," *Bulletin of the John Rylands University Library of Manchester* 78.1 (Spring 1996) 47–61.

[7] Thomas A. Prendergast, *Chaucer's Dead Body: From Corpse to Corpus* (New York: Routledge, 2004).

[8] See the collections of essays such as Thomas A. Prendergast and Barbara Kline, eds., *Rewriting Chaucer: Culture, Authority and the Idea of the Authentic Text, 1400–1602* (Columbus: Ohio State University Press, 1999), or Theresa M. Krier, ed., *Refiguring Chaucer in the Renaissance* (Gainesville: University Press of Florida, 1998), as well as articles by Bowers, Strohm, Spearing, Edwards, Boffey, and Benson, among others: John M. Bowers, "The *Tale of Beryn* and the *Siege of Thebes*: Alternative Ideas of the *Canterbury Tales*," *Studies in the Age of Chaucer* 7 (1985) 23–50; Paul Strohm, "Chaucer's Fifteenth-Century Audience and the Narrowing of the 'Chaucer Tradition'," *Studies in the Age of Chaucer* 4 (1982) 3–32; A.C. Spearing, "Lydgate's Canterbury Tale: The *Siege of Thebes* and Fifteenth-Century Chaucerianism," *Fifteenth-Century Studies: Recent Essays*, ed. Robert F. Yeager (Hamden: Archon, 1984) 333–64; A.S.G. Edwards, "The Early Reception

Conclusion: *Readers Then, Now, and In Between*

such as Charlotte Morse extend studies of Chaucer's audience to the Victorians and nineteenth-century readers, while Steve Ellis and Candace Barrington explore the non-academic twentieth-century responses to Chaucer's works.[9] These studies overlap with general histories of Chaucer criticism and explore the reception of Chaucer's works up to and throughout the twentieth century.

Kittredge, Lewis, and earlier Victorian scholars also studied the responses of successors of Chaucer such as Lydgate, Hoccleve and the writer of the *Tale of Beryn*. What is new and different about the recent studies is the way in which they incorporate insights drawn from the second field of reader-response study that has opened up in the past 25 years: the study of scribal and marginal evidence as extant traces of readers' reactions. Instead of studying the way in which a reader is implicitly "coded" within a text, or a general concept of how readers in a particular society would receive certain texts, these studies focus on the minute traces actual readers left of their readings in the physical books they left behind. A 1979 article by B.A. Windeatt was trend-setting in this regard. Windeatt argues that the scribes of various manuscripts of Chaucer's works, instead of being considered irritating nuisances whose influence the textual critic had to erase in order to discover the author's "real" text, should be valued for the evidence of unique readings of Chaucer's work they provided. Windeatt characterizes scribal transcribing as "active reading," and writes, "the scribes ... can offer us the earliest line-by-line literary criticism of Chaucer's poetry."[10] Scribes were not mere machines, mindlessly transcribing words they did not understand, but were *critics* and *readers*, and incorporated their interpretations into the copies they made. Later scholars echo this insight: Seth Lerer writes, "A manuscript of a given work can represent, potentially, a critical reading of that work, and in manuscripts which are considered textually unreliable we may find evidence for the critical interpretation of Chaucer's poetry."[11] This is true not just of scribal variation, but

---

of Chaucer and Langland," *Florilegium* 15 (1998) 1–22; Julia Boffey, "Richard Pynson's *Book of Fame* and the *Letter of Dido*," *Viator* 19 (1988) 339–53; C. David Benson, "Critic and Poet: What Lydgate and Henryson Did to Chaucer's *Troilus and Criseyde*," *Modern Language Quarterly* 53.1 (March 1992) 23–40.

[9] Charlotte Morse, "Popularizing Chaucer in the Nineteenth Century," *Chaucer Review* 38.2 (2003) 99–125; Steve Ellis, *Chaucer at Large: The Poet in the Modern Imagination* (Minneapolis: University of Minnesota Press, 2000); Candace Barrington, *American Chaucers* (New York: Palgrave, 2007); see also John Ganim, "Mary Shelley, Godwin's *Chaucer*, and the Middle Ages," *Chaucer and the Challenges of Medievalism*, eds. Donka Minkova and Theresa Tinkle (Frankfurt: Peter Lang, 2003) 175–89.

[10] B.A. Windeatt, "The Scribes as Chaucer's Early Critics," *Studies in the Age of Chaucer* 1 (1979) 119–41, 122, 120; cf. 121. For discussion and criticism of this article, see Dane, *Who is Buried?*, 204–10.

[11] Seth Lerer, "Rewriting Chaucer: Two Fifteenth-Century Readings of *The Canterbury Tales*," *Viator* 19 (1988) 1. See also Derek Pearsall, "Texts, Textual Criticism and Fifteenth-Century Manuscript Production," *Fifteenth-Century Studies: Recent Essays*, ed. Robert F. Yeager (Hamden: Archon, 1984) 128; Dane, *Who is Buried?*, 196; John

158   *Twentieth-Century Chaucer Criticism*

of marginal glosses and commentary: Susan Schibanoff remarks, "The anonymous glosses or marginal annotations that appear in almost half of the 58 complete manuscripts of *The Canterbury Tales* provide a rich—but neglected—source of reader response to Chaucer's poetry."[12] Lee Patterson, in his analysis of the Syon manuscript, positions himself among the scholars who share this insight, and who study particular medieval manuscripts and early printed books for evidence of unique instances of reading. Lerer and Schibanoff likewise perform close analyses of specific manuscripts in various articles; other scholars who undertake similar studies include John Bowers, Barbara Kline, Edgar Laird, Julia Boffey, A.S.G. Edwards, Beverly Kennedy, Alison Baker, and Paul Strohm.[13] The *Huntington Library Quarterly* devoted a special issue to such explorations, including studies by Ralph Hanna III, Julia Boffey and David Boyd, while Kathryn Kerby-Fulton and Maidie Hilmo edited a collection of essays on the same topic.[14] David Matthews and Alexandra Gillespie perform similar analyses on printed books, looking for the responses of particular readers in the materiality of specific books in the way

---

Bowers, "Chaucer's *Canterbury Tales*—Politically Corrected" in Prendergast and Kline, *Rewriting Chaucer*, 14.

[12] Susan Schibanoff, "The New Reader and Female Textuality in Two Early Commentaries on Chaucer," *Studies in the Age of Chaucer* 10 (1988) 71. See also Kathryn Kerby-Fulton and Maidie Hilmo, eds., *The Medieval Professional Reader at Work: Evidence from the Manuscripts of Chaucer, Langland, Kempe and Gower* (Victoria: University of Victoria Press, 2001) 7.

[13] Lerer, "Rewriting Chaucer"; Seth Lerer, "Unpublished Sixteenth-Century Arguments to *The Canterbury Tales*," *Notes and Queries* 50.1 (2003) 13–17; Seth Lerer, "Textual Criticism and Literary Theory: Chaucer and His Readers," *Exemplaria* 2.1 (Spring 1990) 329–45; Schibanoff, "The New Reader"; John M. Bowers, "Two Professional Readers of Chaucer and Langland: Scribe D and the HM 114 Scribe," *Studies in the Age of Chaucer* 26 (2004) 113–46; articles by Kline, Laird, Boffey and Edwards, and Kennedy in Prendergast and Kline, *Rewriting Chaucer*; Alison Ann Baker, "Writers as Readers: The Scribes of Chaucer's 'Troilus and Criseyde'," unpublished PhD diss. Purdue University, 2002; Theresa Tinkle, "The Imagined Chaucerian Community of Bodleian MS Fairfax 16," in Minkova and Tinkle, eds., *Chaucer and the Challenges of Medievalism*, 157–74; Julia Boffey and A.S.G. Edwards, "Manuscripts and Audience," Corinne Saunders, ed., *A Concise Companion to Chaucer* (Oxford: Blackwell, 2006) 34–50, especially 44–8; Paul Strohm, "Jean of Angoulême: A Fifteenth Century Reader of Chaucer," *Neuphilologische Mitteilungen* 72 (1971) 69–76. As Joseph Dane notes, Strohm's 1971 article, published well before Windeatt's revolutionizing article, attributes the "specific readership" to the owner of the manuscript, John of Angoulême, and not to the scribe, Duxworth, as later scholars might have opted to do. See Dane, *Who is Buried?*, 199.

[14] See the introduction to this issue, and the essays in the same volume: Seth Lerer and Joseph Dane, "Reading from the Margins: Textual Studies, Chaucer, and Medieval Literature," *Huntington Library Quarterly* 58.1 (1995); Kerby-Fulton and Hilmo, *Medieval Professional Reader*.

Conclusion: Readers Then, Now, and In Between 159

other scholars examine individual manuscripts.[15] Other scholars, especially feminist scholars attempting to discern traces of female readership and women's reading practices, have examined wills and other documents to discover the owners of particular manuscripts.[16] In this way they can discover the actual, specific readers of texts, and, in the way in which books moved, were compiled, were categorized, and were glossed, tentatively trace what some of the reading practices of those individuals might have been.

These scholars, for the most part, perform very detailed, extremely valuable studies of specific, particular instances of reading. Few of them, however, theorize about the implications their endeavours have for the broader field of studies in Chaucer's audience, or theories of audience generally. Like Lee Patterson, they give the student of Chaucer an excellent understanding of the readings of specific individuals without always suggesting a methodology with which to generalize from those local, unique readings. They do not always conceptualize the move from "reader" to "audience," and while they offer a great deal of detailed evidence about the functioning of readers, they are only beginning to draw any abstract conclusions from that evidence. They offer much that is valuable to the student of Chaucer and his readers, but they rarely contribute explicitly to more general theories about the way in which medieval audiences, or audiences in general, function. In many ways this is a welcome development, since it is a reaction against the overly-generalized, overly-abstract theories of critics such as C.S. Lewis or D.W. Robertson. Yet it leaves the student of Chaucer, and indeed of reception-theory in general, in danger of getting lost in the forest because of all the trees.

I have traced, through a study of six specific scholars of different generations, the ways in which the "audience function" has changed over the course of the twentieth century, and we have seen the effects these changes have had on interpretations of Chaucer. Kittredge's and Lewis's image of relatively trusting

---

[15] David Matthews, "Public Ambition, Private Desire and the Last Tudor Chaucer," *Reading the Medieval in Early Modern England*, ed. Gordon McMullan and David Matthews (Cambridge: Cambridge University Press, 2007) 74–88; David Matthews, "Speaking to Chaucer: The Poet and the Nineteenth-Century Academy," *Studies in Medievalism* 9 (1997) 5–25; Alexandra Gillespie, "Caxton's *Chaucer* and Lydgate Quartos: Miscellanies from Manuscript to Print," *Transactions of the Cambridge Bibliographical Society*, 21.1 (2000) 1–25; Joseph A. Dane and Alexandra Gillespie, "Back at Chaucer's Tomb," *Studies in Bibliography* 52 (1999) 89–96; Alexandra Gillespie, *Print Culture and the Medieval Author: Chaucer, Lydgate, and Their Books, 1473–1557* (Oxford: Oxford University Press, 2006) chapter 3.

[16] See Julia Boffey, "'Twenty Thousand More': Some Fifteenth- and Sixteenth-Century Responses to the *Legend of Good Women*," *Middle English Poetry: Texts and Traditions*, ed. A.J. Minnis (York: York Medieval Texts, 2001) 279–97; Nicola F. McDonald, "Chaucer's *Legend of Good Women*, Ladies at Court and the Female Reader," *Chaucer Review* 35.1 (2000) 22–42; Josephine Korster-Tarvers, "'Thys Ys My Mystrys Boke': English Women as Readers and Writers in Late Medieval England," *The Uses of Manuscripts in Literary Studies*, ed. Charlotte Morse *et al.* (Kalamazoo: Western Michigan University Press, 1992) 305–27.

audiences produced criticism which took Chaucer's poetry "straight," giving fairly straightforward, literal readings which did not depend on profound ironies or inversions. Donaldson and Robertson, by contrast, posited audiences which were distanced from the narrators or characters of the text, and their readings were profoundly ironic and at times the direct opposite of the literal meaning of the text. Dinshaw and Patterson produced readings which did not depend as much on the concept of irony, but were alive to the multiplicity of Chaucer's audience, and hence they developed criticism which was less overarching and universal, and more hesitant, contingent and specific. We have also seen a fundamental divide between historicist and cross-historical scholars: the workings-out of this division have undergone much change, but the root issue remains one that faces every critic of Chaucer. Will one restrict the "audience function" to Chaucer's original medieval audience, or will one expand it to include modern as well as medieval audiences? To what extent can modern responses act as indicators of a medieval audience's reactions?

Because of the profound effect assumptions about audience have on one's criticism, it is my conviction that critics must explicitly theorize about the choices they make in defining the "audience function" for their interpretations. Dinshaw and Patterson make gestures towards this kind of theorization. In contrast to earlier scholars, late-twentieth-century scholars are much more self-reflective and conscious about the assumptions they are making and the ways in which their personal subjectivity might affect their interpretations. Nonetheless, as we have seen with Patterson, this consciousness does not always go far enough. In his omission of an explanation of how he generalizes from specific readers to a general audience, Patterson leaves crucial assumptions about the reading process unstated. We have made great steps, as a discipline, in moving away from the overarching, over-generalized theories of the beginning and mid-century critics, which ignored individuals and unique cases in favour of broad images of the "medieval mind." With the excellent work of so many New Historicists, codicologists, and palaeographers, we have redirected our focus on the unique and the specific in a way that does much to redress the oppressions and exclusions of earlier approaches. What is needed now is a renewal of abstraction, without an attendant loss of the material and concrete.

We need to conceptualize our work in two ways. First, as I discussed with reference to Patterson, we need to conceptualize a move from specific to general. In the metaphors drawn from swarm theory which I used in describing Patterson's apparent assumptions about audiences, I raised one possibility for conceptualizing the way in which we might envision the movement from specific cases to general conclusions. More theorizing of this sort is needed. If we wish to read in the way a medieval audience read, we need to develop a way of generalizing from "reader" to "audience" that does not lose the specificity and the uniqueness of the individual reader, or subsume him or her in grand theories that take precedence over concrete examples. While studies of individual readers and specific instances are worthy and interesting in themselves, if these studies are to have any meaning to the

Conclusion: Readers Then, Now, and In Between 161

broader field of Medieval Studies or of audience-reception studies—whether or not we subscribe to a historicist imperative that our own interpretations of Chaucer should be based on medieval readings—we need to be able to theorize on the basis of individual cases. This move must be explicitly conceptualized if the theory is to have any force.

Second, the studies of individual, particular readers of Chaucer open up another, fascinating field of conceptualization. As literary critics, our endeavours often touch on the verges of big questions: how do audiences read literature? How does the communication process function? How do stories mean? How does language work? Why do we love stories? Why are stories and poems meaningful and powerful in a way that facts and data often are not? We cannot answer, and probably never will be able to answer, even a fraction of these questions (indeed, many properly belong more to the work of cognitive psychologists and linguists than to literary critics). What we *can* ask, however, and what we do have a chance at answering, are questions a step removed from these big ones. We can ask these same questions of the readers we study, and explore the ways in which *they* answered them. How did Chaucer's *readers* think stories worked? Why did *they* like his poetry? How did *they* think communication and writing and story-telling and literary transmission and language itself worked? How did this affect the ways in which they read Chaucer? And how did Chaucer himself think all these things worked? How did he think audiences functioned, and what effect did this have on his writing? With the extensive concrete examples of "palpably specific" reading practices which have been unearthed in the past fifteen years and which continue to be developed, we have ways of answering these questions. We have evidence to form the basis for new conceptualizations and theories about the way in which audiences in general, and Chaucer's audience in particular, function.

Bibliography

Akbari, Suzanne Conklin. *Seeing through the Veil: Optical Theory and Medieval Allegory.* Toronto: University of Toronto Press, 2004.

Allen, Judson Boyce. *The Ethical Poetic of the Middle Ages.* Toronto: University of Toronto Press, 1982.

————— and Theresa Anne Moritz. *A Distinction of Stories: The Medieval Unity of Chaucer's Fair Chain of Narratives for Canterbury.* Columbus: Ohio State University Press, 1981.

Allen, Mark and John H. Fisher. *The Essential Chaucer; An Annotated Bibliography of Major Modern Studies.* Boston: G.K. Hall, 1987.

Altick, Richard D. *The Scholar Adventurers.* New York: Macmillan, 1960.

Anderson, Judith H. "Commenting on Donaldson's Commentaries." *Chaucer Review* 41.3 (2007) 271–8.

Augustine. *On Christian Doctrine.* Trans. D.W. Robertson, Jr. Upper Saddle River: Prentice Hall, 1958.

Baker, Alison Ann. "Writers as Readers: The Scribes of Chaucer's 'Troilus and Criseyde'." Unpublished PhD Diss. Purdue University, 2002.

Bal, Mieke. *Narratology: Introduction to the Theory of Narrative.* Toronto: University of Toronto Press, 1985.

Barbour, Brian. "Lewis and Cambridge." *Modern Philology* 96.4 (May 1999) 439–84.

Barthes, Roland. *Rustle of Language.* Oxford: Basil Blackwell, 1986.

Baugh, Albert C. "Fifty Years of Chaucer Scholarship." *Speculum* 26.4 (Fall 1951) 659–72.

Beach, Charles F. "C.S. Lewis, Courtly Love, and Chaucer's *Troilus and Criseyde.*" *C.S. Lewis* 26.4 (February 1995) 1–10.

Beidler, Peter G., ed. *Geoffrey Chaucer: The Wife of Bath: Case Studies in Contemporary Criticism.* Boston: Bedford Books, 1996.

—————. "Teaching Chaucer as Drama: The Garden Scene in the Shipman's Tale." *Exemplaria* 8.2 (1996) 485–93.

Benson, C. David. "The *Canterbury Tales*: Personal Drama or Experiments in Poetic Variety?" *The Cambridge Chaucer Companion.* Ed. Piero Boitani and Jill Mann. Cambridge: Cambridge University Press, 1986. 93–108.

—————. "Critic and Poet: What Lydgate and Henryson Did to Chaucer's *Troilus and Criseyde.*" *Modern Language Quarterly* 53.1 (March 1992) 23–40.

Benson, Larry D. "Courtly Love and Chivalry in the Later Middle Ages." *Fifteenth-Century Studies: Recent Essays.* Ed. Robert F. Yeager. Hamden: Archon, 1984. 237–57.

164   *Twentieth-Century Chaucer Criticism*

————. "A Reader's Guide to Writings on Chaucer." *Geoffrey Chaucer.* Ed. Derek Brewer. London: G. Bell & Sons, 1974. 321–51.

Berggren, Ruth. "Who Really Is the Advocate of Equality in the Marriage Group?" *Massachusetts Studies in English* 6.1 (1977) 25–36.

Birney, Earle. *Essays on Chaucerian Irony.* Toronto: University of Toronto Press, 1985.

Bloomfield, Morton W. "The *Canterbury Tales* as Framed Narratives." *Leeds Studies in English* 14 (1983) 44–56.

————. "Contemporary Literary Theory and Chaucer." *New Perspectives in Chaucer Criticism.* Ed. Donald L. Rose. Norman: Pilgrim, 1981. 23–36.

Bloom, Harold, ed. *Bloom's Modern Critical Views: Geoffrey Chaucer.* New York: Infobase Publishing, 2007.

Boase, Roger. *The Origin and Meaning of Courtly Love: A Critical Study of European Scholarship.* Manchester: Manchester University Press, 1977.

Boffey, Julia. "The Reputation and Circulation of Chaucer's Lyrics in the Fifteenth Century." *Chaucer Review* 28.1 (1993) 23–40.

————. "Richard Pynson's *Book of Fame* and the *Letter of Dido.*" *Viator* 19 (1988) 339–53.

————. "'Twenty Thousand More': Some Fifteenth- and Sixteenth-Century Responses to *The Legend of Good Women.*" *Middle English Poetry: Texts and Traditions.* Ed. A.J. Minnis. York, England: York Medieval Texts, 2001. 279–97.

———— and A.S.G. Edwards. "Manuscripts and Audience." *A Concise Companion to Chaucer.* Ed. Corinne Saunders. Oxford: Blackwell, 2006. 34–50.

Boitani, Piero and Jill Mann, eds. *Cambridge Companion to Chaucer*, 2nd ed. Cambridge: Cambridge University Press, 2003.

Booth, Wayne. *The Rhetoric of Fiction.* Chicago: University of Chicago Press, 1961.

Boswell, Jackson Campbell and Sylvia Wallace Holton. *Chaucer's Fame in England: STC Chauceriana 1475–1640.* New York: Modern Language Association of America, 2004.

Bowers, John M. "The *Tale of Beryn* and *The Siege of Thebes*: Alternative Ideas of *The Canterbury Tales.*" *Studies in the Age of Chaucer* 7 (1985) 23–50.

————. "Two Professional Readers of Chaucer and Langland: Scribe D and the HM 114 Scribe." *Studies in the Age of Chaucer* 26 (2004) 113–46.

Brewer, D.S., ed. *Chaucer: The Critical Heritage,* 2 vols. London: Routledge and Kegan Paul, 1978.

————. "The Criticism of Chaucer in the Twentieth Century." *Chaucer's Mind and Art.* Ed. A.C. Cawley. Edinburgh: Oliver and Boyd, 1969. 1–25.

————. "The History of a Shady Character: The Narrator of *Troilus and Criseyde.*" *Modes of Narrative: Approaches to American, Canadian and British Fiction.* Ed. Reingard M. Nischik and Barbara Korte. Würzburg: Königshausen and Neumann, 1990. 166–78.

————. "The Reconstruction of Chaucer." *Studies in the Age of Chaucer: Proceedings 1* (1985) 3–19.

————. "Review of *Fruyt and Chaf*." *Review of English Studies* 16.63 (August 1965) 304–5.

Brown, Carleton. "The Evolution of the Canterbury 'Marriage Group'." *PMLA* 48 (1933) 1041–59.

Burrow, Colin. "C.S. Lewis and *The Allegory of Love*." *Essays in Criticism* 53.3 (2003) 284–94.

Cai, Zong-qi. "Fragments I–II and III–V in *The Canterbury Tales*: A Re-Examination of the Idea of the 'Marriage Group'." *Comitatus* 19 (1988) 80–98.

Calin, William. "C.S. Lewis, Literary Critic: A Reassessment." *Mythlore* 23.3 (Summer 2001) 4–20.

————. "Defense and Illustration of Fin'amor: Some Polemical Comments on the Robertsonian Approach." *The Expansion and Transformations of Courtly Literature*. Ed. Nathaniel B. Smith and Joseph T. Snow. Athens: University of Georgia Press, 1980. 32–48.

————. *The Twentieth-Century Humanist Critics: From Spitzer to Frye*. Toronto: University of Toronto Press, 2007.

Cantor, Norman. *Inventing the Middle Ages*. New York: William Morris, 1991.

Carruthers, Mary J. "Speaking of Donaldson." *Acts of Interpretation: The Text in Its Context: Essays in Honor of E. Talbot Donaldson*. Ed. Mary J. Carruthers. Norman: Pilgrim Books, 1982. 365–80.

Chatman, Seymour. *Story and Discourse: Narrative Structure in Fiction and Film*. Ithaca: Cornell University Press, 1978.

Chaucer, Geoffrey. *The Riverside Chaucer*. Ed. Larry Benson. 3rd ed. Oxford: Oxford University Press, 1987.

"Chaucer's Audiences: Discussion." *Chaucer Review* 18.2 (1983) 175–81.

Coghill, N.K. "Love and 'Foul Delight': Some Contrasted Attitudes." *Patterns of Love and Courtesy*. Ed. John Lawlor. London: Edward Arnold, 1966. 141–56.

Como, James T., ed. *C.S. Lewis at the Breakfast Table and Other Reminiscences*. London: Collins, 1980.

Cooper, Helen. "Chaucerian Representation." *New Readings of Chaucer's Poetry*. Ed. Robert G. Benson and Susan Ridyard. Cambridge: D.S. Brewer, 2003. 7–29.

————. *The Structure of the* Canterbury Tales. Athens: University of Georgia Press, 1983.

Crane, Susan. *Insular Romance: Politics, Faith, and Culture in Anglo-Norman and Middle English Literature*. Berkeley: University of California Press, 1986.

Dane, Joseph A. "Bibliographical History versus Bibliographical Evidence: The Plowman's Tale and Early Chaucer Editions." *Bulletin of the John Rylands University Library of Manchester* 78.1 (Spring 1996) 47–61.

————. *Who is Buried in Chaucer's Tomb? Studies in the Reception of Chaucer's Book*. East Lansing: Michigan State University Press, 1998.

166 *Twentieth-Century Chaucer Criticism*

————— and Alexandra Gillespie. "Back at Chaucer's Tomb." *Studies in Bibliography* 52 (1999) 89–96.

Delasanta, Rodney. "Chaucer and the Exegetes." *Studies in the Literary Imagination* 4.2 (1971) 1–10.

de Man, Paul. *Allegories of Reading: Figural Language in Rousseau, Nietzsche, Rilke and Proust*. New Haven: Yale University Press, 1979.

Dempster, Germaine. "A Period in the Development of the *Canterbury Tales* Marriage Group and of Blocks B2 and C." *PMLA* 68 (1953) 1142–59.

DeNeef, Leigh. "Robertson and the Critics." *Chaucer Review* 2 (1968) 205–34.

Derrida, Jacques. *Of Grammatology*. Trans. Gayatri Chakravorty Spivak. Baltimore: Johns Hopkins University Press, 1976.

Dinshaw, Carolyn. *Chaucer and the Text: Two Views of the Authors*. New York: Garland Press, 1988.

—————. "Chaucer's Queer Touches/A Queer Touches Chaucer." *Exemplaria* 7.1 (1995) 75–92.

—————. *Chaucer's Sexual Poetics*. Madison: University of Wisconsin Press, 1989.

—————. "Dice Games and Other Games in Le Jeu de Saint Nicolas." *PMLA* 95.5 (October 1980) 802–11.

—————. Email. July 16, 2005.

—————. "Eunuch Hermeneutics." *English Literary History* 55.1 (Spring 1988) 27–51.

—————. "Getting Medieval: *Pulp Fiction*, Gawain, Foucault." *The Book and the Body*. Ed. Dolores Frese and Katherine O'Brien O'Keefe. Notre Dame: University of Notre Dame Press, 1997. 116–63.

—————. *Getting Medieval: Sexualities and Communities, Pre- and Postmodern*. Durham: Duke University Press, 1999.

—————. "A Kiss is Just a Kiss: Heterosexuality and Its Consolations in *Sir Gawain and the Green Knight*." *Diacritics* 24.2/3 (Summer–Autumn 1994) 204–26.

—————. "Margery Kempe." *The Cambridge Companion to Medieval Women's Writing*. Ed. Carolyn Dinshaw and David Wallace. Cambridge: Cambridge University Press, 2003. 222–39.

—————. "New Approaches to Chaucer." *The Cambridge Companion to Chaucer*, 2nd ed. Ed. Piero Boitani and Jill Mann. Cambridge: Cambridge University Press, 2003. 270–89.

—————. "Pale Faces: Race, Religion, and Affect in Chaucer's Texts and Their Readers." *Studies in the Age of Chaucer* 23 (2001) 19–41.

—————. "Quarrels, Rivals, and Rape: Gower and Chaucer." *A Wyf Ther Was: Essays in Honour of Paule Mertens-Fonck*. Ed. Juliette Dor. Liège: Department of Language and Literature, Liège, 1992. 112–22.

Donaldson, E. Talbot. "Adventures with the Adversative Conjunction in the General Prologue to the *Canterbury Tales*; or, What's Before the But?" *So Meny People Longages and Tonges: Philological Essays in Scots and Mediaeval English*

Presented to Angus McIntosh. Ed. Michael Benskin and M.L. Samuels. Edinburgh: Middle English Dialect Project, 1981. 355–66.

—————. "Arcite's Injury." *Middle English Studies Presented to Norman Davis in Honour of His Seventieth Birthday*. Ed. Douglas Gray and E.G. Stanley. Oxford: Clarendon Press, 1983. 65–7.

—————, ed. and tr. *Beowulf*. New York: Norton, 1966.

—————. "Chaucer and the Elusion of Clarity." *Essays and Studies* 25 (1972) 23–44.

—————. "Chaucer in the Twentieth Century." *Studies in the Age of Chaucer* 2 (1980) 7–13.

—————. "Chaucer, *Canterbury Tales*, D117: A Critical Edition." *Speculum* 40 (1965) 626–33.

—————. "Chaucer's Final -e." *PMLA* 63 (1948) 1101–24.

—————. "Chaucer's *Miller's Tale*, A3583–6." *Modern Language Notes* 69 (1954) 310–4.

—————, ed. *Chaucer's Poetry: An Anthology for the Modern Reader*. New York: The Ronald Press Company, 1958.

—————. "Chaucer the Pilgrim." *Chaucer Criticism:* The Canterbury Tales. Ed. Richard J. Schoeck and Jerome Taylor. Notre Dame: University of Notre Dame Press, 1960. 1–13.

—————. "Designing a Camel: Or, Generalizing the Middle Ages." *Tennessee Studies in Literature* 22 (1977) 1–16.

—————. "Gallic Flies in Chaucer's English Wordweb." *New Perspectives in Chaucer Criticism*. Ed. Donald M. Rose. Norman: Pilgrim Books, 1982. 193–202.

—————. "Idiom of Popular Poetry in the *Miller's Tale*." *Explication as Criticism: Selected Papers from the English Institute 1941–1952*. Ed. W.K. Wimsatt. New York: Columbia University Press, 1951. 27–51.

—————. "MSS R and F in the B-Tradition of *Piers Plowman*." *Transactions of the Connecticut Academy of Arts and Sciences* 39 (1955) 177–212.

—————. "Oysters Forsooth: Two Readings in Pearl." *Neuphilologische Mitteilungen* 63 (1972) 75–82.

—————. "*Piers Plowman:* Textual Comparison and the Question of Authorship." *Chaucer und seine Zeit*. Ed. A. Esch. Tübingen: Niemeyer, 1968. 241–7.

—————. *Piers Plowman: The C-Text and Its Poet*. New Haven: Yale University Press, 1949.

—————. *Speaking of Chaucer*. London: Athlone Press, 1970.

—————. *The Swan at the Well: Shakespeare Reading Chaucer*. New Haven: Yale University Press, 1985.

—————. "The Texts of *Piers Plowman:* Scribes and Poets." *Modern Philology* 50 (1953) 269–73.

—————— and George Kane, eds. *Piers Plowman: The B Version*. London: Athlone, 1975.

Eagleton, Terry. *Literary Theory: An Introduction*. Oxford: Blackwell, 1983.

Edwards, A.S.G. "The Early Reception of Chaucer and Langland." *Florilegium* 15 (1998) 1–22.

Edwards, Bruce L. "Deconstruction and Rehabilitation: C.S. Lewis and Critical Theory." *C.S. Lewis* 13.11 (September 1982) 1–7.

————, ed. *The Taste of the Pineapple: Essays on C.S. Lewis as Reader, Critic and Imaginative Writer*. Bowling Green, Ohio: Popular, 1988.

Ellis, Steve, ed. *Chaucer: An Oxford Guide*. Oxford: Oxford University Press, 2005.

————. *Chaucer at Large: The Poet in the Modern Imagination*. Minneapolis: University of Minnesota Press, 2000.

Erler, Mary C. "Fifteenth-Century Owners of Chaucer's Work: Cambridge, Magdalene College MS Pepys 2006." *Chaucer Review* 38.4 (2004) 401–14.

Farrell, Thomas J. "The Persistence of Donaldson's Memory." *Chaucer Review* 41.3 (2007) 289–98.

Faulkner, Peter. "'The Paths of Virtue and Early English': F.J. Furnivall and Victorian Medievalism." *From Medieval to Medievalism*. Ed. John Simons. New York: St. Martin's, 1992. 144–58.

Fichte, Joerg O. "The Reception of C.S. Lewis' Scholarly Works in Germany." *Man's "Natural Powers": Essays For and About C.S. Lewis*. Ed. Raymond P. Tripp, Jr. Church Stretton: Society for New Language Study, 1975. 17–22.

Fish, Stanley. *Is There a Text in This Class? The Authority of Interpretive Communities*. Cambridge, Mass.: Harvard University Press, 1980.

————. *Surprised by Sin: The Reader in Paradise Lost*. Berkeley: University of California Press, 1967.

Fleming, John. *Reason and the Lover*. Princeton: Princeton University Press, 1984.

————. Telephone interview. June 7, 2005.

Forni, Kathleen. *The Chaucerian Apocrypha: A Counterfeit Canon*. Gainesville: University Press of Florida, 2001.

————. "The Chaucerian Apocrypha: Did Usk's 'Testament of Love' and the 'Plowman's Tale' Ruin Chaucer's Early Reputation?" *Neuphilologische Mitteilungen* 98.3 (1997) 261–72.

————. "The Value of Early Chaucer Editions." *Studia Neophilologica* 70.2 (1998) 173–80.

Foucault, Michel. "What is an Author?" *Modern Criticism and Theory: A Reader*. Ed. David Lodge. London: Longman, 1988. 197–210.

Ganim, John M. "Drama, Theatricality and Performance: Radicals of Presentation in the *Canterbury Tales*." *Drama, Narrative and Poetry in the* Canterbury Tales. Ed. Wendy Harding. Toulouse, France: Presse Université du Mirail, 2003. 69–82.

Genette, Gerard. *Narrative Discourse: An Essay in Method*. Trans. Jane E. Lewin. Ithaca: Cornell University Press, 1980.

————. *Narrative Discourse Revisited*. Trans. Jane E. Lewin. Ithaca: Cornell University Press, 1988.

Ginsberg, Warren. "The Lineaments of Desire: Wish-Fulfillment in Chaucer's Marriage Group." *Criticism* 25.3 (Summer 1983) 197–210.

Gillespie Alexandra. "Caxton's Chaucer and Lydgate Quartos: Miscellanies from Manuscript to Print." *Transactions of the Cambridge Bibliographical Society* 21.1 (2000) 1–25.

————. *Print Culture and the Medieval Author: Chaucer, Lydgate, and Their Books, 1473–1557.* Oxford: Oxford University Press, 2006.

Gradon, Pamela. "Review of *Essays in Medieval Culture.*" *Review of English Studies* 34.133 (February 1983) 51–2.

Graff, Gerald and Michael Warner, eds. *The Origins of Literary Studies in America: A Documentary Anthology.* New York: Routledge, 1989.

Gray, Douglas, ed. *The Oxford Companion to Chaucer.* Oxford: Oxford University Press, 2003.

Green, Richard Firth. *Poets and Princepleasers.* Toronto: University of Toronto Press, 1980.

————. "Women in Chaucer's Audience." *Chaucer Review* 18.2 (1983) 146–54.

Green, Roger Lancelyn and Walter Hooper. *C.S. Lewis: A Biography.* London: HarperCollins, 2002.

Gross, John. *The Rise and Fall of the Man of Letters.* London: Macmillan, 1969.

Grudin, Michaela Paasche. "Chaucer Scholarship at the Turn of the Century: Postmodernism, Poetry, and Comfortable Assumptions." *Review* 23 (2001) 107–37.

Gust, Geoffrey. *Constructing Chaucer: Author and Autofiction in the Critical Tradition.* New York: Palgrave Macmillan, 2009.

————. "Revaluating 'Chaucer the Pilgrim' and Donaldson's Enduring Persona." *Chaucer Review* 41.3 (2007) 311–23.

Haahr, Joan G. "Chaucer's 'Marriage Group' Revisited: The Wife of Bath and Merchant in Debate." *Acta* 14 (1990) 105–20.

Hahn, Thomas. "The Premodern Text and the Postmodern Reader." *Exemplaria* 2.1 (Spring 1990) 1–21.

Halverson, John. "Patristic Exegesis: A Medieval Tom Sawyer." *College English* 27.1 (October 1965) 50–55.

Hanna, Ralph III. "Donaldson and Robertson: An Obligatory Conjunction." *Chaucer Review* 41.3 (2007) 240–49.

Harwood, Britton J. "The Political Use of Chaucer in Twentieth-Century America." *Medievalism in the Modern World: Essays in Honour of Leslie J. Workman.* Ed. Richard Utz and Tom Shippey. Turnhout, Belgium: Brepols, 1998. 379–92.

Henderson, Jeff. "Chaucer's Experiment in Narrative Metadrama: The General Prologue as *Dramatis Personae.*" *Publications of the Arkansas Philological Association* 14.1 (Spring 1988) 13–24.

Hewitt, Martin, ed. *Scholarship in Victorian Britain.* Leeds: University of Leeds Press, 1998.

Hinckley, Henry Barrett. "The Debate on Marriage in the *Canterbury Tales*." *PMLA* 32.2 (1917) 292–305.

Hinkel, Cecil Ellsworth. *An Analysis and Evaluation of the 47 Workshop of George Pierce Baker*. Unpublished PhD diss., Ohio State University, 1959.

Hooper, Walter. *C.S. Lewis: A Companion & Guide* (New York: Harper Collins, 1996).

Huppé, Bernard F. and D.W. Robertson, Jr. *Fruyt and Chaf: Studies in Chaucer's Allegories*. Princeton: Princeton University Press, 1963.

Hyder, Clyde Kenneth. *George Lyman Kittredge: Teacher and Scholar*. Lawrence: University of Kansas Press, 1962.

Irigaray, Luce. *This Sex Which Is Not One*. Trans. Catherine Porter. Ithaca: Cornell University Press, 1985.

Irvine, Martin. "Medieval Grammatical Theory and Chaucer's *House of Fame*." *Speculum* 60.4 (October 1985) 850–76.

Jackson, Elizabeth. "The Kittredge Way." *College English* 4.8 (May 1943) 483–7.

Jauss, Hans Robert. *Toward an Aesthetic of Reception*. Trans. Timothy Bahti. Minneapolis: University of Minnesota Press, 1982.

Jeffrey, David Lyle, ed. *Chaucer and Scriptural Tradition*. Ottawa: University of Ottawa Press, 1984.

Johnson, James. "Walter W. Skeat's Canterbury Tale." *Chaucer Review* 36.1 (2001) 16–27.

Kaske, R.E. "Chaucer and Medieval Allegory." *English Literary History* 30.2 (June 1963) 175–92.

————. "Chaucer's Marriage Group." *Chaucer the Love Poet*. Ed. Jerome Mitchel *et al*. Athens: University of Georgia Press, 1973. 45–65.

————. "Patristic Exegesis: The Defense." *Critical Approaches to Medieval Literature*. Ed. Dorothy Bethurum. New York: Columbia University Press, 1960. 27–60.

Keefe, Carolyn, ed. *C.S. Lewis: Speaker and Teacher*. London: Hodder and Stoughton, 1971.

Kelly, Kevin. *Out of Control: The New Biology of Machines, Social Systems and the Economic World*. New York: Addison-Wesley, 1994.

Kenyon, John. "Further Notes on the Marriage Group in the *Canterbury Tales*." *Journal of English and German Philology* 25 (1916) 282–8.

Kerby-Fulton, Kathryn. "'Standing on Lewis's Shoulders': C.S. Lewis as Critic of Medieval Literature." *Studies in Medievalism* 3.3 (Winter 1991) 257–78.

———— and Maidie Hilmo, eds. *The Medieval Professional Reader at Work: Evidence from Manuscripts of Chaucer, Langland, Kempe, and Gower*. Victoria, BC: University of Victoria, 2001.

Kirk, Elizabeth D. "Donaldson Teaching and Learning." *Chaucer Review* 41.3 (2007) 279–88.

Kittredge, George Lyman. *Chaucer and His Poetry*. Cambridge, Mass.: Harvard University Press, 1970.

Bibliography

———. "Chaucer and Some of His Friends." *Modern Philology* 1.1 (June 1903) 1–18.

———. "Chaucer and the *Roman de Carité*." *Modern Language Notes* 12.2 (February 1897) 57–8.

———. "Chauceriana." *Modern Philology* 7.4 (Spring 1910) 465–83.

———. "Chaucer's Alceste." *Modern Philology* 6.4 (Spring 1909) 435–9.

———. "Chaucer's Discussion of Marriage." *Modern Philology* 9.4 (Spring 1912) 435–67.

———. "Chaucer's Envoy to Bukton." *Modern Language Notes* 24.1 (Winter 1909) 14–15.

———. "Chaucer's Medea and the Date of the *Legend of Good Women*." *PMLA* 24.2 (1909) 343–63.

———. "Chaucer's Pardoner." *Atlantic Monthly* 72 (December 1893) 829–33.

———. "Chaucer's *Troilus* and Guillaume de Machaut." *Modern Language Notes* 30.3 (March 1915) 69.

———. "Coryat and the Pardoner's Tale." *Modern Language Notes* 15.7 (November 1900) 193–4.

———. "A Friend of Chaucer's." *PMLA* 16.3 (1901) 450–52.

———. "Guillaume de Machaut and the *Book of the Duchess*." *PMLA* 30.1 (1915) 1–24.

———. "Lewis Chaucer or Lewis Clifford?" *Modern Philology* 14.9 (January 1917) 513–18.

Knapp, Ethan, "Chaucer Criticism and its Legacies." *The Yale Companion to Chaucer*, ed. Seth Lerer (New Haven: Yale University Press, 2006) 324–56.

Kollman, Judith. "C.S. Lewis as Medievalist." *C.S. Lewis* 10.7 (1979) 1–5.

Koonce, B. *Chaucer and the Tradition of Fame: Symbolism in the* House of Fame. Princeton: Princeton University Press, 1966.

Korster-Tarvers, Josephine. "'Thys ys my mystrys boke': English Women as Readers and Writers in Late Medieval England." *The Uses of Manuscripts in Literary Studies: Essays in Memory of Judson Boyce Allen.* Ed. Charlotte Cook Morse *et al.* Kalamazoo: Western Michigan University Press, 1992. 305–27.

Krier, Theresa M. ed. *Refiguring Chaucer in the Renaissance.* Gainesville: University Press of Florida, 1998.

Lawrence, W.W. "The Marriage Group in the *Canterbury Tales*." *Modern Philology* 11 (1912–1913) 247–58.

Lawton, David. "Donaldson and Irony." *Chaucer Review* 41.3 (2007) 231–9.

Leavis, F.R. *The Great Tradition.* London: Chatto and Windus, 1948.

Leicester, H. Marshall. *The Disenchanted Self: Representing the Subject in the* Canterbury Tales. Berkeley: University of California Press, 1990.

Lenaghan, R.T. "Chaucer's Circle of Gentlemen and Clerks." *Chaucer Review* 18.2 (1983) 155–60.

Lerer, Seth. *Chaucer and His Readers: Imagining the Author in Late-Medieval England.* Princeton: Princeton University Press, 1993.

————. "Chaucer's Sons." *University of Toronto Quarterly* 73.3 (Summer 2004) 906–15.

————. "Rewriting Chaucer: Two Fifteenth-Century Readings of *The Canterbury Tales.*" *Viator* 19 (1988) 311–26.

————. "Textual Criticism and Literary Theory: Chaucer and His Readers." *Exemplaria* 2.1 (Spring 1990) 329–45.

————. "Unpublished Sixteenth-Century Arguments to *The Canterbury Tales.*" *Notes and Queries* 50.1 (March 2003) 13–17.

———— , ed. *The Yale Companion to Chaucer.* New Haven: Yale University Press, 2006.

———— and Joseph A. Dane, eds. "Reading from the Margins: Textual Studies, Chaucer, and Medieval Literature." *Huntington Library Quarterly* 58.1 (1996).

Lewis, C.S. *The Allegory of Love: A Study in Medieval Tradition.* Oxford: Clarendon Press, 1936.

————. "The Anthropological Approach." *English and Medieval Studies.* Ed. Norman Davis and C.L. Wrenn. London: Allen and Unwin, 1962. 219–30.

————. *The Discarded Image: An Introduction to Medieval and Renaissance Literature.* Cambridge: Cambridge University Press, 1964.

————. *An Experiment in Criticism.* Cambridge: Cambridge University Press, 1961.

————. *Selected Literary Essays.* Ed. Walter Hooper. Cambridge: Cambridge University Press, 1969.

————. *Studies in Medieval and Renaissance Literature.* Cambridge: Cambridge University Press, 1966.

————. "What Chaucer Really Did to *Il Filostrato.*" *Chaucer Criticism Vol. II: Troilus and Criseyde and the Minor Poems.* Ed. Richard Schoeck and Jerome Taylor. Notre Dame: University of Notre Dame Press, 1961. 16–33.

———— and E.M.W. Tillyard. *The Personal Heresy: A Controversy.* Oxford: Oxford University Press, 1939.

Loomis, R.S. "The Origin of the Grail Legends." *Arthurian Literature in the Middle Ages.* Oxford: Clarendon, 1959. 274–94.

Lumiansky, R.M. *Of Sondry Folk: The Dramatic Principle in the* Canterbury Tales. Austin: University of Texas Press, 1955.

Lusk, Linda. "C.S. Lewis as a Critic 'At the Present Time'." *C.S. Lewis* 22.6 (Spring 1991) 1–9.

Lyons, C.P. "The Marriage Debate in the *Canterbury Tales.*" *English Literary History* 2 (1935) 252–62.

Mann, Jill. "The Authority of the Audience in Chaucer." *Poetics: Theory and Practice in Medieval English Literature.* Ed. Piero Boitani and Anna Torti. Cambridge: D.S. Brewer, 1991. 1–12.

Mariella, Sister. "The Parson's Tale and the Marriage Group." *Modern Language Notes* 53.4 (Spring 1938) 251–6.

Martin, Thomas L. "Is C.S. Lewis Still Relevant to Literary Studies Today?" *Journal of the Wooden O Symposium* 1 (2001) 26–35.

Matthews David. "Foreword: The Spirit of Chaucer." *The Canterbury Tales Revisited—21st Century Interpretations*. Ed. Kathleen A. Bishop. Cambridge: Cambridge Scholars Publishing, 2008. x–xiv.

———. *The Making of Middle English, 1765–1910*. Minneapolis: University of Minnesota Press, 1999.

———. "Public Ambition, Private Desire and the Last Tudor Chaucer." *Reading the Medieval in Early Modern England*. Ed. Gordon McMullan and David Matthews. Cambridge: Cambridge University Press, 2007. 74–88.

———. "Speaking to Chaucer: The Poet and the Nineteenth-Century Academy." *Studies in Medievalism* 9 (1997) 5–25.

McAlpine, Monica E. "Catching the Wave to Canterbury." *College English* 54.5 (September 1992) 595–602.

McDonald, Nicola F. "Chaucer's *Legend of Good Women*, Ladies at Court and the Female Reader." *Chaucer Review* 35.1 (2000) 22–42.

McLaws, Lafayette. "A Master of Playwrights." *North American Review* 200.706 (September 1914) 459–67.

McMillan, Douglas. "Discarded and Reclaimed Images, Natives, and Dinosaurs: C.S. Lewis as Teacher and Literary Historian." *Lamp-Post* 21.3 (Fall 1977) 17–25.

McMurty, Jo. *English Language, English Literature: The Creation of an Academic Discipline*. Hamden, CT: Archon, 1985.

Mehl, Dieter. "The Audience of Chaucer's *Troilus and Criseyde*." *Chaucer and Middle English Studies in Honour of Rossell Hope Robbins*. Ed. Beryl Rowland and Lloyd A. Duchemin. London: Allen and Unwin, 1974. 173–89.

Middleton, Anne. "Chaucer's 'New Men' and the Good of Literature in the *Canterbury Tales*." *Literature and Society*. Ed. Edward Said. Baltimore: Johns Hopkins, 1978. 15–56.

———. "Medieval Studies." *Redrawing the Boundaries: The Transformation of English and American Literary Studies*. Ed. Stephen Greenblatt and Giles Gunn. New York: The Modern Language Association of America, 1992. 12–40.

Mieszkowski, Gretchen. "'The Least Innocent of All Innocent-Sounding Lines': the Legacy of Donaldson's *Troilus* Criticism." *Chaucer Review* 41.3 (2007) 299–310.

Minkova, Donna and Theresa Tinkle, eds. *Chaucer and the Challenges of Medievalism*. Frankfurt: Peter Lang, 2003.

Mooney, Linne R. "Chaucer's Scribes." *Speculum* 81.1 (January 2006) 97–138.

Morse, Charlotte. "Popularizing Chaucer in the Nineteenth Century." *Chaucer Review* 38.2 (2003) 99–125.

Muscatine, Charles. "Chaucer's Religion and the Chaucer Religion." *Chaucer Traditions: Studies in Honour of Derek Brewer*. Eds. Ruth Morse and Barry Windeatt. Cambridge: Cambridge University Press, 1990. 249–62.

Olson, Clair C. "The Interludes of the Marriage Group in the *Canterbury Tales*." *Chaucer and Middle English Studies in Honour of Rossell Hope Robbins*. Ed. Beryl Rowland and Lloyd A. Duchemin. London: Allen and Unwin, 1974. 164–72.

Olson, Glending. *Literature as Recreation in the Later Middle Ages*. Ithaca: Cornell University Press, 1982.

Pakkala-Weckström, Mari. "Discourse Strategies in the Marriage Dialogue of Chaucer's *Canterbury Tales*." *Neuphilologische Mitteilungen* 105.2 (2004) 153–75.

Panofsky, Erwin. *Early Netherlandish Painting.* Cambridge, Mass.: Harvard University Press, 1953.

————. *Gothic Architecture and Scholasticism*. New York: Meridian, 1957.

————. *Studies in Iconology.* Oxford: Oxford University Press, 1939.

Patterson, Lee. "Ambiguity and Interpretation: A Fifteenth-Century Reading of *Troilus and Criseyde*." *Speculum* 54.2 (Spring 1979) 297–330.

————. *Chaucer and the Subject of History*. Madison: University of Wisconsin Press, 1991.

————. "Chaucerian Confession: Penitential Literature and the Pardoner." *Medievalia et Humanistica* 7 (1976) 153–73.

————. "Chaucer's Pardoner on the Couch: Psyche and Clio in Medieval Literary Studies." *Speculum* 76 (July 2001) 638–80.

————. "The Disenchanted Classroom." *Exemplaria* 8.2 (1996) 532–3.

————. "'Experience Woot Well It is Noght So': Marriage and the Pursuit of Happiness in the Wife of Bath's Prologue and Tale." *Geoffrey Chaucer: The Wife of Bath: Case Studies in Contemporary Criticism*. Ed. Peter G. Beidler. Boston: Bedford Books, 1996. 133–54.

————. "'For the Wyves Love of Bathe': Feminine Rhetoric and Poetic Resolution in the *Romance of the Rose* and the *Canterbury Tales*." *Speculum* 58.3 (1983) 656–95.

————. "'The Living Witnesses of Our Redemption': Martyrdom and Imitation in Chaucer's *Prioress's Tale*." *Journal of Medieval and Early Modern Studies* 31.3 (Fall 2001) 507–47.

————. *Negotiating the Past: The Historical Understanding of Medieval Literature*. Madison: University of Wisconsin Press, 1987.

————. "On the Margin: Postmodernism, Ironic History, and Medieval Studies." *Speculum* 65.1 (1990) 87–108.

————. "The 'Parson's Tale' and the Quitting of the 'Canterbury Tales'." *Traditio* 34 (1978) 331–80.

————. "Putting the Wife in Her Place." *William Matthews Lectures*. London. Birbeck College. 1995.

————. "Remainders and Reminders." *Unquiet Spirits: D.W. Robertson's Remains in Medieval Studies Now*. Chair Wesley Yu, International Congress on Medieval Studies, Kalamazoo: Princeton Program in Medieval Studies, July 5, 2004.

Bibliography

————. "The Return to Philology." *The Past and Future of Medieval Studies.* Ed. John Van Engen. Notre Dame: University of Notre Dame Press, 1994. 231–44.

————. *Temporal Circumstances: Form and History in the Canterbury Tales.* New York: Palgrave MacMillan, 2006.

————. "'What is Me?' Self and Society in the Poetry of Thomas Hoccleve." *Studies in the Age of Chaucer* 23 (2001) 437–77.

————. "'What Man Artow?': Authorial Self-Definition in The Tale of Sir Thopas and the Tale of Melibee." *Studies in the Age of Chaucer* 11 (1989) 117–75.

Pearsall, Derek. "Chaucer's Poetry and Its Modern Commentators: The Necessity of History." *Medieval Literature: Criticism, Ideology, and History.* Ed. David Aers. New York: St. Martin's, 1986. 123–47.

————. *Chaucer to Spenser: A Critical Reader.* Oxford: Blackwell, 1999.

————. "The Criticism of Chaucer in the Twentieth Century." *Chaucer's Mind and Art.* Ed. A.C. Cawley. Edinburgh: Oliver and Boyd, 1969. 1–25.

————. "Kittredge, George Lyman," *Dictionary of American National Biography.* New York: Oxford University Press, 1999. 781–2.

————. *Old and Middle English Poetry.* London: Routledge and Kegan Paul, 1977.

————. "Review of *Chaucer's Sexual Poetics.*" *Speculum* 67.1 (January 1992) 134–8.

————. "Texts, Textual Criticism, and Fifteenth Century Manuscript Production." *Fifteenth-Century Studies: Recent Essays.* Ed. Robert F. Yeager. Hamden: Archon, 1984. 121–36.

————. "The *Troilus* Frontispiece and Chaucer's Audience." *Yearbook of English Studies* 7 (1977) 68–74.

Perry, Bliss. "And Glady Teach." *The Origins of Literary Studies in America: A Documentary Anthology.* Eds. Gerald Graff and Michael Warner. New York: Routledge, 1989. 139.

Phelan, James. *Narrative as Rhetoric: Technique, Audiences, Ethics, Ideology.* Columbus: Ohio State University Press, 1996.

Prendergast, Thomas A. *Chaucer's Dead Body: From Corpse to Corpus.* New York: Routledge, 2004.

———— and Barbara Kline, eds. *Rewriting Chaucer: Culture, Authority and the Idea of the Authentic Text, 1400–1602.* Columbus: Ohio State University Press, 1999.

Prince, Gerald. "Introduction à l'Etude Du Narrataire." *Poétique* 14 (1973) 178–96.

Reiss, Edmund. "Chaucer and His Audience." *Chaucer Review* 14 (1980) 390–402.

Richards, I.A. *Practical Criticism.* London: Routledge, 1964.

————. *Principles of Literary Criticism.* London: Routledge, 1970.

Ridley, Florence H. "Questions without Answers—Yet or Ever? New Critical Modes and Chaucer." *Chaucer Review* 16.2 (Fall 1981) 101–6.

————. "A Response to 'Contemporary Literary Theory and Chaucer'." *New Perspectives in Chaucer Criticism.* Ed. Donald L. Rose. Norman: Pilgrim, 1981. 37–51.

————. "The State of Chaucer Studies: A Brief Survey." *Studies in the Age of Chaucer* 1 (1979) 3–16.

Robertson, Alice. *A Biographical Study of George Lyman Kittredge.* Unpublished MA diss. University of Maine, June 1947.

Robertson, D.W., Jr. "'And For My Land Thus Hastow Mordred Me?' Land Tenure, the Cloth Industry, and the Wife of Bath." *Chaucer Review* 14 (1980) 403–20.

————. "Chaucer and Christian Tradition." *Chaucer and Scriptural Tradition.* Ed. David Lyle Jeffrey. Ottawa: University of Ottawa Press, 1984. 3–32.

————. "Chaucer Criticism." *Medievalia et Humanistica* 8 (1977) 252–5.

————. *Chaucer's London.* New York: John Wiley and Sons, 1968.

————. "The Cultural Tradition of *Handlyng Synne.*" *Speculum* 22.2 (April 1947) 162–85.

————. "The Doctrine of Charity in Mediaeval Literary Gardens: A Topical Approach Through Symbolism and Allegory." *Speculum* 26.1 (January 1951) 24–49.

————. *Essays in Medieval Culture.* Princeton: Princeton University Press, 1980.

————. "Frequency of Preaching in Thirteenth-Century England." *Speculum* 24.3 (July 1949) 376–88.

————. *The Literature of Medieval England.* New York: McGraw-Hill, 1970.

————. "The Physician's Comic Tale." *Chaucer Review* 23.2 (1988) 129–39.

————. *A Preface to Chaucer: Studies in Medieval Perspectives.* Princeton: Princeton University Press, 1962.

————. "The Probable Date and Purpose of Chaucer's *Troilus.*" *Medievalia et Humanistica* 13 (1985) 143–71.

————. "Some Disputed Chaucerian Terminology." *Speculum* 52.3 (July 1977): 571–81.

————. "Some Observations on Method in Literary Studies." *New Literary History* 1.1 (October 1969) 21–33.

————. "Why the Devil Wears Green." *Modern Language Notes* 69.7 (1954) 470–72.

Rogers, William. "The Raven and the Writing Desk: The Theoretical Limits of Patristic Criticism." *Chaucer Review* 14.3 (Winter 1980) 260–77.

Rossignol, Rosalyn. *Chaucer: A Literary Reference to His Life and Work.* New York: Infobase Publishing, 2007.

Rudd, Gillian. *The Complete Critical Guide to Geoffrey Chaucer.* London: Routledge, 2001.

Rudy, Jill Terry. "Transforming Audiences for Oral Tradition: Child, Kittredge, Thompson, and Connections of Folklore and English Studies." *College English* 66.5 (May 2004) 524–45.

Ruggiers, Paul G., ed. *Editing Chaucer: The Great Tradition*. Norman, Oklahoma: Pilgrim Books, 1984.

Saunders, Corinne, ed. *Blackwell Guides to Criticism: Chaucer*. Oxford: Blackwell, 2001.

Sayer, George. *Jack: A Life of C.S. Lewis*. London: Hodder and Stoughton, 1997.

Scala, Elizabeth. "Historicists and Their Discontents: Reading Psychoanalytically in Medieval Studies." *Texas Studies in Literature and Language* 44.1 (Spring 2002) 108–31.

Schibanoff, Susan. "The New Reader and Female Textuality in Two Early Commentaries on Chaucer." *Studies in the Age of Chaucer* 10 (1988) 71–108.

Selden, Raman and Peter Widdowson. *A Reader's Guide to Contemporary Literary Theory*, 3rd ed. London: Harvester Wheatsheaf, 1993.

Sharrock, Roger. "Second Thoughts: C.S. Lewis on Chaucer's *Troilus*." *Essays in Criticism* 8.2 (April 1958) 123–37.

Sherbo, Arthur. "More on Walter William Skeat." *Poetica* 36 (1992) 69–89.

Skeat, Walter W., ed. *The Complete Works of Geoffrey Chaucer*, 6 vols. Oxford: Clarendon Press, 1894.

Spearing, A.C. "Lydgate's Canterbury Tale: The *Siege of Thebes* and Fifteenth-Century Chaucerianism." *Fifteenth-Century Studies: Recent Essays*. Ed. Robert F. Yeager. Hamden: Archon, 1984. 333–64.

Speirs, J. *Medieval English Poetry: The Non-Chaucerian Tradition*. London: Penguin, 1957.

Spurgeon, Caroline, ed. *Five Hundred Years of Chaucer Criticism and Allusion, 1357–1900,* 3 vols. London: Cambridge University Press, 1925.

Steeves, Harrison Ross. *Learned Societies and English Literary Scholarship*. New York: Columbia University Press, 1913.

Steinberg, Glenn. "Chaucer and the Critical Tradition." *Approaches to Teaching Chaucer's Troilus and Criseyde and the Shorter Poems*. Ed. Tison Pugh and Angela Jane Weisl. New York: Modern Language Association of America, 2007. 87–91.

Stillinger, Thomas, ed. *Critical Essays on Geoffrey Chaucer*. New York: G.K. Hall & Co, 1998.

St John, Michael. *Chaucer's Dream Visions: Courtliness and Individual Identity*. Aldershot: Ashgate, 2000.

Strohm, Paul. "Chaucer's Audience." *Literature and History* 5 (1977) 26–41.

————. "Chaucer's Audience(s): Fictional, Implied, Intended, Actual." *Chaucer Review* 18.2 (1983) 137–45.

————. "Chaucer's Fifteenth-Century Audience and the Narrowing of the 'Chaucer Tradition'." *Studies in the Age of Chaucer* 4 (1982) 3–32.

————. *Hochon's Arrow: The Social Imagination of Fourteenth-Century Texts*. Princeton, New Jersey: Princeton University Press, 1992.

————. "Jean of Angoulême: A Fifteenth Century Reader of Chaucer." *Neuphilologische Mitteilungen* 72 (1971): 69–76.

————. *Social Chaucer*. Cambridge, Mass.: Harvard University Press, 1989.

Thompson, John J. "Reception: fifteenth to seventeeth centuries." *Chaucer: An Oxford Guide*. Ed. Steve Ellis. Oxford: Oxford University Press, 2005. 497–511.

Trigg, Stephanie. *Congenial Souls: Reading Chaucer from Medieval to Postmodern*. Minneapolis: University of Minnesota Press, 2002.

Utley, Francis Lee. "Anglicanism and Anthropology: C.S. Lewis and John Speirs." *Southern Folklore Quarterly* 31.1 (March 1967) 1–11.

————. "Chaucer and Patristic Exegesis." *Chaucer's Mind and Art*. Ed. A.C. Cawley. Edinburgh: Oliver and Boyd, 1969. 69–85.

Utz, Richard. *Chaucer and the Discourse of German Philology: A History of Reception and an Annotated Bibliography of Studies, 1793–1948*. Turnhout, Belgium: Brepols, 2002.

————. "Enthusiast or Philologist? Professional Discourse and the Medievalism of Frederick James Furnivall." *Studies in Medievalism* 11 (2001) 189–212.

————. "When Dinosaurs Ruled the Earth: A Short History of German *Chaucerphilologie* in the Nineteenth and Early Twentieth Century." *PhiN: Philologie im Netz* 21 (2002) 54–62.

Van Dyke, Carolynn. "Amorous Behavior: Sexism, Sin and the Donaldson Persona." *Chaucer Review* 41.3 (2007) 250–60.

Veldman, Meredith. *Fantasy, the Bomb, and the Greening of Britain: Romantic Protest, 1945–1980*. Cambridge: Cambridge University Press, 1994.

Walsh, Chad. *The Literary Legacy of C.S. Lewis*. London: Sheldon Press, 1979.

Ward, Antonia. "'My Love for Chaucer': F.J. Furnivall and Homosociality in the Chaucer Society." *Studies in Medievalism* 9 (1997) 44–57.

Watson, George. *Critical Essays on C.S. Lewis*. London: Scolar Press, 1992.

Wetherbee, Winthrop. "Convention and Authority: A Comment on Some Recent Critical Approaches to Chaucer." *New Perspectives in Chaucer Criticism*. Ed. Donald Rose. Norman: Pilgrim, 1981. 71–81.

Wheatley, Margaret J. *Leadership and the New Science: Learning About Organization from an Orderly Universe*. San Francisco: Berrett-Koehler, 1994.

Wheeler, Bonnie. "The Legacy of New Criticism: Revisiting the Work of E. Talbot Donaldson." *Chaucer Review* 41.3 (2007) 216–24.

Wilson, A.N. *C.S. Lewis: A Biography*. London: Collins, 1990.

Windeatt, Barry. "The Scribes as Chaucer's Early Critics." *Studies in the Age of Chaucer* 1 (1979) 119–41.

Wood, Chauncey. "In Memoriam: D.W. Robertson Jr., 1914–1992." *Chaucer Review* 28.1 (1993) 1–4.

Yager, Susan. "Boethius, Philosophy and Chaucer's 'Marriage Group'." *Carmina Philosophiae* 4 (1995) 77–89.

Index

Abelard, Peter 124
Adam Scriveyn 1, 7
Aers, David 131n
Akbari, Suzanne Conklin 102n
Alain de Lille 47, 124
alchemy 27, 54
Alighieri, Dante 124
allegory 32, 38, 42–52, 54–6, 59–61, 64,
    75, 85–6, 88–90, 95–100, 102–4,
    107–8, 110, 112, 117–21, 145
America / American 20, 22, 122–3, 126,
    128, 131, 135
Anglo-Saxon *see* Old English
anthropological criticism 41–2, 56n, 86,
    69, 119, 124
anti-semitism 75, 150–52
Apuleius 54
Aquinas, Thomas 124
Aristotle 87
art history 87–8
astrology 54
astronomy 54
audience function x, **3–12**, 16, 25, 35, 45,
    69, 82, 86, 94, 96, 105, 108, 134,
    140, 142–3, 146–7, 150, 152,
    159–60
author function **4–6**, 25; *see also* Foucault,
    Michel

Baker, Alison 158
Baker, George Pierce 20
ballad(s) 20–21, 56n, 100, 102n
Barnett, Allen 127
Barrington, Candace 157
Barthes, Roland 101n, 121, 124, 127,
    140
Baugh, Albert C. 9
de Beauvoir, Simone 124
Bede 98
Beidler, Peter 24n, 134, 137

Benoit 146
Benson, C. David 24
Benson, Larry ixn
bestiaries 53–4
Bhabha, Homi 121, 124, 147
Black studies 109
Boccaccio, Giovanni 113, 117, 124, 146
Boethius 1, 23, 54, 98, 124
Boffey, Julia 158
book history or history of the book 157;
    see also codicology
Boswell, John 8, 127
Bowers, John 158
Boyd, David 158
Brewer, Derek S. 8n, 13n, 21n, 45, 76n,
    85n, 155
ten Brink, Bernhard 32
Bronson, B.H. 9, 67, 69
Brooks, Cleanth 61
Bryn Mawr College 111
Bukton 7
Burlin, Robert 111
Butler, Judith 124

Canada/Canadian 135
Cambridge Companion to Chaucer ix, 111
Cambridge University 40, 45, 52
Capellanus, Andreas 95, 103
careful reading 15, 64, **66–71**, 75, 108
caritas 59, 60n, 64, 86, 95–6, 99, 103–4,
    106–7, 109, 124
charity *see* caritas
Chaucer, Geoffrey
    Anelida and Arcite 146
    Boece 1
    Book of the Duchess 1–2, 26, 29, 32,
        49, 55, 90, 101
    Canterbury Tales 1–3, 23, 25–30,
        33–8, 44, 55–7, 61, 78–81, 99, 104,

107, 115, 117, 120, 129n, 146–7, 158

Characters
Chaucer the Pilgrim 61, 78, 82, 90
Clerk 22–3, 37, 107
Cook 74
Franklin 22–3, 37, 109
Friar 35, 37, 70, 78, 101, 107
Harry Bailey *see* Host
Host 2–3, 27, 36, 56, 106, 141
Knight 2–3, 79, 101
Man of Law 31, 125
Manciple 3, 34
Merchant 22–3, 37, 66, 79
Miller 2, 56, 98, 101–2, 138
Monk 3, 27, 78
Nun's Priest 78, 80, 152
Pardoner 14, 21–2, 24–5, 30, 34–5, 75, 107, 110, 111n, 119–20, 124–8, 129n, 139–42
Parson 30, 101, 107
Physician 100–101
Plowman 100
Prioress 31, 34, 72–3, 75, 78, 151, 152
Reeve 2, 34, 100
Second Nun 152
Shipman 79
Squire 99
Summoner 2, 35, 37, 79
Wife of Bath 14, 22–3, 29, 36–7, 86, 98–9, 101–2, 107, 113, 117, 119, 137, 148
Chaucer's Retractions 3, 80–81
Clerk's Tale 25, 29, 36–7, 66, 98, 101, 104, 113, 117, 119
Cook's Tale 124
Franklin's Tale 37, 94, 99, 102, 105–6
Friar's Tale 66, 107
General Prologue 30, 36, 56, 78, 80, 82, 104, 106, 151
Knight's Tale 27, 67, 79, 99, 102, 138, 146–7
Man of Law's Tale 56, 101, 104, 119, 123–4, 126

Manciple's Tale 3
Merchant's Tale 37, 66–9, 71–4, 79, 99, 101, 106
Miller's Tale 47n, 56, 75
Monk's Tale 3, 27, 75
Nun's Priest's Tale 56, 66, 79, 152
Pardoner's Prologue and Tale 25, 31, 68, 110, 117–18, 124, 126, 133–4, 139, 141–2
Parson's Tale 64, 80, 104, 138
Physician's Tale 99
Prioress's Tale 31, 75, 104, 138, 150–52
Reeve's Tale 102
Second Nun's Tale 56, 104
Summoner's Tale 68, 107
Tale of Melibee 75, 89, 97n, 101
Tale of Sir Thopas 56, 81, 89
Wife of Bath's Prologue and Tale 14, 22–4, 26, 36–7, 56, 86, 98–9, 107, 113, 117, 119, 137–8, 148
"Chaucers Wordes unto Adam" 1
"Envoy to Bukton" 29, 45
House of Fame 1, 30, 32, 35, 55–6, 85
Legend of Good Women 1–3, 7, 21, 115–16, 123
Parlement of Foules 46–7, 55, 105
Troilus and Criseyde 1–2, 27, 29–30, 32–5, 38, 42, 44–6, 49–51, 55, 61, 63–4, 66–7, 69, 72–4, 76–8, 87, 98–9, 101–6, 113–17, 119, 121, 126, 130, 138, 144–6, 149, 152

Chaucerian apocrypha 156
Chaucer Society vii, 13, 19
Chesterton, G.K. 9, 22n
Chalcidius 54
Child, Francis 19–21
Chrétien de Troyes 29, 42–3, 47–8, 95, 103
Christianity 33, 40, 41, 44, 46, 48–9, 57, 63, 88–9, 93–99, 103–4, 105n, 107–8, 125, 127, 138, 151–2
Christine de Pizan 124
Claudian 54
close reading 15, 62, 688–70, 81–2, 86, 121, 131, 155
codicology 13, 19, 109, 144
Coffman, George 87

Columbia University 60
comedy 28, 30, 46, 94n, 105
Consolation of Philosophy see Boethius
courtly love 27, 29, 32–3, 43–51, 53, 56–7,
      63, 76, 88–9, 91, 94, 105
Croce, Benedetto 89
crusade 151
culture wars 128–9, 132
cupiditas 89, 95–6, 99, 103–4, 106, 124
cupidity *see* cupiditas

Dane, Joseph 156, 158n
Dante *see* Alighieri
David of Augsburg 145
Decameron see Boccaccio, Giovanni
deconstruction 108, 136
Derrida, Jacques 109, 124
Deschamps, Eustache 21, 44–45
Dinshaw, Carolyn 2, 15, 16n, 73n,
      109–130, 131–33, 135, 148–52,
      155, 160
    Chaucer's Sexual Poetics 73n, 110–13,
      115, 121, 122n, 124, 126
    Getting Medieval 111, 121–2, 124,
      126–7, 149
    "Pale Faces" 122
Disce mori 145
Donaldson, E. Talbot 9, 15–16, 26, 40,
      43n, 57, **59–83**, 85, 89–90, 105–6,
      108, 110, 112–16, 121, 123, 125–6,
      129–30, 133, 135, 148, 151–2, 155,
      160
    "Chaucer the Pilgrim" 59, 78
    "Effect of the Merchant's Tale" 67,
      69, 71
    "Masculine Narrator and Four Women
      of Style" 72
    Speaking of Chaucer 61, 67n, 110
Donne, John 55n
dramatic principle *see* dramatic theory
dramatic theory 14, 22, 23n, 24n, 25–6,
      29–30, 31n, 33, 36–8, 101–2, 151
dream vision 1–3, 26, 34, 44, 55n, 101, 146
Duke University 135

Early English Text Society 13, 19
early printed books 158

Edwards, A.S.G. 158
Eleanor of Aquitaine 43n
Ellesmere Manuscript 7
Ellis, Steve 157
exegetical criticism 9–10, 15–16, 31, 46,
      57, 59, 61–6, 82, 85–9, 94–5, 98,
      112, 144, 147
exemplum, exempla 31, 87, 96–7, 99, 107,
      118

fabliau 56, 75–6
feminist criticism 57, 73n, 109–10, **111–15**,
      122, 124, 131, 138, 151, 159
fifteenth-century audience 7, 44–5, 144–5,
      149, 156
fin'amor *see* courtly love
Fish, Stanley 71
Fleming, John 85n, 135
Formalism *see* New Criticism
Forni, Kathleen 156
Fortune 47, 94
Foucault, Michel 4–6, 109, 112, 124, 133,
      136–7, 150
fourth Lateran council 138
frame tale 35, 107
Freud, Sigmund 54, 93n, 124, 139–42
Froissart, Jean 47, 54
Frost, Robert 134
Furnivall, F.J. 13, 19, 21

Gilbert, Sandra 124
Gillespie, Alexandra 158
Glück, Robert 126–7, 133
Gower, John 7, 42, 44–5, 124, 129
Gray, Douglas 8n, 13n
Green, Richard Firth 7
Greenblatt, Stephen 136
Gregory the Great 98
ground zero 122
Gubar, Susan 124
Guibert of Nogent 124
Guido delle Colonne 146
Gust, Geoffrey 31, 73n, 118n

Handlyng Synne see Mannyng, Robert
Hahn, Thomas 148
Hanna, Ralph 61, 158
Harvard University 19–20, 21n

182 *Twentieth-Century Chaucer Criticism*

Harwood, Britton 132n
Hengwrt Manuscript 7
Henryson, Robert 2, 8, 114
  Testament of Cressid 2, 114
hermeneutics 65, 106, 110–12, 117–19,
  120–21, 124
Higden, Ranulf 124
Hilmo, Maidie 158
historicism 10, 15, 51, 63, 111–12, 126,
  135–8, 144
Hoccleve, Thomas 7, 8, 29, 44–5, 51, 138,
  143, 157
Holocaust 75
horizon of expectations 5–6; *see also* Jauss,
  Hans Robert
Hugh of St. Victor 98, 106
human comedy 28, **33–8**
humanism 148
Huppé, Bernard 86–8

iconography 65, 87–8, 98, 101, 151
identity criticism 110; *see also* Black
  studies, feminism, masculinism,
  Marxism, Orientalism, post-
  colonialism, queer theory
implicit audiences 3, 55–6
Indiana University 60
individualism 100, 139, 147
Inklings 40; *see also* Lewis, C.S. *and*
  Tolkien, J.R.R.
intentional fallacy 61
Irigaray, Luce 109, 122, 124, 151
irony 5, 16, 30–31, 33, 39, 42, 44–6, 57,
  59, 75–83, 90, 97–8, 102–6, 110,
  113, 151–2, 160

Jauss, Hans Robert 5–6
John of Gaunt 29
Johns Hopkins University 20, 22, 135
Judas 140

Kalamazoo International Congress 135
Kane, George 61
Kennedy, Beverly 158
Kempe, Margery 111n, 122, 126–8, 133
Ker, W.P. 22n
Kerby-Fulton, Katherine 55n, 158

Kittredge, G.L. 9, 12–15, **19–38**, 39, 41,
  45–6, 54, 78–9, 80, 90–91, 106,
  113, 123, 125–6, 129, 143, 151,
  155, 157, 159
  Chaucer and His Poetry 14, 22, 26, 110
Kline, Barbara 158
Knapp, Ethan ixn, 9, 13, 14n, 22n, 110n,
  131n
Kristeva, Julia 124

Lacan, Jacques 124, 141
Lady Philosophy 99; *see also* Boethius
Laird, Edgar 158
Lancastrians 138
Langland, William 8, 55n, 64–5
  Piers Plowman 60–62
Lawton, David 90n
Leavis, F.R. 39, 41, 60–62
Leicester, H. Marshall 79n
Lerer, Seth 155n, 156–8
Lévi-Strauss, Claude 119, 124–5
Lewis, C.S. 14n, 15–16, 23, 29, 32, 38,
  39–57, 61, 63, 70, 74–5, 79–80,
  90–91, 94, 96, 100n, 106, 113, 123,
  135, 134, 137, 143, 145, 149, 152,
  157, 159
  Allegory of Love, The 39, 42–4, 46, 48,
    52, 55, 61, 110
  An Experiment in Criticism 41
  Discarded Image, The 39, 52–3, 143
  fictional writing 40n, 41
  *Studies in Medieval and Renaissance
    Literature* 55
Lollardy 124, 130, 141
London 30, 99, 101, 124, 127, 138
Loomis, R.S. 42
Lounsbury, Thomas 22
Lucan 54
Lumiansky, R.M. 22
Lydgate, John 7–8, 29, 44–5, 51, 143, 157

Mack, Maynard 61
Macrobius 54
Magdalen College 40
Malory, Sir Thomas
  Le Morte Darthur 42
de Man, Paul 107n, 109

Index

manuscripts 1, 7–8, 13, 19, 21, 45n, 71n, 75, 109–10, 144, 147, 157–9
marriage debate *see* marriage group
marriage group 22–3, 36–7
Martianus Capella 47
martyrdom 150–52
Martz, Louis 61
Marx, Karl 54
Marxism 10, 93n, 109–12, 131, 135–6
masculinism 110
Matthews, David 110, 158
medieval "mindset" 27, 39, 41–2, 50, **51–54**, 56, 92, 143
Metamorphoses see Ovid
Middle English (as a language) 19, 21, 26, 39, 65, 68, 75, 111n
Middle English Dictionary 75
Middleton, Anne 7, 10, 136
Milton, John 19, 55n
mimesis *see* mimicry
mimicry 122n, 151
Mooney, Linne 7
Morse, Charlotte 156–7
Morte Darthur see Malory, Sir Thomas
Muscatine, Charles 9

narratology 11
Nature 47, 96, 105
New Criticism 9–10, 16, 46, 59, **60–62**, 91, 111, 135, 155
New Democratic Party 135
New Historicism 109–10, 131, **133–8**
new philology 136
New Troy 99
New York 123

objectivity 15, 48, 68, 86, 100, 114, 132, 134
Occitan literature *see* Provence, Provençal poetry
Oedipus/Oedipal theory *see* Freud, Sigmund
Old English 19, 43, 44n, 68, 88
Orientalism 110, 126
Ovid 54, 98
Oxford Companion to Chaucer ix, 8n
Oxford University 20, 40

paleography 109, 135
Panofsky, Erwin 87–8
Paris, Matthew 52–3
Patterson, Lee 10, 15, 19n, 62n, 63n, 64, 74, 110n, 130, **131–53**, 158–60
 "Ambiguity and Interpretation" 144, 149
 Chaucer and the Subject of History 138–9, 158n
 "Chaucer's Pardoner on the Couch" 133n, 141–2
 "'Living Witnesses of Our Redemption'" 150–52
 Negotiating the Past 10, 19n, 137–8, 142, 144
Payne, Robert 9
Pearsall, Derek ix, 7, 9, 20, 115, 129
Peter Lombard 98
Petrarch, Francesco 29, 36, 97, 113, 116–17, 119, 124
philology 13, 19–20, 61, 68, 135
Piers Plowman see Langland
popular Chaucerianism 22n, 157
post-colonialism 110
post-structuralism 108–9, 112, 131
Prendergast, Thomas 156
Princeton University 87–88, 111, 135
Provence, Provençal poetry 42–3, 50, 53
Prudentius 47
pseudo-Dionysius 54
psychoanalytic criticism 124–5, 133, 140–42
psychological realism 25, 33–5, 48, 145
Pulp Fiction see Tarantino, Quentin

queer theory 110, 111–13, **121–30**, 151

race 122–3, 126, 133
rape 1, 117, 119, 129
reader-response criticism 113, 155, 157
realism 25, 30, 33–6, 39, 44, 80, 92, 97, 101
reception theory 11, 155
Renaissance studies 109, 136
Richard II 138, 146
Richard of Bury 124
Richards, I.A. 39, 41, 60, 61
Ricoeur, Paul 124
Ridley, Florence 9

Riverside Chaucer, The 9n, 21
roadside drama *see* dramatic theory
Robert of Basevorn 124
Robert Mannyng of Brunne 87
Robertson, D.W. 6, 9, 15–16, 23, 31,
    43n, 57, 59–66, 70, 75, 80, 82–3,
    85–108, 109–18, 120–1, 123, 126,
    133–5, 137–8, 143–5, 147, 149,
    151–2, 159–60
    "Allegorist and the Aesthetician" 89,
      102n
    Chaucer's London 86, 93, 143
    "Frequency of Preaching in Thirteenth-
      Century England" 86, 98
    Fruyt and Chaf, 86–7, 97, 103
    "Historical Criticism" 60, 86, 90
    Preface to Chaucer, A 61, 86, 92, 99,
      107, 110, 135
Robertsonianism *see* exegetical criticism
Robin Hood 100
Robinson, F.N. 13, 19–20
romance(s) 19, 40, 44n, 56n, 69, 73, 75–6,
    102n, 124, 146
Roman de la Rose / Romance of the Rose 1,
    29, 42, 47–50, 54, 100n
Roman gods 47, 139
Romantic period 51, 91n, 100, 102
Rowland, Beryl 105n
Rubin, Gayle 124
Rudd, Gillian ix, 8n
Russell, H.K. 87
Rykener, John/Eleanor 122, 127, 148

Said, Edward 126
St. Augustine of Hippo 59, 93, 95–6, 98–9,
    124, 147
St. Francis of Assisi 78
St. Jerome 4, 98, 118
St. Kenelm 152
St. Nicholas and the Jew 152
St. Paul 98
Saunders, Corinne ix, 8n ,9n, 137
Scala, Elizabeth 131n, 137, 141n
Schibanoff, Susan 158
scribes 1, 7, 110, 118, 143–5, 157–8
September 11: 122–3, 126, 128
Shakespeare, William 19, 33, 36–7, 69n
Silvestris, Bernardus 47

Skeat, Walter W. 13, 19, 21
source study 14, 20–22, 38
Speirs, John 9, 42
Spenser, Edmund 19, 42, 55n
Spurgeon, Caroline 155
Statius 54
Stillinger, Thomas 15n
Strode, Ralph 7
Strohm, Paul 7, 131n, 136, 158
subjectivity 10, 15, 48, 68, 86, 114, 132–3,
    136–7, **138–142**, 143, 152, 155, 160
swarm theory 149–50, 160
symbolism 41, 48, 51, 65, 82, 87–8, 90, 96–9,
    102, 111n, 112, 117, 140–41, 152
Syon Abbey 145
Syon reader 145, 150, 158

Tale of Beryn 29–30, 45, 157
Tarantino, Quentin 126
Teseida see Boccaccio, Giovanni
Testament of Cresseid see Henryson, Robert
Thebiad 146
Tillyard, E.M.W. 41n
Tolkien, J.R.R. 40, 53
tragedy 45n, 87, 94
translation 1–2, 113, 117, 119
Trigg, Stephanie 156
troubadours 42–3

United Kingdom 128
United States 121, 126–8, 132
University of California at Berkeley 112
University of Michigan 60
University of North Carolina 87
University of Toronto ix, 135
Usk, Thomas 42, 44–5

Van Dyke, Carolynn 60n, 69n, 70n, 113n
Veldman, Meredith 40
Victorian scholars 13, 19, 42, 86, 156–7
Virgil 54, 98
verisimilitude 101

Wallace, David 131n, 132n
Windeatt, Barry 157, 158n
Wilde, Oscar 125
Wimsatt, W.K. Jr. 61
Wyclif, John 27, 124; *see also* Lollardy

Yale Companion to Chaucer ix
Yale University 60, 61, 73n, 135–6